I dedicate this book to the memory of my father

As you read this book you may well find omissions and inaccuracies, and for these I apologise in advance. However, I have relied for some of the information on the memories of those supporters and players who were connected with Oldham Athletic very many years ago, and it is always possible that you, the reader, have more accurate memories. If so, I would always be pleased to hear from you.

STEWART BECKETT

THE TEAM FROM A TOWN OF CHIMNEYS

forward...

"THE TEAM FROM A TOWN OF CHIMNEYS"

Acknowledgements

J.W. Lees Brewery Limited
Oldham Athletic A.F.C. Limited
Oldham Evening Chronicle
for supplying many photographs printed in this book
The Football League
Manchester Evening News
Daily Express
Daily Telegraph
The Observer
The Local Interest Centre, Oldham
Aston Villa A.F.C. Limited
BBC Times Hulton Picture Library
County Press Photos
Mr. G. Collin (Oldham Chronicle)
Bob Young (Oldham Chronicle)
Paul Hince (Manchester Evening News)
Mr. Harry Wilde
Mr. Albert Birtles
Mr. David O'Shea
Mr. C. Nickson
Mr. R.H. Venables
Mr. Jimmy Naylor
Mr. George Milligan
Mr. Charles Hemsley
Mr. Robert Scholes
Mr. Eric Krieger
Mrs. M. Greaves
Mr. Garth Dykes
Mr. Peter Haslam
Mr. Shaw (Hyde)
Shane Wray McCann
Mr. W. Fulton

and a special thanks to the Skipworth family for the use of material belonging to the late Reg. Skipworth.

EDITED BY BOB YOUNG

Design, Production & Picture Research by Stewart Beckett for
Comprehensive Art Services
Courtlets House
38 King Street West
Manchester M3 2WZ
England

ISBN 0-9516497-0-1

All rights reserved. No part of this publication may be reproduced, stored in a retrieval system, or transmitted in any form or by any means, electronic, mechanical, photocopying, recording, or otherwise, without the prior permission of Comprehensive Art Services.

Setting by Pinnacle Typesetting/City Typesetting, Manchester, England.
Printed by L.V. Lawlor Printers, Oldham, England.

THIS is a most appropriate time for Stewart to be up-dating his book about the club, coming as it does, in the wake of the most eventful season in Athletic's history.

The 1989/90 season saw us win new friends and widespread recognition but not, regretably, promotion to the First Division – an achievement surely within the capabilities of the side in a normal, less demanding season.

Off the field the club faced an equally challenging prospect of ground redevelopment to comply with The Taylor Report's recommendations for all-seater stadia, and other safety measures.

As we go to press, we are awaiting the outcome of the Clayton Playing Fields development scheme, and the method of distributing ground aid via the new Football Trust – both of which (particularly the former) will have a bearing on our ability to create a first-class stadium for spectactors and players.

There is, of course, still much opposition to all-seater stadia and I believe there is a place for a shallow terrace between seats and the perimeter of the pitch. I think we are unlikely to win that argument although, of course, we did – with the considerable help of Lord Justice Taylor and some belated commonsense – win the battle over the Government's compulsory identity card membership scheme.

As recent achievements have prompted Stewart to up-date his book, let us hope the events of the 1990-91 season will force him to do so again.

IAN STOTT Chairman Oldham Athletic A.F.C.
August 1990

Stewart Beckett was born in Chadderton, Oldham, in November 1946, and was a student at the Oldham College of Art and Design.

Between 1964 and 1972 he worked in various advertising agencies in Manchester and Sheffield, before opening his own design company – Comprehensive Art Services – in Manchester in 1972, where he works to this day.

His father first took him to Boundary Park as a small boy way back in 1952, and he has keenly followed the Club's fortunes ever since.

Stewart had been collecting Athletic memorabilia for many years, and in 1982 first produced 'The Team From a Town of Chimneys', which attracted good reviews in both press and T.V.

Once called 'A Romantic' in a T.V. interview with Stuart Hall for believing Athletic might one day reach a Cup Final and gain Division One status!!

Pictured with Sir Matt Busby during a design presentation in 1984

Having been at this club for 14 of its most recent years, I consider myself a "new boy," a small link in its considerable history. So it gives me great pleasure to be asked to write a foreword to this book which tells the story of a lot of people who have contributed to making O.A.A.F.C. one of the most respected and progressive clubs of today.

Oldham is essentially a family club. Even in this competitive age of big business associated with football, it has still been able to retain the charm and background associated with a family. The club in my time has always been noted for its character on and off the field. You only have to ask players from around the League, which is one of the most daunting away fixtures to play in and nearly always Oldham gets a mention. Also in recent years the club has produced many of its own players, due to a successful youth policy, which enables the club to challenge clubs of bigger stature.

I welcome this book which pays tribute to O.A.A.F.C., whose name and reputation past and present has become one of envy throughout the Football League.

IAN WOOD

The club's appearance record is held by defender Ian Wood who played a total of 525 League games in his 14 years with Athletic until given a free transfer prior to the 1980-81 season, when he joined Lancashire rivals Burnley.

Introduction

On July 4, 1899, Pine Villa football team simply ceased to exist. However, there were no downcast faces at this death in Oldham's football family for the occasion also marked the birth of Pine Villa's successors . . . OLDHAM ATHLETIC ASSOCIATION FOOTBALL CLUB.

For the Lancashire mill town this was the logical culmination of over 35 years of slow development of the game — from a time when football was all but illegal and working-class people worked up to 12 hours a day, six days a week, to a society in which the Saturday half-day holiday was a fact of life for everybody.

Since before the Middle Ages, working folk had enjoyed the chance to join in the village football game — one which bore little relation to that we know today except that it was played by two teams with a "ball" . . . usually the proverbial pig's bladder.

The object was for one team to get the "ball" past the opposition to a pre-arranged point, usually more than a mile behind "enemy lines".

So unruly was this rough and tumble that serious injuries, even death, were commonplace among the participants. Several times the games were outlawed — made illegal by a Royal warrant.

The story of football as we know it today does not begin until 1863, by when a more acceptable, less hazardous game had developed. Several clubs decided on a common set of rules for their matches and formed themselves into the Football Association.

Not all the clubs were keen on this Association and progress was slow until 1872 when Old Harrovian C. W. Alcock, the secretary of the Association, adapted, for all its members, the knock-out competition he had known at school. The birth of the Football Association Cup competition not only saw more clubs wanting to join the F.A. but it also led to many more new teams springing up all over the country.

At this time, football was the relaxation of the well-to-do. It was largely the young men of the public schools and Oxford and Cambridge Universities who spread the game in its organised form. The amateur players of the South of England dominated the game.

"THE TEAM FROM A TOWN OF CHIMNEYS"

ASSOCIATION.

GREENACRES ATHLETIC V. MOSSLEY AMATEURS. —At Clarksfield.

Athletic: A Denton, goal; W Smith and G Taylor, backs; F Platt, J Ashworth, and W Richards, halfs; F Richards, W Cox, G Hill, G Sibbles, and A Balmforth, forwards.

OLDHAM NORTH END V. WINDSOR.—At Clarksfield.

North End: H Eastwood, goal; R Platt and A Smalley, backs; W Davies, E Smith, and J Lees, halfs; J Littlewood, W Eckersley, Shaw, Ward, and Whitehead, forwards.. Reserves: Taylor, Gartside, and Mallalieu.

GREENACRES LADS V. MILTON ATHLETIC.—At Royton.

Greenacres Lads: J T Gartside goal; E Ashworth and G W Yates, backs; F Goddard, W Ormrod, F Green, halfs; Hetherington, J Milhench, W Brown, H Ormrod, D Hilditch, forwards. Reserves: D Newton, G Tattersall.

ROCK AMATEURS V. WATERLOO ATHLETIC.—At Alexandra Park.

Rock Amateurs: J Taylor, goal; W Butler and T Riley, backs; E Toole, D Walker, and C Newton, halfs; T Brierley, A Mitchel, J Garth, H Lowe, and D Lowe, forwards. Reserves, J Hall and J Bryan.

UNITY V. FRANKHILL LADS.—At Robin Hill.

Unity: A Lees, goal; Knott and F Shaw, backs; Brierley, H Healey, and Chester, halfs; J Wolstencroft, J Taylor, P Tetlow, O Davenport, and C Partington, forwards.

OLDHAM JUNIOR ASSOCIATION LEAGUE.
FIRST DIVISION.

ALEXANDRA V. OLDHAM UNITED.—At Nether Hey.

Alexandra: Wrigley, goal; P Fairnie and J Stott, backs; V Charnock, C Stock, and W Charnock, halfs; J W Hill, S Davies, A Ashworth, T Royds, T Charnock, and G Lee, forwards.

MIDDLETON JUNCTION RAMBLERS V. WATERHEAD TRINITY.—At Grimshaw Lane.

Ramblers: Mellsom, goal; Fairbrother and W Greenhalgh, backs; S Dixon, K Greenhalgh, and J Dixon, halfs; Jameson, Johnson, Leach, Crabtree, and Ashworth, forwards.

SECOND DIVISION.

LARKHILL V. ALEXANDRA RESERVES.—At Clarksfield.

Alexandra: T Farr, goal; F Parker and S Thornton, backs; A Walsh, D Halstead, and H Slater, halfs; S Bradbury, A Lees, J Shepherd, R Woodhead, B Jones, and J Bailey, forwards.

PINE VILLA V. ROYTON AMATEURS' RESERVES.—

Villa: Green goal; Joe Stafford and J E Clarke, backs; Firth, Griffiths, and G Livesey, halfs; Rowley, Heron, Joe Sankey, Jack Stafford, and F Livesey, forwards. Reserves, Greenhalgh, Marsden, and Avison.

Jack Stafford (Pine Villa)
Joe Sankey (Pine Villa)

It was not until the Saturday half-day holiday came into being that working-class people had time for football. And it was not until the legalisation of professional players in 1885 that they could really afford to play at the top level.

These two factors enabled football to spread quickly, and by 1888, the Football League had been formed.

Despite the fact that in those days a player had to provide his own outfit, pay all incidental expenses and even subscribe towards the up-keep of the pitch, such was the eagerness of team members that when evening matches were on they hurried to the ground at the end of their working day carrying their supper baskets.

They were, indeed, hardy men who worked hard for their daily bread and who played football like demons on match days.

They also drank hard and our story begins in 1897 at the Featherstall and Junction Hotel, Oldham.

OLDHAM COUNTY v. OSWALDTWISTLE ROVERS.—About 2,000 spectators were present at this match in the first round of the qualifying competition of the English Cup, on Saturday, the game being described as the "first English Cup tie played in Oldham." Oswaldtwistle started with ten men. Furniss set the ball in motion for the County, and the home forwards at once proceeded in the direction of the Rovers' goal. Wilson hit the post with a shot, and Shaw had to use his hands. After some neat passing Sharpe put one past Shaw, and the goalkeeper had all his work cut out to stop one from Furniss. Sharpe shot, and the ball hitting the post, Cunliffe placed it in the net. Ireland, the visitors' centre, now made his appearance, but the Oldham men still held the advantage, and Wilson obliged with goal No. 3. Shaw stopped an effort of Sharpe's, and the same player and Furniss successively placed the sphere over the goal Free kicks for fouls were awarded both sides in quick succession. Carman put in a good kick from the line, but Shaw saved, and Mackay was tested for the first time. One of the Oswaldtwistle players got injured, and had to retire. Shaw was again visited, and he had to negotiate shots from Furniss and Wilson. Sharpe sent in a smart shot, and the visitors' custodian was deservedly applauded for a splendid save. Just before half time Cunliffe put another in the met, and the homesters led at the interval by four goa's to nil. Ireland kicked off, and the home team at once began to press. From a good kick the Rovers' went off in the direction of the home goal, but Mellors robbed, and dribbled to the opposition end, finishing up with a shot that nearly scored. After Wilson had had hard lines, Cunliffe put one past Shaw after a round of passing. From a free kick by Mellors, the Rovers' goal had a narrow escape, and Wilson made an unsuccessful attempt at scoring. Furniss made the score into the half-dozen, and Mackay and Gaskell changed places. After Cunliffe had shot over the top, the Oldham centre forward again beat Shaw, and Wilson, Cunliffe, and Mackay each tested him. The home team pressed to the finish, when the score was:—Oldham County, seven; Oswaldtwistle Rovers, none. Teams:—

County: Mackay, goal; Gaskell and Mellors, full-backs; Foster, Errentz (captain), and Stevenson, halfs; Carman, Cunliffe, Furniss, Sharpe, and Wilson, forwards.

Oswaldtwistle Rovers: Shaw, goal; Livesey and Yarwood, backs; Savage, Caughey, and Nuttall, halves; Rushton, Bradley, Ireland, Richmond, and Macdonald, forwards.

OLDHAM JUNIOR ASSOCIATION LEAGUE.
FIRST DIVISION.
GREENACRES ATHLETIC v. MIDDLETON JUNCTION RAMBLERS.—At Middleton Junction.
Athletic: W Cox, goal; W Smith and G Taylor, backs; W Richards, F Platt, and J Ashworth, halfs; Balmforth, F Richards, Hargreaves, G Hill, and G Sibbles, forwards.
Ramblers: Mellsom, goal; Fairbrother and W Greehalgh, backs; S Dixon, K Greenhalgh, and J Dixon, halfs; Jameson, Johnson, Leach, Crabtree, and Ashworth, forwards.

HATHERSHAW v. HOLLINWOOD ATHLETIC.—At Honeywell Lane.
Hathershaw: Brooks, goal; W Bennett and J Greaney, backs; T Wild, H Lindley (captain), and A Garrison, halfs; J Blunn, Yarwood, Acton, G Tilsley, and R Dalton, forwards. Reserves: Cooke, W Stott, and Corbishley.

ALEXANDRA v. ROYTON AMATEURS.—At Royton.
Alexandra: Wrigley, goal; P Fairnie and A Ashworth, backs; J Slater, W Charnock, and C Stock, halfs; J W Hill, S Davies, H Heyworth, T Royds, and J Stott, forwards. Reserve 1st, G Lee.

SECOND DIVISION.
LARKHILL v. WOODFIELD.—At Clarksfield.
Woodfield: P Wolstencroft, goal; J Wolstencroft and Naylor, backs; Wrigley, Cox, and Aspinall, halfs; Hall, Jackson, Clark, Wood, and Wilde, forwards. Reserves, Warwick and Newton.

PINE VILLA v. ALEXANDRA RESERVES.—On Berry's Field. Referee, Mr. Clegg.
Villa: A N Other, goal; Green and Marsden, backs; Griffiths, Livesey, and A N Other, halfs; Hermon, Joe Sankey, Joe Stafford, Rowley, and Jack Stafford, forwards.
Alexandra: T Farr, goal; Beckett and E Fairnie, backs; A Walsh, H Travis, and H Slater, halfs; S Bradbury, A Lees, J Shepherd, R Woodhead, F Parker, Thornton, Jones, and Halstead, forwards.

Alexandra, four goals; Pine Villa, three goals. At Pitses. Taylor kicked off for Alexandra, and the Villa soon pressed, Clayton scoring within ten minutes. Owing to smart passing they scored two more goals before the interval. Caffrey restarted for the Villa, and the game ruled somewhat even till about twenty minutes from the finish, when Alexandra completely outplayed their opponents, Taylor scoring three goals and Wroe another.

The Pine Mill, Oldham, where our story begins . . .

In the beginning...

In 1897, the licensee of the Featherstall and Junction Hotel was one John Garland and it is to this man that all who now enjoy Oldham Athletic football should turn to offer their thanks.

It was John Garland and his son, Fred, who, together with a few of the Junction's regulars, decided to form a football club.

While this was nothing unusual — and still isn't today — no other pub team in the area has had quite the same startling success as John Garland's.

Keen they certainly were, for they went out and rented a ground at the nearby Pine Mill and under its foreboding shadows, Pine Villa was born.

Their first season of competitive football, 1897-98, began in the second division of the Oldham Junior League — and from that humble beginning they never stopped moving upwards.

By the end of the season they were top of the table with 24 points, one more than Greenacres Lads.

Pine Villa moved on to pastures new, the first division, with high hopes, and their enthusiasm was well rewarded.

Dogged all the way by their old rivals, Greenacres, the Villa continued to thrive. At the end of the season they had 25 points, only one less than the champions — none other than Greenacres.

Still, Villa's efforts in those first two seasons can only be described as creditable in the least.

During these two seasons, however, there was another Oldham team whose performances had been anything but creditable.

Oldham County were a professional team who played at Sheepfoot Lane. After only one season they found themselves in great financial trouble and went into liquidation.

One of the liquidators was George Elliot and he was interested in what he saw at Pine Villa. He suggested that they make use of County's ground and the scene was set for the red and white shirts of Villa to disappear and for a new team to make an entrance.

OLDHAM ATHLETIC ASSOCIATION FOOTBALL CLUB.
MANCHESTER ALLIANCE JOINED.

Pine Villa, having taken to the ground previously held by the Oldham County Football Club, have decided to alter their name, and in future they will be known under the title of the Oldham Athletic Association Football Club. A general meeting of the members was held on Tuesday night, at the Black Cow Inn, Burnley Lane, Chadderton, principally for the purpose of deciding what league the club should become associated with during the ensuing season. Mr. G. T. Elliot (president) occupied the chair, and there was a good attendance of members. The secretary read the minutes of a general meeting held on the 4th inst., at which it was resolved that the name of the club be as above stated; also that the terms as arranged between the secretary and Mr. Elliot for the Oldham Athletic Ground be accepted. The minutes further stated that Mr. Elliot had been elected president and Mr. S. Taylor vice-president, and that members' fees for the season be 3s. It was also decided that all players should be free from paying contributions. The minutes were adopted, and a committee consisting of Messrs. H. Lees, G. Worsley, F. Marsland, F. Brooks, J. Schofield, J. Bell, W. Taylor, and F. Sinkinson, which had previously only been elected *pro tem*, was appointed to manage the affairs of the club for the ensuing year.—The Chairman, in introducing the question as to which league the club should join, said that, as they were all aware, the club last season was affiliated with the Oldham Junior League. The committee had now received an invitation from the Manchester and District Alliance to join that combination. The Oldham Junior League consisted of only nine clubs, whilst the Manchester Alliance consisted of at least fourteen, which would mean five more home matches than the former. Moreover, the Manchester Alliance clubs would draw better gates than the Oldham Junior League clubs, and they would have a better opportunity of distinguishing themselves. The winners of the championship of the league received a silver cup and gold medals, and the runners-up silver medals with gold centres—Ultimately it was unanimously decided to join the Manchester Alliance, and the appointment of the club's representative on the league was left in the hands of the committee. Mr. J. Finney was appointed as the club's referee on the league.

The Oldham Athletic Club, previously known as Pine Villa, opened its season under very auspicious circumstances on the new ground. Berry's A team was entertained, and some exciting play was witnessed, the home eleven only gaining the verdict by a goal to nil. The Athletic team contains players of much promise, and they gave a good exposition of the game. They should make themselves felt in their new surroundings by a little practice.

OLDHAM ATHLETIC
Association Football Club.
SEASON 1899-1900.

President: GEO. T. ELLIOT, ESQ.
Vice-Presidents:
F. ALDRED, ESQ.   DR. HASLOP,
H. CAFFERY, ESQ.   DR. CLEGG,
H. ROWLEY, ESQ.   DR. HEARNE,
A. HOWARTH, ESQ.   A. RAYNOR, ESQ.
T. JACQUES, ESQ.   J. WINTERBOTTOM, ESQ.
Committee:
MR. G. WORSLEY,   MR. J. BELL,
  " F. BROOKS,   "   H. LEES,
  " W. TAYLOR,   "   F. SINKINSON,
  " F. MARSLAND,   "   J. SCHOFIELD,
MR. H. GARLAND.
Secretary:
MR. W. PLATT, 5, Cambridge Street, Werneth
Fin. Secretary:
MR. H. LEES, 45, Cottam Street, Oldham.
Treasurer:
MR. G. LIVSEY, 395, Burnley Lane.
Headquarters:
Willow Bank Hotel, Featherstall Road.
Club Colours:
Red and White Shirts, Dark Blue Knickers.
This Card admits to all Football Matches during Season (except Cup Ties).

NOT TRANSFERABLE.

NOTE. Should any person use this card but

Mr. R. NUTTALL.

same to be forfeited without question.

MEMBERS' CARD
1899 - 1900

FIXTURES (Manchester Alliance).

DATE.	CLUB.	GR'ND.
1899		
Sept. 2	Berry's Association	Home
" 9	*Nook Rovers	Home
" 16	*Hollins Ramblers	Home
" 23		
" 30	*Lower Crumpsall	Home
Oct. 7	Manchester All. Cup 1st R'nd.	
" 14	*Knutsford	Away
" 21	*Heathfield	Home
" 28		
Nov. 4		
" 11		
" 18	*Nook Rovers	Away
" 25	*Springfield	Home
Dec. 2	Manchester All. Cup 2nd R'nd.	
" 9	*Berry's Reserve	Home
" 16	*Moston	Away
" 23		
" 30	*Hollins Ramblers	Away
1900		
Jan. 6	*Heathfie'd	Away
" 13		
" 20	*Moston	Home
" 27	*Springfield	Away
Feb. 3	*Berry's Reserve	Away
" 10	*Manc'r. All. Cup Semi-Final	
" 17	*Lower Crumpsall	Away
" 24	Hollins Ramblers	Away
Mar. 3	Springfield	Away
" 10	Hollins Ramblers	Home
" 17	Manchester All. Cup Final	
" 24	Springfield	Home
" 31	Moston	Home
Apl. 7	*Knutsford	Home
" 14	Moston	Away
" 21		
" 28		

* Alliance Matches

FIRST FIXTURES
1899 - 1900

Top: Oldham Chronicle, Wednesday July 19th 1899

Oldham Chronicle, Saturday ◄ September 9th 1899

"THE TEAM FROM A TOWN OF CHIMNEYS"

FOOTBALL.

The Pine Villa A. F. C. has secured the Oldham Athletic Grounds, and the club will be known in future as the Oldham Athletic Club.

Oldham Standard, Monday July 10th 1899

Enter Athletic

Just as Pine Villa had been born among the beer and skittles of the Featherstall and Junction Hotel, so Oldham Athletic carried on the tradition and came into the world at the Black Cow Inn on Burnley Lane, Chadderton, July 4, 1899.

George Elliot became the first president, Mr. F. Marland the treasurer and Mr. W. Platt the secretary.

Like any other infant Oldham Athletic had teething problems, but George Elliot and his committee dug deep into their own pockets several times to keep the club alive.

Despite this, they never thought of giving up and, having applied to join the Manchester Alliance League, they collected a good team of amateurs around them and set off with a vengeance.

Their first match of 1899-1900 was against Berry's Reserves, the second team of Berry's Blacking Works, Blackley, Manchester.

That first-ever Oldham Athletic team was:— Johnson, Dickinson (captain), Kelly, Charnock, Cox, Heyworth, Sankey, Brooks, Whitmore, Ramsden, Jones.

The "Latics" as they were nicknamed, won their first match and in their first season maintained the tradition of Pine Villa by finishing as runners-up in the League.

They had truly answered an article which appeared in the local newspaper, the *Oldham Chronicle*, shortly after their formation, which commented:—

'It is really surprising that a first-rate Association Football Club cannot be run in Oldham for there is plenty of room for one without crippling the leading rugby club and, in addition, there is a demand for good soccer.'

With their taste for success hardly satisfied, the Latics were now ready for bigger game and the following season joined the Manchester League.

Their first match was at home to Middleton and drew a sizeable crowd to set the trend for encouraging shows of support for the Oldham side.

"THE TEAM FROM A TOWN OF CHIMNEYS"

However, halfway through the season came a setback. Trouble arose with the ground landlords over the rent and terms of lease. No compromise could be reached and the only answer was for Latics to find another ground to play on.

Hudson Fold enclosure was chosen but the move proved to be a costly one. A stand had to be erected for members and for a time it seemed the task would be too great and that the club would go down. However, plenty of willing helpers were found and, although a struggle, the job was finished and the club kept alive.

In all, the Latics spent four years in the Manchester League and for much of the time the club's energies were devoted to fund raising, with schemes such as summer band concerts and factory and workshop competitions all bringing in money.

The frantic off-field efforts didn't seem to disturb Athletic's traditionally high standards of football and in 1902-03 they won the Manchester Junior Cup.

The foundations were laid for success, but the ambitions of the eager committee were nowhere near satisfied.

OLDHAM ATHLETIC 1902/03
(Winners of the Manchester Junior Cup)

T. WORSLEY . R. NUTTALL . H.M. JONES . J. STAFFORD *(Capt.)* . G. WORSLEY . R. NEWTON . J. HILL . A. TETLOW . H. CHADWICK . G. TRAVIS
T. WHEAL . R. BRIERLEY . G. GASKELL . H. BOOTH . J. WINTERBOTTOM . E. BUCKLEY . F. HOLT . J. SCHOFIELD . J. BELL
J. HULME . J. SANKEY . W. PEPPER . D. McDERMOTT . P. MOULT

League status

Season 1904-05 saw a period of further advancement with Athletic securing a place in the "B" Division of the Lancashire Combination.

Alderman J. Crossman took over the presidency from George Elliot while Mr. W. C. Brierley became chairman and Mr. J. Schofield secretary.

Promotion was again achieved at the first attempt and, in retrospect, it is clear that this was the time when the club began to have serious thoughts about League soccer.

Christmas time of the following season saw two major, important decisions taken.

The first was to engage Jimmy Hanson as trainer and the second was to form the club into a Limited Liability Company with a capital of £2,000 divided into 10-shilling shares.

Mr. E. Thompson, an accountant, was appointed secretary pro tem and the new company was floated at his offices in Union Street, Oldham.

It was at this time that J. W. Lees Brewery, from nearby Middleton Junction, began an involvement with the club.

They leased out the present site of the ground at Sheepfoot Lane to the club — and that was the beginning of an association which has blossomed to this day when J. W. Lees are now the major shareholders.

The first directors of the new company were Messrs. J. W. Mayall, A. Barlow, S. Carter, A. Pellowe, W. Shone, T. Johnson, H. M. Jones and A. Tetlow.

During the summer months other influential Oldham business men were invited to join the board and before long, Alderman J. Grime, W. Heath, H. Cooper, T. Hilton, G. Morton and C. E. Sutcliffe had enlisted in the club's cause.

A referee from Waterford, Mr. David Ashworth, became the club's first manager and, with results going well in the Lancashire Combination, a determined campaign began to get Athletic in the Football League.

OLDHAM ATHLETIC 1905/06
(*Lancashire Combination 'A' Division*)

Every town now visited by Oldham supporters began to boast small stickers declaring "Oldham wants League football".

More legitimately, canvassing of all the League clubs began to secure votes for their annual election. So promising were their reactions that success seemed certain for Athletic.

However, when it came to the day of the voting, Athletic were in for a rude surprise. They missed election by just one vote.

Undeterred, they embarked on the 1906-07 season in the Combination in high spirits. A fine side was gathered together, including five players retained from the previous season — Fay, Hodson, Shadbolt, Stafford and Wright.

It was in this season that a memorable half-back line of Fay, Walders and Wilson emerged and, if they couldn't succeed in winning votes, Athletic certainly could succeed at football.

They ended the season winning the Combination championship and managed to survive all the qualifying rounds to reach the second round proper of the F.A. Cup.

Followers of the game began to take notice of Oldham Athletic.

All the celebrating was tinged with sadness, however, as a highly successful season closed with Athletic amazingly winning fewer votes than the previous year at the Football League election.

They say every cloud has a silver lining — and so it proved for Athletic.

Resigned to spending another season in the Combination, Athletic suddenly found their dreams of League soccer turned into reality.

Sadly, it was at the expense of Burslem Port Vale who were forced to resign from the Second Division because of financial troubles.

Into the Second Division for the start of season 1907-08 in place of Burslem, came Oldham Athletic. By default it may have been — but nobody really cared.

It is incredible to think that only ten years earlier, John Garland and his son Fred had held that fateful first meeting to start a football team in the Featherstall and Junction Hotel.

Who could have guessed that in just one decade the embryo that was Pine Villa would hatch into a team preparing for their first match in Division Two of the Football League?

The Great Adventure was about to begin.

OLDHAM ATHLETIC 1906/07)
(Lancashire Combination Champions)
FAY . HODSON . SLATER . D. WALDERS . WILSON . DAW
SHADBOLT . WALDERS . HANCOCK . ASHWORTH *(Manager)* . BRUNTON . RAMSEY . STAFFORD

OLDHAM ATHLETIC 1907/08
HANSON *(Trainer)* . HODSON . FAY . SHUFFLEBOTTOM . HEWITSON . HAMILTON . STAFFORD
KELLY . HESHAM . DODDS . WALDERS . HANCOCK . WILSON . SWARBRICK

The Big Match

As reality replaced the euphoria which surrounded Athletic's admission to the League, it began to dawn on the club directors that, as well as they had done in the Combination, the side would need to be strengthened considerably to meet the increased demands of the Second Division.

Two of the now defunct Burslem Port Vale side, Hamilton and Dodds, had already joined the Latics and both proved to be excellent acquisitions.

But, more were needed and the directors had no hesitation in giving manager David Ashworth the princely sum of £20 with instructions to buy a winning team.

With the cash he signed Swarbrick, Shufflebottom, Newton, Hesham, Waites and Bottomley — and still gave the directors 2/6d change!

So, Athletic were ready for their onslaught on the Second Division.

Their historic first game was away to Stoke City and, on the face of it, it was to be one of the mis-matches of the season.

Little Athletic, unheard of only a few years previously, against a Stoke side which had spent the majority of its professional life in the First Division. It was lambs to the slaughter — but somebody forgot to tell the lambs!

Athletic's team on that momentous day was:— Hewitson, Hodson, Hamilton, Fay, Walders (captain), Wilson, Ward, Dodds, Newton, Hancock and Swarbrick.

The *Oldham Evening Chronicle* of September 7, 1907, tells the story of the big match.

'Oldham had an exceptionally large following who were very enthusiastic and had travelled on full or half-day trips from Clegg Street at eight o'clock and mid-day respectively.

The Victoria ground looked in splendid condition. Athletic were first to enter the field, being loudly cheered by their supporters. Walders won the toss and elected to play towards the town goal.

Watkins commenced the game for Stoke, the ball going out to the left, but Fay robbed Coxon and sent into touch.

"THE TEAM FROM A TOWN OF CHIMNEYS"

FIRST SEASON IN FOOTBALL LEAGUE, PROGRAMME V BURNLEY, NOVEMBER 1907

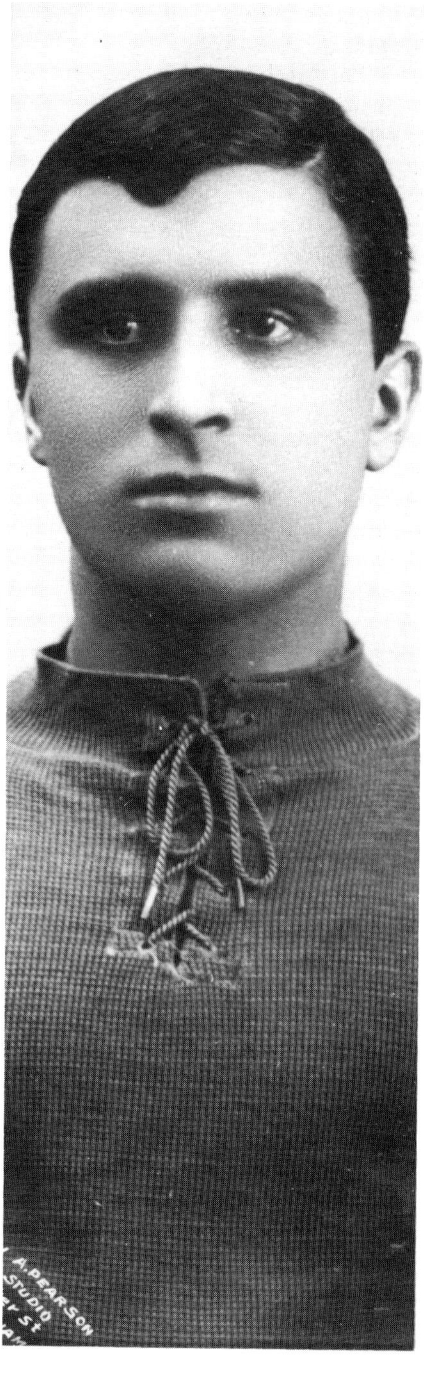

W. DODDS, scorer of Athletic's first ever Football League goal ▶

Play was getting very exciting, Walders clearing a very dangerous ball.

The Oldham forwards were going nicely, but off-side spoiled them. Swarbrick put in a good run which Burgess checked. A moment later, Box just managed to clear from Hancock.

The home forwards forced a corner which was well put into Fielding who found the net, but off-side marked the effort.

The Potters were attacking in vigorous fashion and the Oldham defence stood out splendidly.

Athletic forwards paid a visit to the other end but Mollinoaux drove them back. Stoke forwards, who were showing great cleverness, bore down on the Oldham goal many times, Wilson stopping a fine rush.

Stoke now changed the tempo and forced a corner, but nothing came of it. A moment later, Holford got in a terrific drive just grazing the crossbar.

Ward and Dodds tried to make headway on the right but Mollinoaux stopped them. They came again, however, and the ball going across to Hancock, that player drove in across to Dodds who beat Box with a clinking shot. The goal evoked loud cheers from the Oldham followers.

On play being resumed, the Potters were first to get away but found the Oldham backs fully alive, Hodson playing grandly.

The Athletic forwards were showing grand combination and the home goal had a miraculous escape from Dodds, who sent a shot just behind the goal.

The game was being hotly contested, both teams putting in all they knew. Oldham were more than holding their own and there was great excitement.

Play went wide, Newton, who had been playing well, tested Box with a grand drive which he cleared nicely.

Oldham now pressed hotly, Wilson sending over. The play was very keen, Hancock and Dodds having hard lines.

Half-time: Stoke 0 — Oldham Athletic 1.

The attendance had increased to about 12,000 when Newton opened the second half for Athletic. Coxon, on the home left, soon tried to get away but Fay pulled him up. From the free kick, Baldsley placed well and Watkins, rushing in, completely beat Hewitson, levelling the scores.

On resuming they quickly returned and Sturgess shot wide. Athletic now worked their way down the left, this time Sturgess cleared.

In the next few minutes, Newton headed Athletic into the lead and, in the final minute, Dodds capped a fine individual performance by shooting past Box for the third goal.

Final Score: Stoke 1 — Oldham Athletic 3.

"THE TEAM FROM A TOWN OF CHIMNEYS"

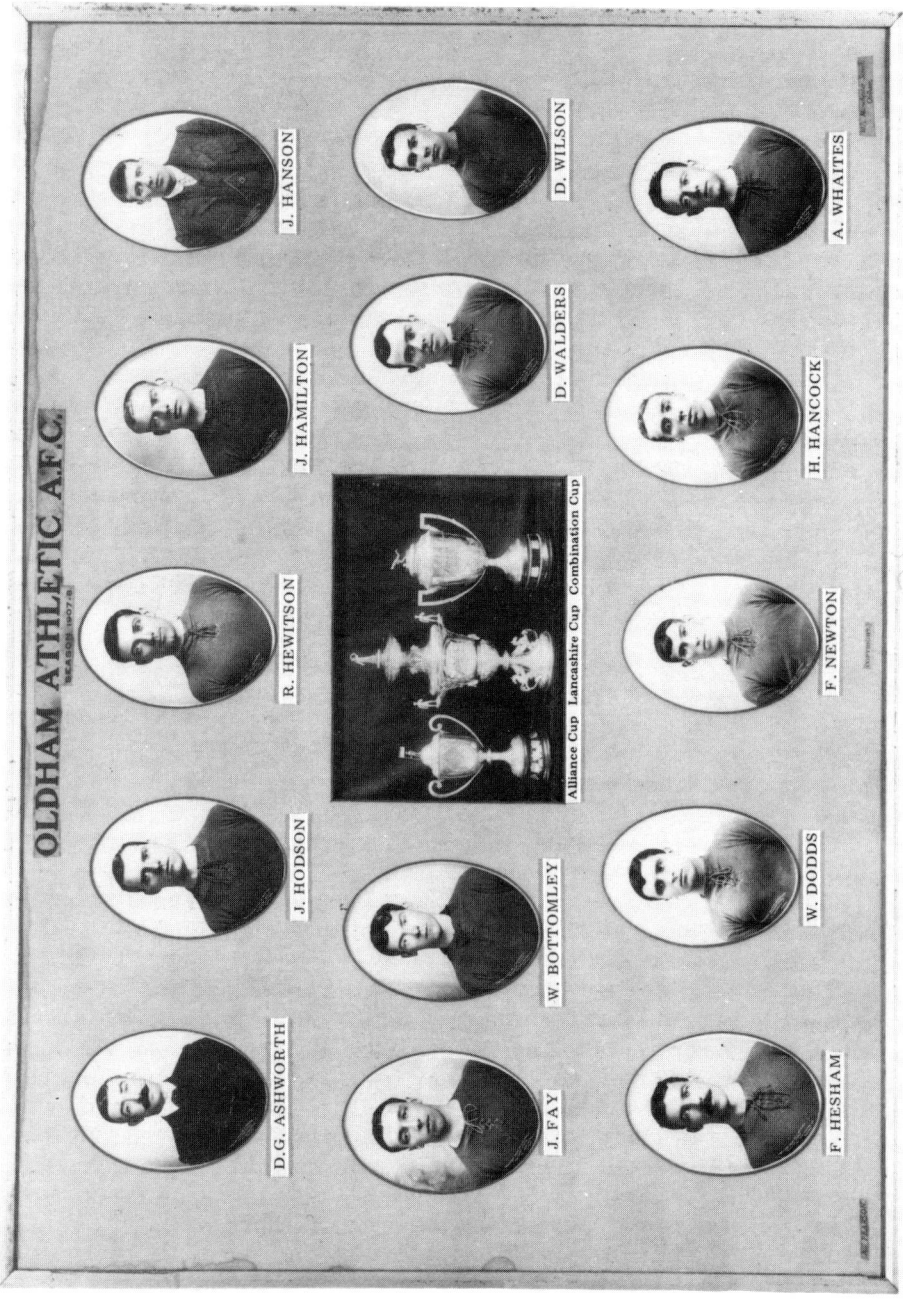

Rising Stars

It was, without doubt, the most sensational result of the day. But this inexperienced Latics side, which soon earned the nickname of the "Babes", proved it was no flash in the pan.

The fans in the newly-erected North Stand witnessed a string of stirring performances that season as the Latics made a brave bid to become the first side in history to win promotion to the First Division in one season of League football.

A glance at the top three teams in the Second Division (two promoted) at the end of the season shows just how close Athletic came to achieving the seemingly-impossible.

SECOND DIVISION
1907-08
Top three positions

1. Bradford City .... 54 points
2. Leicester Fosse .... 52 points
3. Oldham Athletic .... 50 points

Still, the Latics had made a memorable start to League life. And there was consolation in that season in the shape of the Lancashire Cup which Athletic won by beating Preston North End in the final at Hyde Road — then the home of Manchester City.

Clearly, Athletic's directors now had the smell of "the big time" in their nostrils and, during the close season, again instructed manager Ashworth to engage the services of more top players.

The players chosen both came from Newcastle United, centre-forward Will Appleyard and inside-forward Finlay Speedie. Both arrived with enormous reputations but, sadly, neither lived up to their advance billing. Speedie was eventually transferred to Bradford Park Avenue and Appleyard was politely shown the door at the end of the season.

In fact, Athletic's second season in Division Two was bitterly disappointing. Only 40 points were won to fuel the cynical idea that the first year had, indeed, been a flash in the pan and the Latics had now found their true level.

"THE TEAM FROM A TOWN OF CHIMNEYS"

OLDHAM'S TRIUMPH OVER HULL CITY

By their brilliant victory over Hull City on Saturday, Oldham Athletic ensured their election into the premier division of the League. The illustrations convey some idea of the strenuousness of the game. (1) Headwork by Walders (Oldham) from a corner by Broad. (2) An anxious moment for Oldham — Matthews fisting away. (3) A clearance by Roughley (Hull).

(Thompsons Weekly News 29/4/1910)

If anything, the early results the following season, 1909-10, merely strengthened that belief. On October 9, the Latics were bottom of the Second Division with just two points from their opening five matches.

With the club's reserve team also bottom of the Lancashire Combination at this stage, you could have cut the gloom with a knife.

But fate was waiting in the wings to write one of the most incredible chapters in Athletic's story.

By Christmas of 1909, spirits had lifted a little with 17 points now obtained from as many matches.

Incidentally, it was at this time that the club appointed its first permanent secretary — Mr. Robert Mellor who took up his duties on January 1, 1910.

On the playing side, the Latics went from strength to strength. Jimmy Fay was moved out of defence to bolster the attack and the results were remarkable. In best "Roy of the Rovers" style, Jimmy banged home 26 goals in 21 matches, including a hat-trick at Barnsley which earned him a new overcoat from a local tailor.

The misery of those early results was now forgotten as Athletic soared up the Second Division table. Another 21 League games were played with only one defeat — at Stockport County on Good Friday.

And so they arrived at the heart-stopping last match of the season, against Hull City.

Before the game, Hull had 53 points for second place in the table behind Manchester City. Athletic were third with 51 points but a vastly superior goal average.

Hull knew that a win or draw would see them promoted. For Athletic it was win or bust — and 29,083 fans crowded Boundary Park to witness the dramatic final act.

THE "BABES" NO LONGER

DAME FOOTBALL: Good gracious, how that baby's grown!
(Manchester Evening News 26/3/1910)

Oldham Athletic are still rising.
(Manchester Chronicle 2/4/1910)

"THE TEAM FROM A TOWN OF CHIMNEYS"

To add extra spice to the drama, Derby County were playing at West Brom that day and, if they won, they would finish the season with one more point than Athletic, even if the Oldhamers won.

The Boundary Park result was never in serious doubt as Athletic, captained by Alec Downie, ran out comfortable winners by 3-0.

Now players, officials and fans held their breath waiting for the Derby result.

Finally it came . . . West Brom 0 . . . Derby County 0.

ATHLETIC HAD WON PROMOTION ON GOAL AVERAGE AND BOUNDARY PARK ERUPTED IN A COLOURFUL SEA OF REJOICING.

The players hardly had time to finish their baths before they were called out with trainer Jimmy Hanson to acknowledge the acclaim of the delighted fans.

The Manchester City airship, steered by Lot Jones, was the first to accomplish the flight into the First Division. Was much speculation to-day whether Derby County, Oldham Athletic, or Hull City will secure the remains.

(Manchester Evening News 30/4/1910)

The directors and players are supposed to have adjourned later to the Reform Club where tea was taken. But it's a fair bet that there were stronger beverages than tea that memorable night!

Just how desperately close the finish to the promotion race had been can be judged from the final figures of the leading teams:—

SECOND DIVISION 1909-10 Final positions

	P	W	L	D	F	A	Pts
1. Manchester City	38	23	7	8	81	40	54
2. Oldham Athletic	38	23	8	7	79	39	53
3. Hull City	38	23	8	7	80	46	53
4. Derby County	38	22	7	9	72	47	53

Athletic had achieved their ambition by the skin of their teeth — and after only three seasons in the League, at that. It wasn't too far removed from the days of Pine Villa either. Even by the less demanding standards of the early 1900's it was a phenomenal rise.

Behind the scenes at Boundary Park, a number of changes had been made on the board during the previous four years. Messrs. Sutcliffe, Cooper and Parker had resigned as directors but the board had been strengthened by such well-known local figures as Messrs. L. R. Stanton and J. W. Mayall.

Mr. William Heath had taken over as chairman from John Grime and Mr. T. W. Hilton resigned to be replaced by Mr. C. H. Pickford.

This then, was the position at Athletic as they prepared to launch their challenge on the elite of the Football League.

Practically all the players who had helped win promotion were retained, although it was clear that some of them, like the admirable skipper Alec Downie, were nearing the end of their career.

Only two new players were secured as Athletic prepared for life in the top flight — inside-right J. McTavish from Falkirk and goalkeeper Hugh McDonald from Woolwich, Arsenal.

But, could Oldham Athletic, a club still in its infancy, possibly hope to compete with the elite of soccer.

Oldham Athletic still fancy their chance of promotion.
(Manchester Chronicle 2/4/1910)

D.G.A. (to the trainer): You seem to have freshened him up Jimmy. What's his chances for the First Division Stakes?
Hanson (the trainer): Oh, I think he's the pick of the outsiders.
(Manchester Chronicle 12/3/1910)

Oldham Athletic are waiting for Hull and Derby to make a slip.
(Manchester Chronicle 16/4/1910)

"THE TEAM FROM A TOWN OF CHIMNEYS"

Oldham Athletic have been waiting since Monday to avenge themselves on Glossop. Have they done it?
(Manchester Chronicle 1/1/1910)

Cook made it hot for the City forwards at Oldham
(Manchester Chronicle 20/11/1909)

D.G.A. (to the trainer): You seem to have freshened him up Jimmy. What's his chances for the First Division Stakes?
Hanson (the trainer): Oh, I think he's the pick of the outsiders.
(Manchester Chronicle 12/3/1910)

Athletic's Promotion Year 1909/10
as seen through the eyes of local cartoonists...

AN AS(S)TONISHING MISHAP.

Oldham Athletic upset Manchester City's apple-cart at Oldham last Saturday.
(Manchester Chronicle 20/11/1909)

"THE TEAM FROM A TOWN OF CHIMNEYS"

"Now which way are you going, David — up or down?"
(Oldham Athletic are struggling to get in the First Division).
Manchester Evening News 23/4/1910

Ye "Mariners" of Grimsby,
From off the Eastern Shore,
Your one goal would have won the match,
But Oldham scored four more.
(Manchester Chronicle 26/3/1910)

Toward, toward a goal always — at Oldham last Saturday.
(Manchester Evening News 26/3/1910)

Oldham Athletic are waiting for Hull and Derby to make a slip.
(Manchester Chronicle 16/4/1910)

Fay and Toward are the crack marksmen of Oldham Athletic.
(Manchester Evening News 26/3/1910)

Jimmy Fay performed the hat-trick for Oldham Athletic against Barnsley.

Oldham Athletic have not lost a League match this year.
(Manchester Chronicle 26/2/1910)

Cook is now taking an enforced holiday.
(Manchester Chronicle 29/1/1910)

It is hoped that Mr. D.G. Ashworth, the Oldham Athletic manager, will have hooked the first class centre forward in time for the Cup-tie with Aston Villa.
(Manchester Chronicle 18/12/1909)

"THE TEAM FROM A TOWN OF CHIMNEYS"

MONDAY, NOVEMBER 15 1909.

Manchester City Succumb at Oldham

One of City's goal chances.

Cook scored from a penalty at the second attempt.

Eadie headed clear from under Newton.

Kelso curbed Miller's speed.

Hodson was too heavy for Conlin.

"THE TEAM FROM A TOWN OF CHIMNEYS"

The Big Time

It was clear from their first-ever match in the top flight that Athletic were not going to be overawed. They secured a creditable 1-1 draw against Aston Villa at Villa Park.

The historic first home game in Division One took place the following week — September 10, 1910, when the visitors to Boundary Park were Newcastle United, one of the strongest teams in the country and the F.A. Cup holders at the time.

It was a glorious day. Clear blue skies and warm sunshine brought the fans out in their thousands with 34,000 crowded into Boundary Park to watch the kick-off. That "gate" remained a club record for a home League match until April 1930, when 45,120 saw a Second Division game against Blackpool. With the crowd limit long-since reduced, that is a record which will never be bettered.

The notes in the official programme for the Newcastle game seem to reflect the atmosphere of the times:—

'The long sought for honour has at last been attained. The

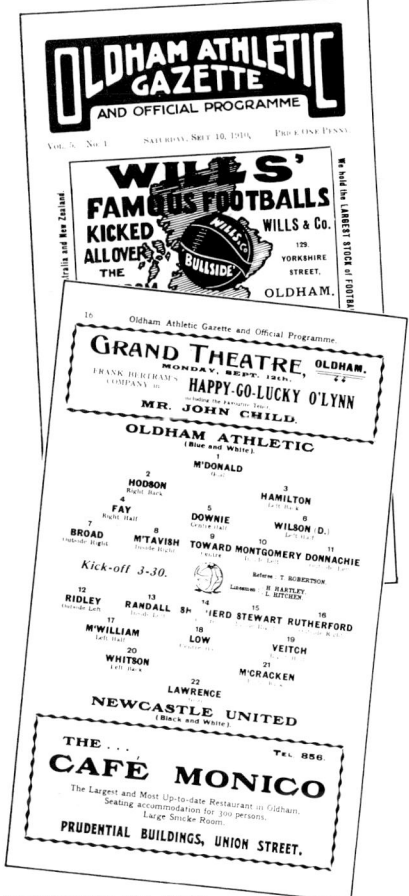

SEPTEMBER 10th 1910
V NEWCASTLE UNITED PROGRAMME
FROM THE FIRST HOME GAME IN DIVISION 1

OLDHAM ATHLETIC.

Their Debut in the First Division.

Probably the career of no club during the forthcoming season will be watched with greater interest than that of Oldham Athletic, who now, in the fourth season of their existence as a combination to be reckoned with, find themselves among the elect of the football world. Last season they made football history; the sensational circumstances of their ascent to the First Division, after a gallant struggle, and against what at one time seemed overwhelming odds, will be fresh in the memory of all who take an interest in the game.

How they will fare in first-class company is a matter about which the writer will venture no prediction. It may be said, however, that the directorate are sanguine, and, on the face of it, there would seem to be ample justification for their optimism. The team has been strengthened by the

J. M'TAVISH.

addition of several players of established reputation, while others who show decided promise have also been secured during the past few months. The general opinion, however, appears to be that the directors will be well advised in relying, at least for the opening matches, on the team who did so well last season, and this is probably the course that will be pursued.

SEASON TICKETS SELLING WELL.

That the club will do well financially is regarded as certain; indeed, it is anticipated that, in this respect, the ensuing season will be conspicuously the most successful the club has yet experienced. In this connection an eloquent fact may be mentioned. Last year, up to the beginning of the season, the number of guinea tickets sold was about 300; this year, up to August 9, the number sold was 530.

Among the "captures" are Hugh M'Donald, late goalkeeper for Woolwich Arsenal; J. M'Tavish, the Scotch international forward (inside right), late of Falkirk, and Alec Wilson, who has been secured from Preston North End, and who can play at either right or left half.

M'Donald has a big reputation, which it is hoped he will fully uphold with his new club. He is 23 years of age, stands 5ft. 11½in., and weighs 14 stone. M'Tavish is a class of player of whom much is expected. He is 23 years of age, stands 5ft. 8in., and turns the scales at about 11 stone. Alec Wilson, whose cleverness is undoubted, is a brother of David Wilson, another of Athletic's half-backs, and of Andy Wilson, who is one of Sheffield Wednesday's stalwarts. Alec is only 22, and he weighs about 11 stone 8lb., his height being 5ft. 8in.

The other new men are: Rowley (late of Farnworth Wednesday), age 20; height 5ft. 9½in.; weight 11 stone; Pilkington (Salford United), 20, 5ft. 9in., 10st. 9lb.; Muskett (Marsden, Yorkshire), 19, 5ft. 8½in., 11 stone; Brennan (Hollinwood United), 19, 5ft. 9in., 10st. 5lb. Rowley plays at centre half, Pilkington at inside right or centre forward; Muskett, who is an amateur, at outside left forward, and Brennan at half.

FULL LIST OF PLAYERS.

The club's players now are:—
Goalkeepers.—Matthews, M'Donald, Green.
Full-backs.—Cook, Hodson, Hamilton, Hope, Stafford.
Half-backs.—Downie, Fay, Walders, D. Wilson, Alec Wilson, Rowley, Bunting, Doughty, Brennan.
Forwards.—Broad, M'Tavish, Toward, Montgomery, Donnachie, Miller, Wolfenden, Pilkington, Muskett, Watts.

The dressing rooms on the ground have been enlarged, and the stands re-painted and otherwise improved. In addition the bottom bank has been tipped up, so that the enclosure is now capable of holding comfortably a crowd of 45,000.

Altogether, with the energetic Mr. Ashworth as manager, and Mr. R. Mellor as secretary, and with a committee whose activity and enthusiasm have been increased by recent happenings, the club may, we think, look forward to a satisfactory season with no little degree of confidence.

OLDHAM ATHLETIC 1910/11 *(First Season in Division One)*
WOLFENDEN . MATTHEWS . BUNTING . STAFFORD
A. GRIME *(Director)* . J. HANSON *(Trainer)* . FAY . WALDERS . MacDONALD . HODSON . HAMILTON . LAMB . WILSON
D.G. ASHWORTH *(Manager)* . BROAD . McTAVISH . TOWARD . DOWNIE . A. WILSON . MONTGOMERY . DONNACHIE . MILLER
ROWLEY . PILKINGTON . WATTS . COPE

J. Fay. (Oldham Athletic, 1910)

First Division of the Football League, so eagerly sought for by all Association followers has now among its select crowd, a new face . . . a young face . . . in fact, a mere baby.

Intentions and promises are easily said and made and don't always fulfil expectations. But we are entitled to say that now the Latics have joined the seniors, the directors intend to leave no stone unturned to keep up with them.

To face such a start at Aston Villa, on the beautifully-appointed enclosure at Villa Park is terror-striking enough to any young club and especially when it is followed by a visit from the cup winners — no less a team than Newcastle United.

But terror seemed to be far enough away from our boys that Saturday and they tackled the problem of the Villa in no half-hearted fashion. And let us say right here and now that Villa were mighty lucky to escape defeat.

Today we have another huge task and football of the brightest should be on show — such as only Newcastle can show when at their best. We have a sincere regard for Shepherd as a goal scorer, but for our sake we hope he has left his shooting boots on Tyneside.'

They certainly don't write programme notes like that any more. But, unfortunately, it was Newcastle who seemed to draw inspiration from the words as they ran out comfortable 2-0 winners.

However, that opening season in the First Division was far from disastrous for Athletic.

(Thompsons Weekly News 20/11/1909)
ATHLETIC V MANCHESTER CITY

Lyall again kept a splendid goal for Manchester City against Oldham. Our photo shows him dealing with a nasty shot.

◄ D.G. ASHWORTH *(Manager)*

34

"THE TEAM FROM A TOWN OF CHIMNEYS"

OLDHAM'S STALWART DEFENDERS.

MATTHEWS.

GALLAHER'S CIGARETTES.

ALEX. DOWNIE,
OLDHAM ATHLETIC, 1909-10.

Moffat, Hunter, Wilson, and Mr D. G. Ashworth.

Oldham Athletic's Mid-Line and Manager.

Broad. Montgomery. Jones. Woodger. Donnachie.

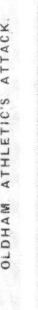

OLDHAM ATHLETIC'S ATTACK.

G. WOODGER
OLDHAM ATHLETIC F.C.

35

New players were signed, among them Walter Rowley, Evan Jones and George Woodger, the wily inside-forward signed from Crystal Palace who went on to prove himself one of the club's finest servants.

By the end of the campaign Athletic had proved they could hold their own in the top flight. Their 41 points gave them seventh place.

One major disappointment was in the F.A. Cup where Athletic surrendered tamely to Hull having disposed of Birmingham in a first-round replay.

One thing did puzzle the directors during the first season. Although the attractive opposition had kept the Boundary Park crowds at a healthy level, the "gate" receipts had taken an alarming nose-dive.

A member of the board was asked to investigate and posted himself outside the ground for the next home game. He discovered, to his amazement, that young men, clearly well beyond school-leaving age, were passing through the boys' entrance for half price.

For the next home match, the following notice appeared:

BOYS ENTER HERE
ADMISSION 3d

BOYS WITH WHISKERS —
TWO TURNSTILES UP
ADMISSION 6d

Receipts quickly soared back to their previous level.

At the end of the season, the club acknowledged the efforts of the players by arranging a tour abroad — something of a novelty in those days.

Sensational Football Offer to Oldham Clubs

Overcoats for Goals and Tries.

We will present one of our Famous Winter Overcoats to any Oldham Athletic Player who scores Two Goals in a single Second Division League match; or to any Rugby player who scores three tries in a Northern Rugby League game, at home or away, and, in addition, but at home matches only, we will present an extra Coat to any spectator the successful player brings along with him.

Our offer commenced on Saturday last, so it's more than probable that a few coats have already been won by Oldham Players and Spectators. We sincerely hope it is so. You see, our advertisement has to be written some days in advance; but any local successes can easily be traced through the columns of Saturday's "Evening Chronicle". We would once again remind our readers that no limit whatever is placed on the number of Overcoats which may be won by Oldham Players and Spectators. In fact, the more the merrier, say we, and that the Players will make full and good use of our offer is a thing we greatly desire.

STEWARTS

THE KING TAILORS,
83, Yorkshire-street, Oldham.

This was the first time an Athletic team had played on foreign soil and the players carried the town's colours with great credit on their three-week, six-match trip to Budapest and Vienna.

Hardly had the tour party arrived back in England than it was time to prepare for the new season, 1911-12. Again the directors were determined to

"THE TEAM FROM A TOWN OF CHIMNEYS"

ATHLETIC V SHEFFIELD WEDNESDAY, NOVEMBER 1911, Division One
Brothers Wilson (David of Athletic, left, and Andy of Wednesday) toss for choice of ends at Boundary Park

strengthen the team, to build on the foundations of the previous season.

Outside-right T. Marrison was signed from Nottingham Forest and Arthur Gee was engaged as a junior from Earlestown for a grand fee of £20. Clare Wilson came from Glossop, goalkeeper Ted Taylor from Balmoral and centre-half George Hunter became the clubs first four-figure signing when they paid a record of £1,250 to Aston Villa.

Hunter's signing was significant in a troubled season.

David Walders was nearing the end of his career and Athletic badly needed a new, dominant centre-half.

There had also been a sad break in that tried and trusted half-back line when Jimmy Fay left Latics for Bolton Wanderers after a disagreement about him continuing to live in Southport. The Fay-Walders-Wilson half-back line, which had been the backbone of the team, was broken and, by the time Hunter signed in January 1912, Athletic were next to bottom of the table with 13 points from 20 games.

Hunter's arrival duly strengthened the team and Athletic had pulled steadily away from the relegation zone by the time the season ended with Preston and Bury going down.

In the F.A. Cup, the Latics reached the third round where they were beaten by Everton at Boundary Park before a then club record cup crowd of 35,473.

Special mention must go to goalkeeper Ted Taylor who arrived from Balmoral as an amateur. He

J. FAY

D. WALDERS

D. WILSON

quickly made the position his own and went on to become an established England international — another feather in the cap of the First Division newcomers.

Without too many frights, Athletic had survived two seasons in the top flight and more new faces arrived at the club as they prepared for their third campaign. Oliver Tummon came from Gainsborough Trinity, Joe Walters from Aston Villa, W. Bradbury from Aberdare and Gilbert Kemp from Wallasey Rovers.

There was an air of confidence for season 1912-13 and that confidence was well-founded as Athletic finished in a comfortable mid-table position.

The side had never looked like winning the title, nor had relegation been a threat. On the face of it it was an average, run-of-the-mill season with little to live on in the memory.

However, nothing could be further from the truth. 1912-13 was to be remembered for years to come as the season when the Boundary Park "Babes" were just 90 minutes away from striding out in the F.A. Cup final.

E. TAYLOR
OLDHAM ATHLETIC

Athletic's goat mascot 1912/13, photographed before the semi-final at Blackburn

"THE TEAM FROM A TOWN OF CHIMNEYS"

THE LAST TURN.

THE OLDHAM ATHLETE: "And now Ladies and Gentlemen, before the curtain drops, I will conclude my performance by extracting a couple of league points from this ball of cotton.

ATHLETIC V MANCHESTER UNITED, APRIL 1913

"THE TEAM FROM A TOWN OF CHIMNEYS"

HOT STUFF FOR BOTH.

THE OLDHAM ATHLETE:—"Trotters Eh! Are they very hot, Walter?" 1st Waiter: "Not too hot for you, Sir."
THE BOLTON BOUNDER:—"H'm, Old Ham, not TOO tough I hope." 2nd Waiter: "Not too tough for you, Sir."

ATHLETIC V BOLTON WANDERERS, JANUARY 1913

THE OLDHAM ATHLETE'S BID FOR FAME.

OLDHAM SUPPORTER:—"Now whatever you do, keep your nerve, he's a big fellow certainly, but if you land him your 'Bradford City' punch, the points are ours."

ATHLETIC V BLACKBURN, DECEMBER 1913

"THE TEAM FROM A TOWN OF CHIMNEYS"

CHELSEA V ATHLETIC, SEPTEMBER 1912

Stage Manager: "Ladies and Gentlemen, the Oldham Athlete will now show you, using the Chelsea Pensioner as an example, how he put it across the Northern Champions."

THE ATHLETE'S EASTER EGG.

THE OLDHAM SUPPORTER: "Well you ought to be able to break through it, with that little lot."

Cup Glory

There was little indication of the drama to come when Athletic were drawn at home to neighbours Bolton Wanderers in the third-round of the F.A. Cup.

The match took place on a bitterly-cold Saturday in January, 1913, with a snow-covered ground making conditions tricky for both teams. However, the Latics adjusted better and won 2-0 with both goals from Oliver Tummon.

Fortune again favoured Athletic with a home draw against Nottingham Forest and that home advantage was put to full use as the Boundary Park lads romped home 5-1.

In the fifth round, Athletic were paired against Manchester United and it looked as if this would be the end of the road when the sides drew 0-0. at Boundary Park on February 22.

Four days later, Athletic made the short trip to Old Trafford and put up a tremendous, battling display to pull off the shock result so far in the competition . . . a 2-1 win with goals from Gee and Toward.

For reasons never fully explained, it was immediately after this match that Athletic transferred centre-half George Hunter to Chelsea for an undisclosed fee.

Hunter had been worth every penny of that record fee paid to Villa three years before and Latics fans were stunned at his departure. In fact, for years afterwards, many maintained that if he had not left the club at that time, the F.A. Cup would have been in the Boundary Park trophy cabinet that season.

So, minus Hunter, Athletic prepared for the sixth round . . . a tough trip to Goodison Park to face Everton.

Again the form books were upset as Athletic turned in a stirring rearguard action after Arthur Gee had "pinched" a goal. Matthews and Cook, in particular, were outstanding as Athletic reached the semi-finals for the first time in their history.

F.A. CUP SEMI-FINAL AT EWOOD PARK, BLACKBURN. ASTON VILLA V OLDHAM ATHLETIC 29TH MARCH 1913
Howard Matthews tips a header from Villa's Halse over Athletic's crossbar

"THE TEAM FROM A TOWN OF CHIMNEYS"

The four teams left in the competition were Athletic, Aston Villa, Sunderland and Burnley. Given a choice, Athletic would have settled for any side other than Villa who had slammed them 7-1 in the League on Boxing Day.

Sadly, you can't pick your opponents and it was Villa with whom Athletic were paired in the semis, the game to be played at Blackburn on March 29, 1913.

Clearly, Athletic were the underdogs. Even the venue seemed against them for they had travelled to Ewood Park only a week earlier and had lost 7-1 to Blackburn.

And, it seemed that many Latics fans had decided in advance that this was a lost cause. Three special trains were laid on from town with another in reserve. But it wasn't needed. Only one train was full and one of the others steamed out with only 50 people on board.

One of the reasons for the poor turnout was probably the early time of departure. Remember, most men still had to work on Saturday mornings, but only one of the trains left after noon.

As the *Oldham Chronicle* pointed out: "There was no occasion for the trains to be timed so early for the last of them reach the destination an hour and three-quarters before the match was due to start which is an unnecessarily long spell and is not in the interest of temperance."

It was also clear that there was little local interest in the match, with the Blackburn folk probably frightened off by the minimum admission charge of one shilling. As it was only 22,616 paid £1,560 to see the following teams take the field:

ATHLETIC: Matthews, Cook, Cope, Moffatt, Toward, Wilson, Tummon, Walters, Gee, Woodger, Donnachie.

ASTON VILLA: Hardy, Lyons, Weston, Barber, Harrop, Leach, Wallace, Halse, Hampton, Stephenson, Bache.

In setting the scene for the match, the *Oldham Chronicle* gravely informed readers that . . . "Athletic's mascot the goat, was in attendance but did not appear on the ground as the authorities had banned any such demonstration and the unfortunate beast was stabled in a cottage nearby."

From the start the game was a typical English cup-tie with the action coming thick and fast at both ends. However, the game was settled in the 32nd minute when Stephenson scored the only goal of the match for Villa.

Athletic had been far from disgraced and had the satisfaction of going out to the eventual winners of the F.A. Cup, Villa beating Sunderland 1-0 in a disappointing final watched by a crowd of 121,000 at the Crystal Palace.

A club still very much in its infancy had, in a few short years, forced its way into the First Division . . . come tantalisingly close to actually winning the League title . . . and now had got to within one game of the F.A. Cup final.

The future looked gloriously rosy.

Oldham Chronicle, Monday, March 21st. 1913

THE CUP SEMI FINALS

In the two semi-final ties in the English Cup competition on Saturday, only one goal was forthcoming, and that was scored by Aston Villa and had the effect of dismissing Oldham Athletic from the tournament. In the other match Burnley and Sunderland struggled for 90 minutes in the mud and rain at Sheffield without either side being able to score and they will replay on Wednesday at Birmingham. Sunderland have done very well financially out of the Cup ties and have certainly had their fill of drawn games and replays.

ATHLETIC'S HARD FIGHT

It was the prevailing impression that Aston Villa would beat Oldham Athletic in their tie at Blackburn, but the event proved that it was by no means a foregone conclusion. There was nothing between the two teams, and no superiority on the part of the winners. A draw or a win for Athletic would have been just as true a reflection of the game as was the narrow victory of the Midlanders. The much-vaunted brilliance of the Villa forwards was not seen and whether in working up the field or at close quarters, they were well held by the Oldham defenders. They got one goal, to be sure — and a right good one it was — but beyond that the losers were every bit as good as the winners. In the defensive parts of the team Athletic, although beaten were quite superior, and this in spite of the fact that Hodson was missing and that Cope was injured early on in the game, and suffered from it all through. Matthews gave another brilliant exhibition in goal, stopping shots of all kinds in the same electrifying style that he showed at Everton in the previous round. He was, I must confess, beaten once, but it was by a shot with which he had no chance whatever, it was from very close range, and was a hard low drive of which he probably never got a proper sight owing to the bunch of players in front of him. In such a scrimmage in the goalmouth, it is a thousand to one that if the backs are beaten the keeper will be, for he has no room to work in or time to see the ball. One cannot blame Matthews for the goal, and his work throughout the game was perfect. As to the forwards, they all did well but not well enough, inasmuch as they failed to score. Moreover, their attempts at scoring were not the best we have seen from them. The shots lacked sting, and Hardy had nothing like so difficult a task as Matthews. It was the only defect in the forward work, that they did not shoot dangerously enough, nearly all were long range shots with which any decent goalkeeper can deal if he gets a sight of the ball.

This comparative harmlessness of the shooting was the adverse criticism which could be made fairly on the Athletic team. Apart from it they played splendid football and stayed through the length of the fast hard game in a way which bore credit to their fit condition. It was

F.A. CUP SEMI-FINAL AT EWOOD PARK, BLACKBURN. ASTON VILLA V OLDHAM ATHLETIC 29TH MARCH 1913
A hard cross from Villa's Stephenson is missed by Wallace as Athletic's keeper Matthews watches anxiously

a great game for the spectators, even though goals were so scarce. The first half-hour or so was one of the fastest games I have ever witnessed, and the football in it was of a very high class, and one excellent feature about the whole match was the cleanness of the play. There were plenty of free kicks for what are technically called 'fouls' mostly trivial, accidental things, but there was a marked absence of the deliberate rough, 'dirty' work, such as tripping or kicking an opponent, which has been frequently known to mar these important matches. There might have been a strong suspicion against Halse in one of his numerous bouts with Cope when the forward raised his foot so high that when he missed the ball he kicked the full-back in the chest. It may not have been intentional, but it could easily have been avoided. Cope was the most unlucky man on the field and had to be attended to on about half-a-dozen occasions. Mr. Bamlett is to be congratulated on the way he controlled the game though some of his offside decisions were not in accord with the views of the crowd, which is, of course, nothing new.

In point of attendance the match was disappointing. Three special trains were run from Oldham and another was held in reserve but was not required. Only one of the trains was full, the earlier two being very badly patronised, one going out with only some 50 passengers. Probably the reason for this lack of patronage was the early time of departure. Only the third train went after noon, so that the working public could not avail themselves of them. There was no occasion for the trains to be timed so early, for the last of them reached the destination an hour and three-quarters before the match was due to start, which is an unnecessarily long spell, and is not in the interest of temperance. It was evident that there was no great local interest in the match, and the Blackburn people were probably kept away by the shilling minimum. The official figures are given as 22,616 spectators and £1,560 so that the experience is not very encouraging to the F.A. to take a semi-final to Ewood Park again for another eighteen years. That Athletic had the bigger following was abundantly proved by the welcome which greeted the entrance of the teams and the Oldham goalkeeper came in for a special little ovation on his own when he took up his position, whilst Mr. Bamlett's popularity was also marked by a round of applause.

Owing to Hodson having developed a bad cold a couple of days before it was deemed advisable not to play him, and Cope was called upon, Cook taking the right-back position, and Cope the left. Otherwise the Oldham representatives were at full strength, though Gee in the centre forward position was an experiment, and for one period he and Walters exchanged places. Aston Villa were able to put forward their strongest eleven on the field.

Athletic's mascot the goat, was in attendance but did not appear on the ground as the authorities had banned any such demonstration, and the unfortunate beast was stabled in a cottage nearby. This will, of *course, be set down by the superstitious as quite sufficient to account for Athletic's defeat. There were, however some blue and white umbrellas and a pierrot dressed in the Athletic colours, and these amused the crowd with their antics before the match. There was a big array of photographers and kinomatograph operators and at one stage of the game proceedings had to be stopped whilst a number of them removed themselves and their gear a little further back from the side of the goal.*

The weather was splendid there being very little wind, and the ground was in good condition though a little on the soft side. As the match progressed the sky became overcast and threatening, and the rain only just managed to hold off until the match was barely over, when it set in a business like fashion and made a night of it.

The wind seems to be funny at Ewood, for it happened just as on the previous Saturday, that it blew almost from the Darwen end of the start and very nearly boxed the compass before the match was over. Wilson won the toss and had the wind behind his men at the opening. Villa were the first to be dangerous and a shot from Bache struck the post, and the Oldham goal had one or two narrow escapes, after which Athletic got away and Moffat shot wide. Then Matthews had another busy few minutes the game being flashed from one goal to the other every moment and some beautiful play all went for nought until the game had been in progress thirty two minutes when a centre, right from

KISS-IN-THE-RING.

The choice of Miss English Cup has now been narrowed down to five, and there is much public concern as to who will be the person favoured to receive her embrace.

a corner was made by Wallace and Stephenson got the ball in a splendid position in front of the Athletic goal, and with a quick low shot he drove the ball just wide of Matthews who flung himself prone but could not reach it. This proved to be the only score. There was plenty of good work by both sides afterwards and each keeper had to stop shots galore, though those with which Matthews had to deal were generally more of a scoring character. There was nothing between the two teams to enable one to say that either was better than the other, though I must say that the Athletic forwards did not take the full advantage of all the openings which were offered and there were several cases where the pass might have been better tactics than the shot. The progress of the game was described in detail in our Saturday evening edition and we need not follow it through again but suffice it to say that there was not a dull moment from start to finish and right to the very last kick the issue was in doubt. It was good football throughout and I suppose it should be described as typical Cup football. There was not so much of the pretty individual work as we saw in the Everton match, but the general level was higher, and Athletic have no cause to be ashamed of their share of the game. They were beaten, but not disgraced as the common saying goes, and they have achieved a very high position, on which I hope they will improve next season. They have almost topped the league tables, and almost reached the Cup-final. Next season I hope to see them quite do both.

TEAMS:

Aston Villa: Hardy; Lyons; Weston; Barber; Harrop; Leach; Wallace, Halse; Hampton; Stephenson and Bache.

Oldham Athletic: Matthews; Cook; Cope; Moffat; Toward; Wilson; Tummon; Walters; Gee; Woodger and Donnachie.

Referee: H.S. Bamlett, Gateshead-on-Tyne. (Bamlett later became Athletic's team manager).

In the other semi-final at Sheffield, Sunderland and Burnley fought a goalless draw, the replay at Birmingham saw Sunderland win by 3-2.

The Cup-final, produced a win for Aston Villa by 1-0, Barber scoring direct from a corner kick in a disappointing final played at Crystal Palace. Attendance: 121,000.

Football Results

HALF-TIME
AND
FINAL SCORES
OF THE
OLDHAM

AND
OLDHAM ATHLETIC
MATCHES WILL IN FUTURE
BE EXHIBITED
IN THE WINDOW OF THE
"STANDARD" OFFICE EVERY SATURDAY.

WHAT HAPPENED AFTER LATICS WON THE CUP
'A Wembley Fantasy'

An April Friday dawned bright and crisp on the Lancashire side of the Pennines, and an unusually early curl of blue smoke coiled its way heavenwards from innumerable chimneys in an industrial town northeast of Manchester.

Thousands of happy faces greeted this pleasant morn so long anticipated. This was the day before the momentous occasion when the Blue Riband of English soccer was to be determined in the Metropolis, the day when the North always journeyed South to claim her undisputed right to battle for soccer's most coveted trophy. As the day wore on the chimney spirals were superseded by the vapours of interminable lanes of automobiles purring, chugging and puffing out their chorus of merriment in harmony with the morning. Soon Oldham would be silent, for the Latics were in the final and all Oldham was "going to town".

All the automobiles pointed their snouts to London laden with hilarious enthusiasts. No less spectacular were the scenes at Mumps as train followed train bulging with happy carefree followers (and families) on their way to London.

TEAM RUMOURS

Never had such things happened in Oldham before, the town was crazy. Rumour of course held sway, "So-and-so had the flu", and another team change was necessary, nevertheless everyone seemed confident of victory.

By noon the town was almost deserted except for a few sport-starved stragglers at traffic cross-roads ventilating their objections to an enforced holiday consequent on the industrial rupture. It is true that at points of vantage such as Rhodes Bank, Star Inn and Market Place, workmen were hurriedly erecting temporary arrangements for the public broadcast of the match on the following day.

Never before did workmen ply their craft with greater eagerness without counting their pay.

By 11 p.m. the various houses of entertainment and refreshment had disgorged their excited crowds of exuberant followers, who, mingling with the more dignified element swelled the throngs en route for the railway stations.

The souvenir men were coining money as the crowd clamoured for outsized rosettes and other symbols of their soccer faith.

IN THE MOOD

Everybody was in the mood and as the trains roared South beflagged in blue and white, Oldhamers sang themselves to sleep to the echoing wheels, "Two-three-FOUR, we want more! Two, Three FOUR, we want more!"

The following morning held its usual attractions in London, in an atmosphere somewhat subdued after the effervescence of the provincial merrymaking, emphasised no doubt by the enormity of the Metropolis. Nevertheless the 'Latics' were at Wembley and everyone had to know it.

For an hour before the kick-off strains of "Lassie from Lancashire" vied with "Owdham Edge bout' at" in an atmosphere of broad vowels and beaming faces. Blue and white balloons were being released every few minutes bearing cunning reference to the 'Latics' capabilities, and these hovered in the sunlight to taunt and tantalise the opposition until carried away by a friendly breeze probably back home to welcome victory.

It was all great fun culminating in a tumultuous cascade of applause as the Boundary Park boys tripped onto the field. The Green Final photographer worked feverishly, his camera shutters clicking like a morse tapper for the benefit of people at home.

The play was worthy of the occasion. At half-time a draw was a fitting result, three-quarter time arrived and there still was no score. The pace had been gruelling and none but the fittest could stand up to the ordeal. Then the "champagne air" of the Pennines swung the balance. Gradually the Latics gained the ascendancy and with loud and repeated requests to "Bang one in!" the call was answered five minutes from time.

HATS ALOFT

Pandemonium broke loose and never before have so many hats and caps been in the air at the same time, nor did their owners care much about their recovery. Nothing now mattered but the space of five minutes, a nerve-racking, heart-throbbing five minutes during which time ten thousand Oldham watches held by ten thousand trembling Oldham hands were eagerly scanned at least twenty times. The longest time has an ending, and as the final whistle blew the field was besieged by an army of wildly cheering Oldhamers intoxicated with indescribable joy as they carried their team shoulder high from the field.

What a time everyone had had! Now they had won, the rosettes were not big enough and they of a sensitive retiring nature now sported a miniature F.A. Cup. Oldham was certainly on the map! Didn't the

"THE TEAM FROM A TOWN OF CHIMNEYS"

Mayor say so when he spoke after the match? Charas from Royton, Shaw, Failsworth and surrounding districts jammed the nearby garages all impetuous it seemed to bound forward and convey the good news home.

The journey home was interspersed with hectic accounts of individual merit on the field. The trains ploughed North, the travellers sang, the bells rang as Derby, Nottingham and Rugby shot through the midnight air like camps in the Klondyke Goldrush.

Policemen on duty in Oldham the following morning had an unusually large and good natured crowd of early-risers, who cheerfully made their respective ways homeward and the better part of that day saw hundreds of tired fans deep in a sleep that was memorable if only for the fact that every sleeper had a smiling face.

Sport had its psychological reactions on the daily lives of everyone in various ways and many reports testified to larger Church collections, presumably from those zealous sportsmen whose gratitude on this particular Sunday found expression in thanksgiving. Few people would have begrudged a 'penny on the rate' as preparations for the Civic Reception grew apace.

It was arranged that the victorious team should be met in Manchester and proceed by road to Oldham arriving at 6.30 p.m., a token of respect to their Failsworth and Hollinwood supporters.

Discreet managements of industry turned a diplomatic blind eye on Monday to glaring examples of diplomatic colds and sudden onsets of lesser-known ailments. Shopkeepers relaxed their under-counter technique and cigarettes were as plentiful as aluminium pans. Even the august assembly within the Town Hall itself dispensed justice this morning with the generosity of a Royal amnesty. As the historic fingers of St. Mary's clock crept round and round to 6.30 p.m., the hooters and buzzers signalled the first relief of all this emotional tension. Some workers rushed home, others had tea in town, many had gone to work ready dressed for the evening, but all were obsessed with one intention to take up a point of vantage and make as much noise as human lungs would permit.

Slowly, too slowly it seemed, the cavalcade of victory coaches wormed its way townward, coiling round King Street, where the Cup was triumphantly held on high from top of a motor coach owned by a local gentleman who cared little tonight if they tore the top off. Star Inn was negotiated with a greater dignity though the narrow footpaths were inadequate to cope with the sightseers who thronged the adjoining buildings and even perched on the roof tops. Again the band struck up a march and again the Cup was held aloft until its bearer was limbweary.

At the G.P.O. a huge banner bearing the final score fluttered vigorously in the breeze with the caption "Good Old Latics" in letters a foot deep. So the victors pressed on, flushed, excited and proud, the bands played, the crowds roared along the last lap up Yorkshire Street.

"THE TEAM FROM A TOWN OF CHIMNEYS"

The air was now electric with irrepressible jubilation and the "iron rails" presented a scene of colourful animation with scores of blue and white balloons suspended from their moorings.

The Mayor and the civic dignitaries stood in their robes beaming a sincere welcome, as the procession came to a halt beneath a banner inscribed "Well done lads!" Bells clanged as the leading figures climbed cautiously down from the coaches. Press photographers bobbed up and down like fairground marionettes and a strange hush came over the scene as the Mayor in a voice of restrained emotion read a message of praise.

Then a voice clear and unmistakable shouted, "Come on Albert Birtles, this five-day week's made thee lazy, dost know what time it is, it's gone ten o'clock — if Latics 'ad bin at whoam tha'd a bin up long sin!" "By crikey", replied Albert, rubbing his eyes, "if they'd a bin at Wembley today tha'd a bin sleepin' bi thi sel last neet".

OLDHAM ATHLETIC 1913/14

TUMMON . J.W. MAYALL *(Director)* . COOK . G.H. MORTON *(Director)* . DONNACHIE . MATTHEWS . J. HANSON *(Trainer)* . GEE . MOFFAT
WILSON . HODSON . ROBERTS *(Capt.)* . BROAD . DIXON . WOODGER

"THE TEAM FROM A TOWN OF CHIMNEYS"

Troubled times

The 1913-14 season brought with it yet more surprises. Few would have guessed that Manchester United would find themselves starting without Charlie Roberts. For £1,750, Charlie had transferred to Athletic and went on to become possibly one of their best ever centre-halves.

Together with Oliver Tummon and Dave Wilson — still going strong in his eighth season at the club — Roberts played in all 38 first-team League games.

Another Latics centre-half, Arthur Dixon, became a professional soon after the season got under way. A local-born player, he later went on to join Glasgow Rangers where he became a great favourite.

Jimmy Broad had also begun to put in appearances at practice games, playing originally as a goalkeeper. He was taken on as a professional, but it was soon found that he had "feet like cannons" and he switched to centre-forward with great success. He would surely have gone on to great things had not the Great War intervened.

The team finished fourth in the table, eight points behind champions Blackburn Rovers, with only one point between second, third and fourth clubs.

However, it was a poor season financially, due in part to a disappointing cup competition in which they went out at the first hurdle to Brighton and Hove Albion, leaving a few Saturdays free.

Although a £250 profit was made by playing at Belfast Distillery and Cardiff City in friendlies, it was poor consolation.

During the close season of 1914, team boss David Ashworth resigned to join Stockport County and in his place came well-known referee Mr. H. S. Bamlett.

On the eve of the season opening, Britain found herself at war and transfers were no longer allowed after the season began. Just in time, Athletic signed A. Cashmore from Manchester United and W. Goodson and H. Grundy.

OLDHAM ATHLETIC 1914/15 (FOOTB
W. COOK · Mr. A. CLEGG (Director) · H. MOFFATT · H. MATTH
O. TUMMON · E. PILKINGTON · C. ROBERTS (Ca

EAGUE DIVISION ONE · RUNNERS-UP)
. KEMP · D. WILSON · H.S. BAMLETT (Manager) · J. DONNACHIE
J. HODSON · A. CASHMORE · J. HANSON (Trainer)

(22) BRIGHTON V OLDHAM CUP REPLAY JAN 14 1914

ROBERTS. OLDHAM.   LEEMING. BRIGHTON

BRIGHTON V OLDHAM CUP REPLAY JAN 14 1914. THE MEETING OF TWO CAPTAINS.

"THE TEAM FROM A TOWN OF CHIMNEYS"

Oldham Athletic Gazette
AND OFFICIAL PROGRAMME
Edited by REM.

VOL. 9. NO. 14. SATURDAY, FEBRUARY 27, 1915. PRICE ONE PENNY.

GETTING HIS HOUSE IN ORDER.

THE ATHLETE:—"Make a nice pair of ornaments, wont they?"
THE PENSIONER:—"I don't know much about the League one, but I rather fancy the other one myself, and I hope we may meet in the Final when our claims to ownership can be fully discussed."

This 1914-15 season was to be the closest Athletic have ever come to winning the championship. Success depended on their last two games, both at home. However, they lost both and Everton took the title by just one point.

At the end of the season, official football was suspended for the duration of the war and it is interesting to wonder just how good Athletic might have been had the hostilities not halted their progress.

As it was, they went through a trying time with team manager Mr. Bamlett and secretary Mr. Mellor volunteering for military service along with many players.

The club carried on in a fashion during these troubled times, playing regional soccer, and won the Lancashire Subsidiary Tournament "B" in 1918-19.

However, these were desperately hard times and only the marvellous work of chairman William Tetlow and directors Messrs. Stanton, Pickford and Grime, prevented the club going bankrupt on numerous occasions.

When football again came into its own there was little raw material with which to fashion a top-class team.

Dixon, Donnachie and Broad had been sold to keep the club alive, Charlie Roberts had been crippled by a serious injury, Cook and

MANCHESTER CITY AT THE OLDHAM TOLL GATE.

MANCHESTER CITY "What d'yer say? Give yer two points before yer opens the gate?"
THE OLDHAM ATHLETE: "Yes, that's the usual thing here. Of course, sometimes I lets them off with one point when they're hard up or out of luck, but I see yer've been in clover, so I wants the maximum from yer."

"THE TEAM FROM A TOWN OF CHIMNEYS"

HOW LONG WILL HE KEEP IT?
(N.B. No Prizes given for the correct Solution).

EVERTON :—"I've come to wish you a Happy New Year, and to collect the two points."
THE OLDHAM ATHLETE :—"You're too late sonny, read this notice."

Hodson had reached the end of their playing days and David Wilson retired, although he was later persuaded to make a comeback.

By the end of season 1919-20 only 38 points had been won — and Notts County had been relegated with 36.

Thomas Norcliffe, Fred Dawson, Herbert Mills and Thomas Stott all joined the board at this stage and the directors set about trying to rebuild the side.

Reuben Butler cost £1,850 from Middlesbrough and Alf Marshall came from Fulham. During the season the spending was boosted to £8,020 by the signing of J. Marshall, W. Taylor and J. Byrom from Rochdale. But again, Athletic just managed to avoid relegation.

Changes continued to be made and, before 1921-22 season kicked-off, A. Cashmore left for Cardiff City, J. Walters went to Southend United. A. Wolstenholme was transferred to Newport County and A. Dolphin joined Notts County.

The board changed too, with new additions being Frank Platt, Thomas Howe and Harry Davies.

Athletic were set to creep quietly into the otherwise "Roaring Twenties".

WE HOPE SO.

BURNLEY: "I've a jolly good mind to break this Record for you."
THE ATHLETE: "You can have a try, but I fancy you'll find it's an unbreakable one."

OLDHAM ATHLETIC 1916/17, WARTIME LEAGUE, LANCASHIRE SECTION

R. MELLOR (Sec.) . S. TAYLOR . A. WOLSTENHOLME . E. CAVANNAGH . E. PILKINGTON . J. ALDRED . H. GRUNDY
A. CASHMORE . A GEE . J. CUFFE . D. WILSON . E. DYKE

(David Wilson's only appearance as goalkeeper!)

OLDHAM ATHLETIC 1919/20, DIVISION ONE

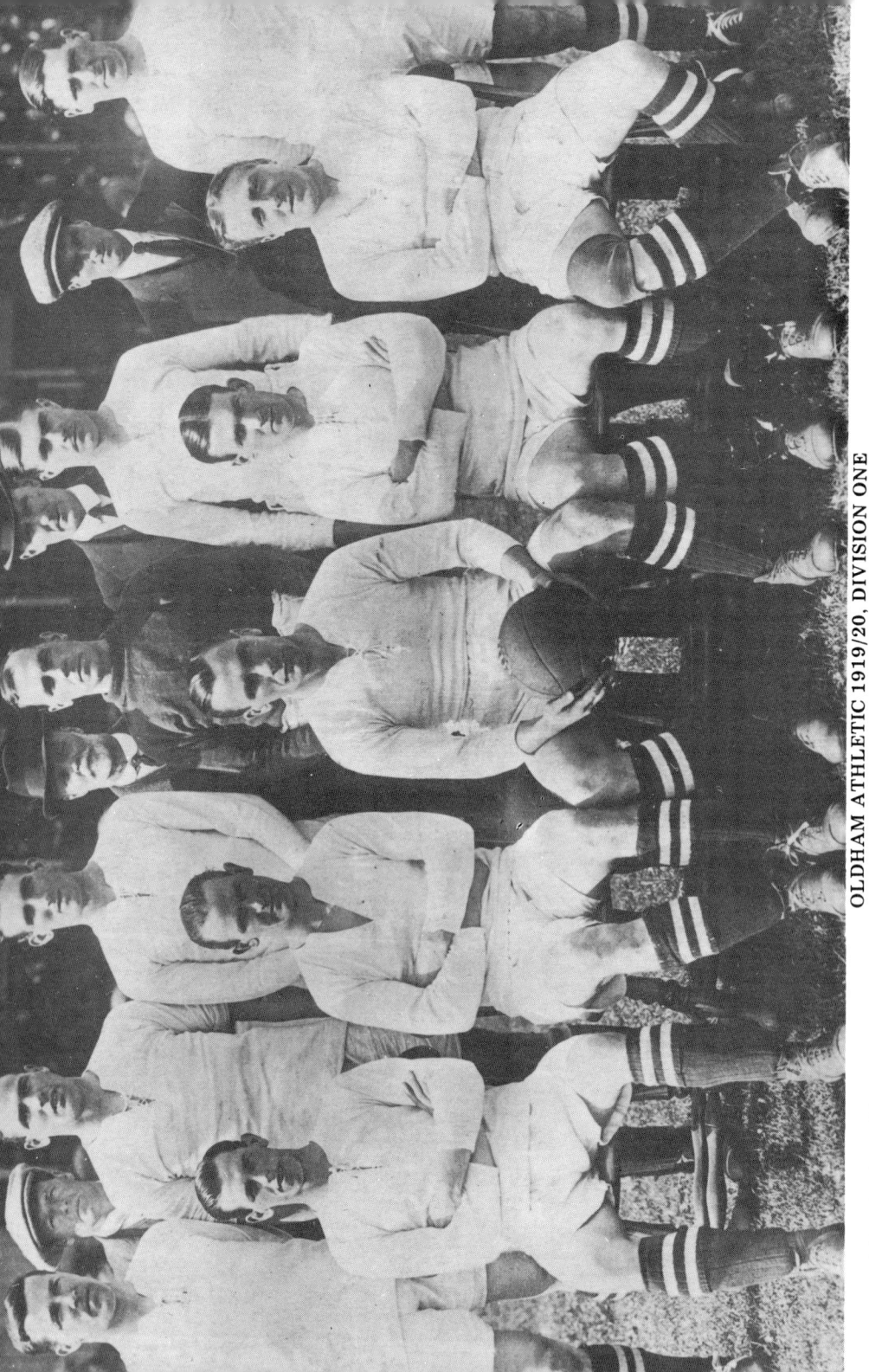

GOODWIN . J. HANSON (Trainer) . DOUGHERTY . STEWART . Mr. TETLOW (Chairman) . MATTHEWS . H. BAMLETT (Manager) . PILKINGTON . CUNLIFFE . WALL

Almost the End

The close season of 1921 saw the resignation of team manager Herbert Bamlett, who later managed Manchester United, and his replacement by the club's old friend Charlie Roberts.

Great things were anticipated but the club was stuck firmly in a rut.

Despite spending more money on new signings, Athletic again struggled and ended the season fifth from bottom on 37 points. They also slipped out of the F.A. Cup at the second round stage, beaten by Barnsley after seeing off Gillingham.

The 1922-23 season came and went — and with it went Athletic.

Halfway through the campaign, team boss Roberts resigned and David Ashworth was persuaded to return to see if his old magic could save Athletic from continuing on the downward path.

Unfortunately, "too late" was the cry and Ashworth found himself back with a Second Division Athletic.

Many clubs have found it harder to get back to the First Division than to reach those dizzy heights for the first time — and so it was with the Latics.

Although setting out on the road back in high spirits, confident they could regain their lost place quickly, Athletic found it as difficult as their countrymen had to "win the war by Christmas" in 1914.

Athletic managed only seventh place with 45 points, despite signing top amateur Johnnie Blair just before Christmas. Blair scored 14 goals in 17 matches and, if he had arrived earlier, might just have helped the club to promotion.

As it was, receipts from the "gate" had been steadily dwindling and, at the end of the season directors faced the now familiar pile of debts.

Previous solutions had been the transfer of Taylor to Huddersfield in 1922 and Freeman to Middlesbrough in 1923. This time Hargreaves went and the playing staff was cut to a minimum. At the start of 1924-25 only 19 professionals were engaged of whom Yarwood was unfit to play and Naylor and Bassendale were so seriously hurt in pre-season games that they missed the early part of the campaign.

"THE TEAM FROM A TOWN OF CHIMNEYS"

In the first two matches, Gillespie and Wilkinson were injured and, as if to knock the last nail in Athletic's coffin lid, the following week saw top scorer Blair break his leg against Clapton Orient at Boundary Park.

If things hadn't looked too healthy at the start of the season, they now looked hopeless.

No longer planning to regain senior status, Athletic were now involved in a desperate fight to avoid further relegation.

Their fate rested on the final match of the season against Crystal Palace and victory saved Athletic for another season while condemning Palace to the drop.

With attendances continuing to plunge during the season, it was obvious the club would fold through lack of interest unless something could be done.

It was decided to call a meeting in Oldham's Baptist Schoolroom which was addressed by the Mayor, Alderman Broadbent.

As a result, the proprietors of the *Oldham Evening Chronicle* "Green Final" — their Saturday Sports edition — took up the cause and launched "The Green Final Appeal Fund." £2,000 was raised by the

---

OLDHAM ATHLETIC 1920/21

G. WALL . W. TAYLOR . L. CHORLTON . MR. DAVIES *(Director)* . G. PILKINGTON . J. HANSON *(Trainer)* . H. MATTHEWS . MR. STOTT *(Director)* . R. FREEMAN
J. TATTON . A. CAMPBELL . P. BELL . D. WILSON . R. JONES . R. BUTLER

"THE TEAM FROM A TOWN OF CHIMNEYS"

CHARLIE WALLACE (Oldham). Born at Sunderland, and has been a big noise in footer for years. Was once with the Villa, and has three caps. Height, 5 ft. 7 ins. Weight, 11 st.

Charlie Wallace
Oldham Athletic

OLDHAM ATHLETIC GAZETTE
AND OFFICIAL PROGRAMME

Vol. 16 No. 18.   FRIDAY, APRIL 2nd, 1926.   ONE PENNY

FRIDAY, APRIL 2nd & SATURDAY, APRIL 3rd.

"DON Q" SON OF ZORRO

Matinee Daily at 2-45.

GROSVENOR SUPER CINEMA

CIRCLE 1/6 — ONE OF THE MOST BEAUTIFUL CINEMAS IN ENGLAND

LOUNGE 1/- — SCRUPULOUSLY CLEAN, PERFECTLY VENTILATED, LUXURIOUS SEATING

Box Office open daily 11 to 4 & 6 to 9

Old and New Stories from the best there is in Literature.

ALLIED NEWSPAPERS LTD., Printers, Withy Grove, Manchester.

Oldham take the field. They're having a hard fight in the League, but they're not going down if they can help it. Reading from the back: Watson, Bassindale, Broadbent (W. H.), Horrocks, Taylor, Staniforth, Matthews, Grundy, Douglas, Pilkington and Freeman   *By Jos. Walker*

club directors giving up debentures to this amount and contributing 10 guineas each. Altogether more than £4,000 was raised and that paid off outstanding debts and helped towards the summer wage bill.

One of the "spin-offs" of the appeal was the idea of a bazaar and a meeting was held at the Cafe Monaco on February 19, 1925. Mr. G. K. Bell presided and a bazaar was organised in the Town Hall. It was a modest success.

The 1925-26 season opened with the shadow of bankruptcy considerably paler and Athletic managed to sign Albert Pynegar from Coventry, Arthur Ormston from Wigan Borough, Ted Goodier from Lancaster Town and C. Hey from Hurst.

The team finished seventh on 44 points and, along the way, won the now defunct Midweek League.

It wasn't such a rosy picture in the F.A. Cup, Athletic going out 1-0 at home in a replay against Millwall. However, a preliminary round 10-1 win over Lytham at Boundary Park set the club's cup scoring record which stands to this day.

Next season, Athletic won seven of their first 11 matches and, with attendances averaging 15,000 it looked as if they had turned the corner.

OLDHAM ATHLETIC 1921/22, DIVISION ONE

"THE TEAM FROM A TOWN OF CHIMNEYS"

R. FREEMAN, OLDHAM ATHLETIC 1922

OLDHAM ATHLETIC AT BLACKPOOL, AUGUST 25TH, 1923
LONGMUIR . GRUNDY . PILKINGTON . WATSON . BASSINDALE . MATTHEWS . FLEETWOOD . YARWOOD . NAYLOR . HEATON . DOUGLAS

However, things suddenly turned sour and the team won only three of the next 12 games. Attendances slumped, money was once again scarce and Athletic's popular full-back Sam Wynne had to be transferred, along with Gray, for a combined £4,500 fee.

A third-round cup defeat, 4-2 at home by Brentford, didn't boost confidence and Athletic scored only one win in the next seven games.

Support was now thin on the ground but the newly-formed Supporters Club did quite invaluable work, raising much-needed finance through garden parties, firework displays at the ground, jazz band contests, boxing, Christmas draws etc.

Athletic's half-back line, 1925. Adlam . Armitage . Naylor
Athletic players celebrate a 10-1 victory over Lytham in the F.A. Cup, 1925/26

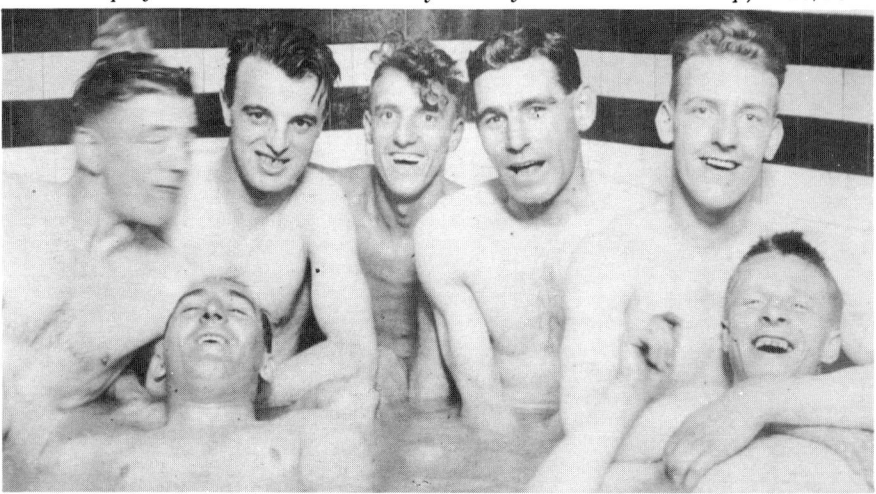

However, not even five wins in the last seven games could win back lost support, though the team survived in a mid-table position — Pynegar finishing as top scorer with 18 League and one cup goal.

Despite the Chadderton Road end stand suffering the indignity of being blown down on its completion in October 1927, Athletic fared much better when the new season began.

However, the good ship once again began to flounder after making good headway.

First Division chances faded, as did cup aspirations when Athletic lost 3-0 to Tottenham in a bruising fourth round clash, having at one stage only eight players on the pitch — two of them injured.

The season finished with them lying seventh on 46 points — Pynegar again topping the scoring charts with 18 goals.

Season 1928-29 was little better, the first 19 games yielding only three wins — including a 2-0 F.A. Cup defeat by the eventual winners Bolton Wanderers.

However, Athletic pulled themselves out of trouble with 25 points from the last 13 home games, ending the season three points clear of relegation in 18th place.

At last, season 1929-30 saw Athletic pull out of the doldrums.

With new boys S. King from Sheffield United, L. Cummings from Huddersfield and W. Finney from Bury, Athletic's performances were once more something to admire.

Stewart Littlewood set the individual scoring record for the club with 28 goals and, in doing so, contributed handsomely to the club total of 90.

The team collected 20 away points which compares favourably with the 1910 total of 21 when they won promotion, and goal average was among the best in the League.

In the F.A. Cup, Athletic beat Wolves 1-0 to earn a Boundary Park meeting with League leaders Sheffield Wednesday. They lost a tremendous game 4-3 and the Battle of the Roses clash brought a club record attendance of 47,671 which still stands.

Over the season the average "gate" rose by 5,142 and gross receipts by £274. The only disappointment was the final League placing — third on 53 points behind Chelsea (55) and Blackpool (58).

But, the Athletic sun was beginning to rise again, it seemed.

When you buy the "GREEN FINAL" you obtain all the latest results.

OLDHAM A

Back row (left to right): L. ADLAM · W. TETLOW (Director) · G. WALKER · S. WYNN

Front row (left to right): G. DOUGLAS · A. PYNEGAR

IC 1925/26
NSON (Trainer) · H. MATTHEWS · G. GILLESPIE · J. NAYLOR · H. DAVIES (Director)
STON · H. GRUNDY (Captain) · H. BARNES · R. WATSON

OLDHAM ATHLETIC 1929/30
E. IVILL . J. HACKING . W. PORTER
F. WORRALL . J. DYSON . S. LITTLEWOOD . M. GRAY . W. HASSON . S. KING
L. ADAM . E. GOODIER
(With the exception of F. Worrall, this was the side fielded in the epic cup-tie against Sheffield Wednesday, January 25th 1930)

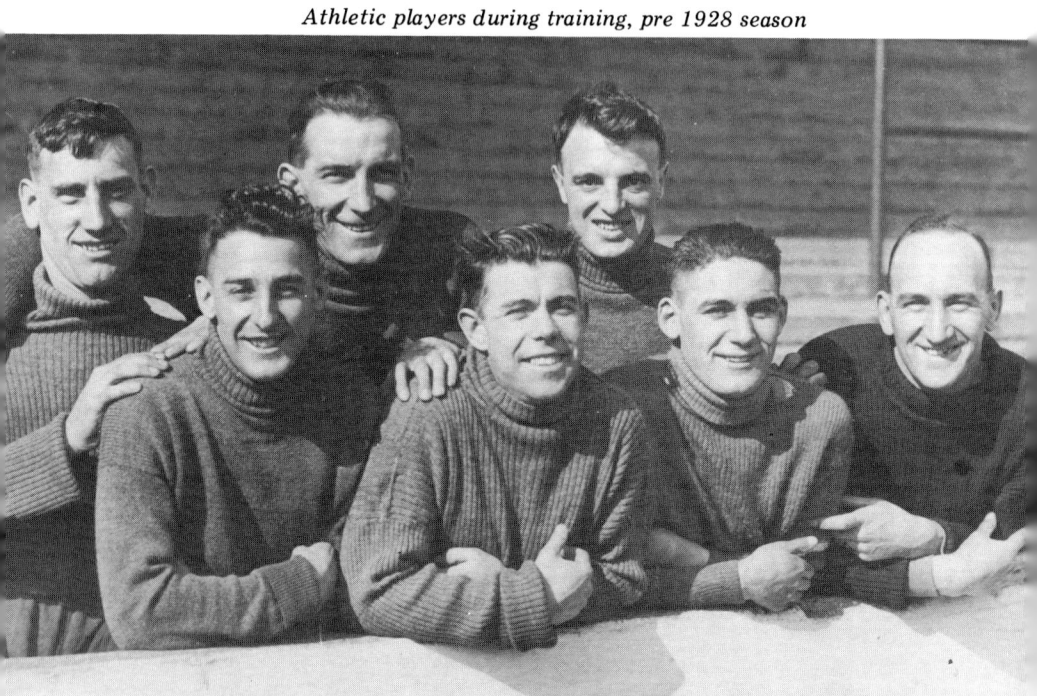

Athletic players during training, pre 1928 season

"THE TEAM FROM A TOWN OF CHIMNEYS"

CUP-TIE DRAMA AT OLDHAM

SHEFFIELD WEDNESDAY snatch victory in final fleeting seconds. Thrilling climax to a thrilling game. Thousands who missed it. Seed's wonder goal. Honour to all twenty-two. Records made and broken.

By TAURUS.

Littlewood.

Oldham Athletic 3, Sheffield Wednesday 4.

IT seems that Oldham Athletic were destined to be the central figures in the Cup-tie dramas of 1930. They scraped through the third round at Boundary Park by a sensational last-minute goal against Wolverhampton Wanderers, and on Saturday, again at Boundary Park, there was another dramatic goal in the fleeting seconds of the game against Sheffield Wednesday, the Athletic this time being the vanquished instead of the victors—a great climax to a great game. I have seen many better games for football artistry and skill, but never one so chock full of thrills, pulsating incidents, and excitement.

Consider the closing scene. Mr. Josephs, the referee, watch poised in hand, a matter of seconds to go—thousands leaving the ground—rival managers, mentally, and actually, I believe, making arrangements for the mid-week replay—the score 3–3—both sides almost spent of effort, fit only to drag themselves to the dressing-rooms. The ball goes out to Rimmer, who takes advantage of a slackness in defence and shoots, Hacking parries the shot, and Jack Allen, ever on the spot, finds himself with the ball at his feet and the goal gaping at him. You've guessed the rest. Thousands who had squeezed out of the ground had to be told about that amazing winning goal by the thousands that had to stay squeezed in. Mr. Josephs told me that no extra time been necessary for stoppages the final whistle would have blown immediately after Allen had scored.

SORRY FOR OLDHAM.

I cannot help feeling sorry for Oldham. Twice were they behind, the first time five minutes after the start, and twice did they draw level, and once actually held the lead. They fought so well that they fully earned the right to a replay that every one must have made up their minds they were going to get.

Speed was the keynote of the game. I counted only twelve corners, and few more throws in, which must give a fair idea of how much the ball was in play. The start was electrifying. The Oldham inside men cut through the defence like a knife, and Taylor nearly scored a magnificent first-minute goal, his breath-taking header being marvellously punched over the bar by Brown.

"Can they keep it up?" asked an Athletic reserve player sitting behind me after five minutes of sustained Oldham pressure. It seemed hardly possible. The answer was swift and emphatic. Sheffield swept to the other end, and in this their first real advance took the lead, Hooper catching a Rimmer centre on the volley. Littlewood squared things up sixteen minutes later when he headed in from a corner. Hasson took this, and the ball touched the heads of Gray and Littlewood and into the net. Excitement alone must have caused Littlewood to miss a great chance of giving Oldham the lead a minute later, but no such feeling communicated itself to "on-the-spot" Allen when, ten minutes before the interval, there was a misunderstanding between Ivill and Hacking. He scored.

RARE OCCURRENCE.

Littlewood made things right with his conscience just before half-time when he equalised with a volley from a corner. Oldham's two goals had come from corners—a rare occurrence, surely!

Half-time, the score 2–2, and the stage set for a thrilling second half, and it came all right. Ten minutes only had gone when the Oldham "fans" were sent into a frenzy of wild delight. Adlam's shot was a harmless looking affair and was well covered by Brown, but Leach, who always hangs back, ever ready to help the defence, diverted it out of the goalkeeper's reach.

Then followed a goal that deserves to land the Wednesday at Wembley. Nobody will ever forget it. It was a goal of a goalkeeper's lifetime. Jimmy Seed was the scorer. Rimmer with the ball had a flying start, so that it seemed no one was up to take his centre, but Seed dashed up like a sprinter from the mark, and the ball whizzed from his head into the net from a distance of at least twenty yards.

All honour to each of the twenty-two players for a football treat. There was not a single deliberate foul in the game.

There is no knowing how much the Wednesday can do. They must be strong favourites for the Cup and League double, and who can say they are not worthy of the position? All played well, and if Hooper was again starred for long periods, Burgess missed an open goal, and Leach put through his own goal, these were but defects that show up in greater relief the remaining perfection.

Oldham can point to no weaknesses apart from occasional lack of coolness near their own goal, and over-eagerness near their opponents. Footballers are but human, and they must be forgiven. For the rest they were valiant.

A few records: Attendance and receipts; Sheffield have not lost to a Lancashire club this season, and this was their first win at Oldham at their tenth visit.

ATHLETIC
V
SHEFFIELD
WEDNESDAY

F.A. CUP 4TH RD.
JANUARY 1930

75

"THE TEAM FROM A TOWN OF CHIMNEYS"

OUR VISITORS TO-DAY HOLD A PROUD POSITION IN THE LEAGUE TABLE.

NOT THE LEAST IMPORTANT OF THEM IS HACKING WHO KNOWS THE WAY TO 'OLD 'EM

A WORD TO OUR BOYS BEFORE THE BATTLE

REMEMBER WHAT YOU DID TO BLACKPOOL'S KEEPER

F.A. CUP 4th ROUND. TOTTENHAM HOTSPUR V ATHLETIC, JAN. 1928
Hacking saves a shot from a Spurs forward with Ivill in close attendance

TOTTENHAM V ATHLETIC DIVISION 2, WHITE HART LANE, OCTOBER 1932
Hasson (Athletic) puts the ball past the Spurs keeper Nicholls to score

"THE TEAM FROM A TOWN OF CHIMNEYS"

JACK HACKING · OLDHAM ATHLETIC & ENGLAND 1928/29

"THE TEAM FROM A TOWN OF CHIMNEYS"

Palladium

Union Street — Oldham

Manager: ALFRED M. LOADER.

The Old-Established House with a reputation for High-Class Consistency.

The Management desire to notify their many Patrons that some of the

Very Best of the .. World's Pictures

Have been secured for screening at the Palladium during the season.

LOOK OUT FOR

HAROLD LLOYD in "Girl Shy,"
MAE MURRAY in "Fashion Row,"
BETTY BLYTHE in "Southern Love,"
SESSUE HAYAKAWA in "The Battle,"
IRENE RICH in "Flaming Passion,"
ANITA STEWART in "The Great White Way."

These are just a few of the good things to whet the appetite for the veritable feast of star attractions to follow

**MARK SENNETT COMEDIES.   HAL ROACH COMEDIES.
POPULAR INTEREST PICTURES.
GOOD MUSIC.**

All the Best in Entertainment at Lowest Possible Prices.

Former Athletic wing-half Jimmy Naylor shakes hands with King George V before the start of the 1930 F.A. Cup Final, Huddersfield v Arsenal
Inset: Jimmy Naylor in 1981, still an Athletic player at heart.

Down again

Full of hope and bathing in the soft light of the previous season's good form, Athletic began the 1930-31 season with a short burst of good results.

The club broke no records, but showed nothing of the terrible luck which had dogged them so often since 1919.

Attendances of around 14,000 meant they could pay their way with receipts averaging £650.

In the first seven games, Athletic notched up five wins. However, the memory of Athletic failing to achieve the First Division goal the previous season seemed to nag at the faith of supporters.

Seven more games brought only one win and support fell away at an alarming rate until, by the time they faced Bristol City, the gate yielded only £111.

Athletic lost to Watford 1-0 in the F.A. Cup third round and this was the last straw. Attendances dropped well below 10,000 for six of the remaining nine home games.

The following season saw support dropping off even further, particularly after Athletic took

JIMMY HANSON WITH THE LATIC'S MASCOT 'DINKY'

"THE TEAM FROM A TOWN OF CHIMNEYS"

CHELSEA V ATHLETIC, DIVISION 2 STAMFORD BRIDGE, JANUARY 1930
Seth King, Athletic's captain shakes hands with Andy Wilson the Chelsea captain with H. Thomas (Referee) looking on.

CHELSEA V ATHLETIC, 1930
Stamford Bridge
Division 2. Result 1-1

only seven points from the first nine games.

It needed some superb play and victory in a game just to halt further decline and the only bright spot was a crowd of 30,607 for the 1-1 cup draw with Huddersfield Town. The Yorkshiremen won the return 6-0.

Financial problems forced the departure, without replacement, of Fred Worrall, one of Athletic's best-ever outside-rights to Portsmouth, Ted Goodier and Les Adlam to Q.P.R. F. Moss to Arsenal and J. Dyson to Grimsby.

Things were no better after trainer Jimmy Hanson retired at the start of 1932-33, to be replaced by Harry Tuffnell, who scored Barnsley's extra-time winner in the 1912 F.A. Cup final replay with West Brom. at Bramhall Lane.

The lack of support which had dogged the club for three seasons was now shown to be deeper rooted than many people had feared.

Less than 9,000 saw the last five home games, the bank put the brake on spending and much-maligned directors had to dig deep into their own pockets to keep the club going.

Out of a total of 33 playing staff, only 14 were retained at the end of the season.

Athletic scraped together enough to buy W. Johnstone from Manchester United and A. Agar from Accrington Stanley but had to part with Ted Ivill who joined Wolverhampton Wanderers after a tremendous 244 consecutive appearances — just missing Dave

FRED WORRALL, OLDHAM ATHLETIC 1930

TEDDY IVILL, OLDHAM ATHLETIC 1930

"THE TEAM FROM A TOWN OF CHIMNEYS"

A group of Athletic player's, pictured before a Division 2 match at Bury, October 1932
Left to right: SEYMOUR . AGAR . BRUNSKILL . TAYLOR

STEWART LITTLEWOOD, OLDHAM ATHLETIC 1930   MATT GRAY, OLDHAM ATHLETIC 1930

85

Season 1935/36 — 3rd Division North · December 25th & 26th 1935

13 GOALS FOR TRANMERE

ATHLETIC'S RECORD DEFEAT, BUT HOME POINTS WON ON CHRISTMAS DAY!

Christmas Day:
Athletic 4, Tranmere 1

Boxing Day:
Tranmere 13, Athletic 4

BUNNY BELL
His 9 goals sent Athletic crashing to their heaviest ever defeat

Athletic completed their 1935 Christmas holiday programme in a manner that will not readily be forgotten. In two matches against Tranmere Rovers an amazing 22 goals were scored. On Christmas Day Athletic completed an excellent performance in defeating the Rovers at Boundary Park by 4-1, and everything looked rosy for the return fixture 24 hours later. What a rude awakening lay in store. Records were broken as Athletic crashed 13-4 with the Rovers centre forward 'Bunny' Bell, a young shipping clerk from Liverpool, crashing home nine goals, and missing a penalty to boot! Prenton Park rang to the shouts of 'We want Bell', as the Rovers player was chaired off the field at the whistle by exhilarated Tranmere supporters. When Athletic's centre-half Brunskill left the field for 15 minutes suffering from a broken nose the scoreline read 1-0. In that period Rovers added 5 goals. Brunskill was instructed when re-entering the arena with his face heavily bandaged, to avoid using his head, about the first thing he did was head a goal!

The goals came as follows: 2 mins-Urmson; 7 mins-Bell; 11 mins-McDonald; 14 mins-Woodward; 16 mins-Bell; 19 mins-Bell; 35 mins-Bell; 38 mins-Brunskill (Ath); 40 mins-Bell; 46 mins-Bell; 50 mins-Woodward; 63 mins-Davis (Ath); 68 mins-Bell; 69 mins-Walsh (Ath); 71 mins-Walsh (Ath); 87 mins-Bell; 89 mins-Bell.

A Tranmere director suggested the run of the game would have been best underlined by a 17-10 scoreline, for in addition to Bell's penalty miss, a number of 'sitters' went begging, while there was some excellent goalkeeping at both ends. In all, Athletic were to be commended on their sporting attitude whilst suffering such a defeat.

Tranmere: Gray, Platt, Fairhurst, McLaren, Newton, Spencer, Eden, McDonald, Bell, Woodward, Urmson.

Athletic: Caunce, Seymour, Talbot, Williamson, Brunskill, Schofield, Jones, Davis, Walsh, Leedham, Buckley.

Wilson's record 264 in his 14 years with the club.

Throughout the 1930's, Athletic continued in much the same vein, seemingly doomed to life in the lower divisions while their Manchester neighbours City were entering a golden era of F.A. Cup success and runners-up followed by a championship win.

In 1933-34, Athletic finished ninth in Division Two thanks to the influence of new manager Jimmy McMullen. But, the following season, Athletic dropped to next-to-bottom with 26 points and were relegated to Division Three along with Notts County. A sign of the times was the loss of manager McMullen without replacement.

Manchester United, then living in the shadows of arch-rivals City, just missed the drop with Athletic by winning their last game at Millwall when Athletic loaned them goalkeeper Jack Hacking who played a big part in a 2-0 victory.

Athletic's first season in the lower division saw them finish seventh on 45 points with William Walsh scoring a record 32 goals. Another record of dubious distinction was the 13-4 defeat at the hands of Tranmere on Boxing Day, 1935 which remains the club's worst League beating.

Meanwhile the reserve team was struggling in the Central League, having been re-elected three years running.

The end of the following season saw them finish bottom and they were kicked out — never to return.

The first team fared better, finishing fourth in Division Three

W.A. HILTON *(Athletic captain — 1936/37)*

with 51 points, and the goalscoring record was advanced again — this time by Tommy Davies whose 35 goals have yet to be bettered. Don Travis (34) came close in 1954-55 and Bert Lister reached 33 in 1962-63.

Although the team was improving, financially the situation could not have been worse.

The Supporters Club executive worked wonders but Athletic owed an enormous debt to an anonymous friend of the Supporters Club, who, with wages overdue, lent the money and saved an embarrassing collapse.

By the end of season, Athletic were again in fourth place on 51 points.

As the start of the 1938-39 season loomed closer, outside events intruded on Athletic's world when local appeals for volunteers for the national armed services were made. Adolf Hitler's armies had occupied Austria and bankruptcy was not now the only black cloud on the horizon.

With the season under way it became apparent that the Oldham public were only interested in watching a winning team. After a home defeat by Rochdale left them 13 points behind leaders Barnsley, support drifted away rapidly.

Although finishing in fifth place, Athletic's "gate" money dropped over £2,000 and there were 43,810 fewer paying customers.

August, 1939 also brought tragic news for Athletic — the death of Charlie Roberts the club's legendary former defender. *The Manchester Guardian* obituary described him as the greatest captain Manchester United and Athletic ever had. He was also a leading figure in the Players' Union dispute of 1909.

"Today," wrote the paper, "the Union flourishes. Roberts became its first chairman and later vice-president and trustee. It is a worthy memorial to a great player and a great sportsman."

As the 1939-40 season opened, events were moving quickly abroad. On September 4, 1939, Athletic's secretary Robert Mellor told the Boundary Park players that, due to international tension, their contracts had been terminated.

The same applied to all other clubs from the week ending September 1.

Once again, the dark days of World War were about to settle heavily on the country.

Charlie Roberts

"THE TEAM FROM A TOWN OF CHIMNEYS"

THE BLACKOUT OF SPORT

Hitler is causing a blot-out and black-out of sports and pleasures.

—and the "All Blacks" had an "all-black" welcome.

Football acts as a sort of safety-valve.

It played a big part in the Great War.

Werneth finished on their pedestal.

OLDHAM ATHLETIC 1936/37
W.A. HILTON . L. CAUNCE . N. PRICE
T. WILLIAMSON . B. RATCLIFFE . G.H. MILLIGAN . N. BRUNSKILL
A. JONES . P. McCORMICK . T.L. DAVIES *(Record goalscorer to 1980)* . P. ROBBINS . P. DOWNES

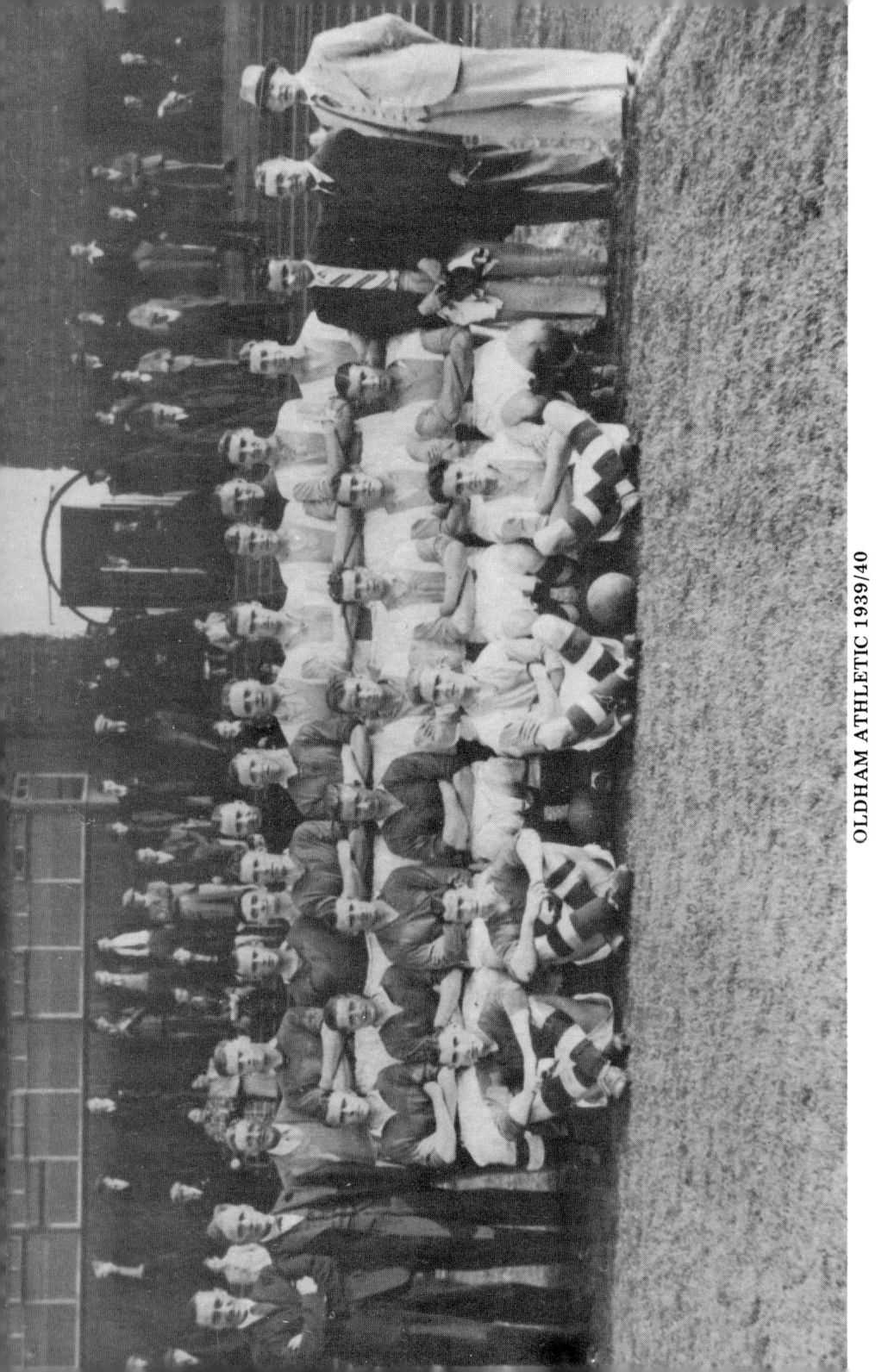

OLDHAM ATHLETIC 1939/40

Going Public

During the six years of hostilities, Athletic played in the war-time Northern League.

Most of their playing strength was drawn from guest players such as George Milligan from Everton, Arthur Buckley (Leeds United), Bill Porter (Manchester United), Fred Worrall (Portsmouth) and Tommy Butler (Middlesbrough) - all of whom had had previous connections with the club.

At last, those dark years were over and Athletic came out to do a more gentle type of battle in a period of football mediocrity in those immediate post-war years.

Athletic's first major attempt to secure financial bouyancy came with the decision to sell club shares to the public.

Club secretary Robert Mellor, when asked what Athletic planned to do with the £6,000 they hoped to raise, denied that it would all be used to pay off debts. Indeed, Athletic were so confident of raising the full amount that they had already decided to mortgage some of the amount to buy well-known players for vital positions.

After Athletic struggled in the 1945-46 season manager Frank Womack pledged to get them back in first-class football.

However, as the new season got under way there was a call from the Oldham town clerk for a ban on the showing of all horror films in the town — which could well have applied to Boundary Park. Athletic finished 19th in the Third Division and Womack resigned.

Despite the lack of success, Athletic's 24 home games were watched by more than 250,000 people and almost 30,000 saw a benefit game for popular defender Tommy Williamson in which the legendary Stanley Matthews, Stan Mortensen and Frank Swift took part.

In June of 1947, former Port Vale player and Northwich Victoria manager Billy Wootton took over the reins at Athletic but the first season was no great shakes.

Season 1948-49 saw an improvement, Athletic finishing sixth, but 49-50 was back to mediocrity and, by the end of it, a storm was raging over the so-called "Ginger Group" of the Shareholders Association whose published aim was to attempt changes in the constitution of the board of directors.

The group snapped up as many shares as possible and hoped to force voting decisions through at the club's annual meeting.

However, on the night, at a rowdy meeting of 600 shareholders, the three retiring directors, Arthur Barlow, Herbert Shepherd and William Bloor were all re-elected.

Despite all the off-field rows, things were about to take a turn for the better on the field.

Oldham Chronicle, July 1948

SPADE WITH SOCCER HISTORY

Athletic Get Valuable Memento

MORE than fifty years ago—on July 18, 1896—the first sod was cut on what is now Athletic's ground at Boundary Park by the late Alderman Thomas Bolton, who afterwards became Mayor, and to commemorate the occasion he was presented with a silver spade beautifully scrolled and engraved.

The movements of the spade in the intervening years are shrouded in mystery, writes Donald Cameron, but recently Mr. J. A. Ogden, executive Officer for the Oldham District of the North Western Area of the Electricity Board, had it brought to his notice, and he mentioned it to director Percy Skipworth, who is the oldest serving member of Athletic's board.

For sentimental reasons Mr. and Mrs. Skipworth decided to purchase the spade, and they have now passed it on to the club so that it can be permanently displayed in the directors' room at Boundary Park.

The spade is a beautiful piece of work. It has a solid silver blade, and an ebony handle and shaft circled by two silver bands.

Engraved on the blade are the Oldham Coat of Arms and the words:

"Presented to Alderman Thomas Bolton by the members of the Oldham Association Football and Athletic Club on the occasion of the cutting of the first sod of their new ground at Westhulme, Oldham, July 18, 1896."

The spade is now to be hung on the wall of the board room in a case which is to be inscribed, "Presented to Oldham Athletic Association Football Club, Ltd., by Mr. and Mrs. Percy Skipworth, May 12, 1948."

Thus, at a time when Athletic are putting in a tremendous amount of spade work to lift the club to a higher sphere of soccer, the spade which originated the whole up-and-down career of Boundary Park is back to the fold.

Athletic's three longest-serving officials examine the historic spade. Secretary Robert Mellor, (left), who has 42 years service, and scout Jimmy Hanson (43 years) look on as director Percy Skipworth (24 years), holding the spade.

"THE TEAM FROM A TOWN OF CHIMNEYS"

Athletic to Ask Middlesbrough for Mannion

OLDHAM ATHLETIC directors decided at their meeting today that they would approach Middlesbrough to explore the possibility of terms being discussed for the probable transfer of Wilfred Mannion to Athletic.

The statement issued by a deputation of the Board was, "We are contacting Middlesbrough for the time asking for an appointment to discuss the probable transfer of Wilfred Mannion, and we are arranging to send a deputation of directors if Middlesbrough give a favourable answer.

"If Middlesbrough would agree to transfer Mannion for a reasonable figure for a player of that calibre, means would be found to raise the necessary capital.

It is common knowledge that Athletic are not in an affluent position. At the moment they have an over-draft of a substantial amount, and while the directors would not disclose where the money would come from...

Mannion May Join Oldham

"Daily Dispatch" Reporter

WILF MANNION may soon be playing for Third Division North team Oldham Athletic.

These were the developments yesterday in the Mannion story...

Mannion: "We'll Wait," Say Shareholders

THOUGH the "ginger group" of the Oldham A.C. Shareholders' Association want the directors of the club to move quickly in making an offer for Wilf Mannion, it is not likely that anything definite will be done this week as Mr. Percy Skipworth, chairman of the Oldham Athletic board, is on holiday.

Tom Mellor, secretary of the Shareholders' Association of the club, says no further move will be made...

THE DAILY DISPATCH, Friday, October 29, 1948

CASH OR PLAYER-CASH NOW, SO—

More Mannion Offers Wanted

By ARCHIE LEDBROOKE

WILF MANNION, the greatest English scheming inside forward of the day, is to be transferred. Middlesbrough directors last night reviewed the offers they had received to date, and also a letter from Oldham Athletic asking whether a deputation would be received.

After a debate lasting for 2½ hours, they announced their decision in the following terms:

"It was resolved by the Middlesbrough F.C. Board that they are open to receive offers for Mannion..."

Oldham Athletic Association Football Club, Ltd.

REGISTERED OFFICE,
BOUNDARY PARK FOOTBALL GROUND,
OLDHAM.

Application for Shares

To the Secretary (Mr. R. Mellor). Please allot to me .... 10s.* shares in the above
                   number
Company. I enclose £   :   s.   d.

Name (in full) ....

Address ....

Occupation ....

        * Minimum number of shares—TWO.

GEORGE HARDWICK 'TALKS TACTICS' — 1952/

GEMMELL SCORES V LINCOLN CITY, 1951/52

ATHLETIC V GATESHEAD, MARCH 1953

Delight, then Despair

Determined to get out of Division Three North, Athletic gambled on paying £15,000 to Middlesbrough to get George Hardwick as player-manager in November of a moderate 1950-51 season.

With Hardwick at the helm, Athletic's sagging fortunes were dramatically revived.

In his first full season, 1951-52, Hardwick guided Athletic to an exasperating fourth place after they had topped the table for a while before hitting an unlucky run of injuries.

Public interest had been sparked again and when the next season began there were some excellent attendances — and results.

Before a crowd of 17,808, Athletic thrashed Darlington 5-0; 22,876 saw them beat Rochdale 1-0; 25,840 watched them dispatch Mansfield 1-0 on Boxing Day and 26,840 turned up for the 1-1 draw with Grimsby.

But, perhaps the most remarkable game of the season came on January 19 against Chester.

Chester took an early lead, Eric Gemmell quickly equalised, Chester went back in front and Syd Goodfellow levelled again. Then all hell broke loose on the Chester goal as Gemmell ended up scoring an amazing seven goals as Athletic won 11-2.

The following week they lost 5-0 at York City!

The top League crowd of the season was 27,521 for the 1-1 draw with Stockport · County and, at the end of a highly entertaining campaign, Athletic were worthy champions and on their way up to the Second Division.

The glory days were back — but all too briefly.

Relying largely on the players who had won promotion, Athletic managed to win only eight matches in the 1953-54 season and, with a mere 25 points, promptly plummeted back down to the Third Division.

Manager Hardwick was not too despondent, believing that the experience would not be lost on the younger players. However, he was to be disgruntled by falling attendances as the team made no progress. Indeed by the end of 1955-56, they were going backwards.

Seven points from their last six games had saved Athletic from the indignity of applying for re-election for the first time in their history.

Hardwick resigned as manager on April 21, 1956, and seven days later played his last match for Athletic against Wrexham at Boundary Park.

New boss Ted Goodier inherited no easy task and, at the end of his first season, Athletic struggled to improve their position by one place to 19th.

With support falling away the outlook was bleak. The playing staff had to be pruned and further problems loomed in the shape of a new Fourth Division.

"The Spectator" wrote in the *Oldham Chronicle* towards the end of 1957-58 season:—

'Never in its history has the Third Division seen such a breath-taking finish. Almost every club has, at some time during the past few weeks, found itself fighting either to avoid a fall from grace or gain promotion. And, in my opinion, this frantic free-for-all should have shown the Football League one inescapable fact — a four-up, four-down policy will be a boon to English League football and a financial saviour for many of the smaller, struggling Cinderellas.

This coming season, 12 clubs from the Third Division North will be dropping into a Fourth Division. Athletic maybe one of them and to me it seems grossly unfair that they will only have a 12-1 chance

---

7-GOAL GEMMELL —OLDHAM NET 11

MY BEST FOOTBALL STORY
I lost count of score

'FELT SOMETHING WAS GOING TO HAPPEN' —Says 7-goal Gemmell

ERIC GEMMELL, Oldham Athletic centre-forward, is today's contributor to our new sporting series. Next: BRIAN LUNDGREN, of Wigan.

GEMMELL IN GOAL RIOT

OLDHAM ATH. 11, CHESTER 2

OLDHAM ATHLETIC, entertaining Chester, had McKennan back at inside left, but McIlvenny was unfit. Munro moved to outside right, and Leslie Smith came in at inside right. Sixteen-year-old Eddie Hopkinson retained his place in goal, thus making his home debut. Chester had Jones for Fletcher at outside right.

OLDHAM ATHLETIC.—Hopkinson; Bell, Hardwick; Warner, White, Goodfellow; Munro, Smith, Gemmell, McKennan, Ormond.

CHESTER.—Threadgold; Molyneux, Morment; Morris, Lee, Astbury; Jones, Whitlock, Coffin, Greenwood, Windle.

After four minutes Hardwick missed a "sitter." Gemmell placed a perfect pass to Ormond, whose centre left Gemmell and there his own 10 yards out, and for his miss.

After 34 minutes, Gemmell scored a wonderful goal to give Oldham the lead. Receiving the ball on the half-way line, the outside right beat three men before placing the ball past Threadgold.

After 36 minutes, WARNER put Oldham further ahead following a free kick.

Four minutes later, SMITH headed in an Ormond centre, to make it five.

A minute from the interval GEMMELL headed in, to put Oldham further ahead. So half-time came with Oldham leading 6—2.

Threadgold made a brilliant save from a flashing header by McKennan, and then Gemmell beat Lee for speed, only to shoot just over the bar.

McKennan, who was limping, tried to walk the ball into the net instead of shooting, and was dispossessed.

After 53 minutes GEMMELL easy task in scoring his

...go for football. We had to play two officers as "passengers" on the wings to stop the game developing into a roughhouse.

But maybe playing under Arctic conditions had something to do with the greatest day of my career, which was when Oldham Athletic played Chester last season.

We won 11-2, and the goals came so fast that I lost count of my personal score—Peter Greenwood, the Lancashire cricketer, who was playing inside-left for Chester, said: "I think you need two more for a collection"—and in one hectic spell I was quite out of breath running back to the centre-circle after a goal.

Altogether I scored seven. Maybe there was nothing in it, but it was a typical Archangel pitch that day—deep in snow.

Eric Gemmell

OLDHAM ATHLETIC, CHAMPIONS DIV. 3 (N), 1952/53
BELL . WARNER . BURNETT . WHYTE . GOODFELLOW . GRAINGER . THOMAS (Trainer)
MUNRO . McKENNAN . HARDWICK . GEMMELL . McLIVENNEY

of fighting back to third grade football. If a club had a 6-1 chance of getting back then there would not only be more incentive and keeness for the players, but for 'Mr. Football' himself.'

When the season closed, with Athletic's average attendance only 7,464, the *Chronicle* was moved to write:—

'Oldham Athletic are in the Fourth Division as founder members. Soccer prestige in the town is at its lowest ebb and the question everyone is asking is 'What are the club going to do about it.' The directors must be prepared to spend money — where the money is to come from is for the board to decide, but it must be begged or borrowed somehow. The first move must be to introduce a proper coaching system'

Ironically, it was this four-up, four-down system that the *Oldham Chronicle* had argued for, that nearly brought about Athletic's downfall.

They finished the 1958-59 season in the bottom four of Division Four and had to apply for re-election.

Despite criticism heaped on manager Norman Dodgin, he had been instrumental in bringing promising players such as Robinson, Stringfellow, Mallon, Beswick and Elder onto the staff. Where Athletic would have been if these players hadn't turned up and asked for trials is anybody's guess.

Dodgin left at the end of 1959-60 and Athletic were really at their lowest ebb.

"THE TEAM FROM A TOWN OF CHIMNEYS"

The *Oldham Chronicle* commented in April 1960:—

'. . . any responsible person who could help the club over its crisis period would be more than welcome at Boundary Park. Being blunt, the days of life-saving appeals by Athletic are finished. The general public cannot come to Athletic's aid with donations.

I am not being pessimistic, therefore, when I say that unless some responsible help can be found, Athletic are on the brink of closing down.

For the club's sake, and for the sake of soccer in Oldham, I hope something will happen. I hope help will come forward. I hope a solution can be found.

The coming weeks could decide whether football is played at Boundary Park next season.'

Re-Birth

Season 1960-61 could have seen the death of Oldham Athletic. Instead, it turned out to be the re-birth of the town's soccer hopes.

It became known as the most adventurous season in the club's history, beginning and ending on an ambitious note.

In July 1960, a new manager was appointed — Jack Rowley — and the directors each agreed to buy £250 worth of the club's available shares.

New players made their appearance — full-back Johnny McCue from Stoke, Ken Branagan and Bert Lister from Manchester City, Bobby Rackley from Bristol, George Greenall from Southampton, Jimmy Frizzell from Morton and Bobby Johnstone from Hibernian.

Athletic felt they were a soccer power again; the team quickly found a good blend; ten successive victories bore testament to their new-found courage — and Athletic literally put themselves in the spotlight with plans to install floodlights at the ground.

The run of wins couldn't last, but Athletic had achieved their ambition — they had made their mark. With an average attendance of 12,305 over the season, Athletic rested until the next campaign in a respectable 12th place.

Unfortunately, season 1961-62 presented unexpected problems. Chances of promotion slipped away alarmingly as simultaneously, the promise of cup success beckoned.

Athletic enjoyed a fine F.A. Cup run, ending in January 1962 with a 2-1 home fourth-round defeat by Liverpool in front of 41,733 spectators. However, once out of the cup, they were unable to rejoin the promotion chase and finished 11th.

It had to be "promotion or bust" in 1962-63, according to club chairman Mr. Frank Armitage. But it ended up as promotion and bust-up!

Athletic finished the season in second place and on their way up to the Third Division but, behind the scenes, a row had been simmering which ended with the board voting 6-4 to ask for manager Jack Rowley's resignation by midnight, May 11, 1963.

"THE TEAM FROM A TOWN OF CHIMNEYS"

BOBBY JOHNSTONE
during his days at Manchester City

OLDHAM ATHLETIC 1961/62
A. WILLIAMS . J. SCOTT . J. BOLLANDS . J. McCUE . J. COLQUHOUN . P. PHOENIX
J. FRIZZELL . B. JOHNSTONE . K. BRANAGAN . B. LISTER . B. JARVIS

ATHLETIC V YORK CITY 1962/63
Bobby Johnstone scores with a spectacular overhead kick

ATHLETIC V CHESTERFIELD 1962
A fine action photo of Bert Lister scoring v Chesterfield 1962

"THE TEAM FROM A TOWN OF CHIMNEYS"

OLDHAM EVENING CHRONICLE, Thursday December 27th 1962

Goal No. 1—Colin Whitaker blasts home a right-footer.

There's another one! Southport's keeper looks back bewildered, as Lister hits No. 7.

Goal No. 3—and the first of Lister's half dozen, as he hooks the ball past Harris.

Colquhoun joins in the revels as he cracks home goal No. 4.

Whitaker completes his hat-trick with a spectacular cross-shot.

And now Ledger (left) gets in the act with a flashing drive.

8...9...10—it's 11-goal Latics in record win

OLDHAM ATHLETIC 11, SOUTHPORT 0

THE ardent rugby supporter summed it up in a sentence . . . . "But somebody told me this team had no punch in front of goal!" Yes, Athletic really confounded their critics with their Boxing Day bonanza. Producing a goal avalanche to match the Arctic weather conditions at Boundary Park they wrote themselves a new page in the soccer record books.

by GEOFF WELLENS

With the tousle-haired, double-hat-trick-man, Bert Lister, leading the goal riot, they laid on a Christmas feast to end all feasts.

For 15,000 fans this fantastic football fiesta left even the turkey and stuffing in the shade. Poor Southport never knew what hit them.

I suppose you could say it was to happen sometime. Athletic, with nothing better than a three-goal win to their credit so far this term, just had to hit the golden goal trail sooner or later.

But not even the most fanatical fan could have expected this 11-goal

BIGGEST WIN

Athletic's win was a record for the Fourth Division and the club's biggest-ever win, beating the 11—2 defeat of Chester ten years ago. It was Southport's biggest defeat.

soccer spectacle. Not only were Athletic in blistering goal form, they were brilliant in every department.

Under conditions which at best could only be described as atrocious, Athletic skated over the snow to the proudest moment in the club's history.

Yet even this glorious win in the performance of the defence. a brought its disappointments. Firstly, with a seven-goal lead at half-time, Athletic went all out to create a new club record.

One short

They did their utmost to better the 11-goal tally notched against Chester back in 1952—and no one tried harder than Ken Lister, who hit four of his six goals in that final 45-minute period.

In the closing minutes, Athletic raged even fiercer than the driving snowstorm, which threatened to wipe out the game. But they couldn't make the dozen.

Disappointment No. 2 was for schemer-in-chief Bobby Johnstone. While he watched his fellow forwards take large helpings of the goal feast, Bobby just couldn't get his name on the scoresheet.

One block-buster of a goal

disallowed and two great saves from goal-keeper Joe Harris almost added up to a conspiracy to cheat Athletic's top - class architect.

But if Bobby didn't get among the goals, he had his share of the glory. Like an impudent snowman, he was all over the snow-covered pitch, prodding and probing, reducing the shattered Southport defence to a state of total collapse.

This wasn't one man's day, however. Not even Lister, with his superb six-goal haul, could claim that.

Narrow angle

There were the brilliant efforts of flying winger Colin Whitaker. He started the fun with a first half hat-trick that soon had the icicles melting on the terraces.

There was the non-stop display from his inside partner, Johnny Colquhoun. What a great first half this terrier-like little Scot had!

There was an equally great first-half display by Bob Ledger, crowned with a gem of a goal, which he crashed home at an angle through the narrowest of gaps between goal-keeper and post.

And then, of course, there was the performance of the defence, a complete unit, which never gave the Southport attack so much as the hint of a chance, a unit which provided a solid springboard for the incessant Athletic attacks.

While we are mentioning the glories, spare a thought for Southport 'keeper Joe Harris. How he took back-breaking, heart-rending times he picked that ball out of the back of his net, yet, on the whole, he played a fine game. He pulled off a number of remarkable saves to double pneumonia in his role as Athletic's coldest spectator.

Packed with punch

At the same time, spare a thought for Athletic 'keeper Johnny Bollands. Often a lone figure in the Athletic half, he came near to double pneumonia in his role as Athletic's coldest spectator.

Yes, this was a rip roaring team

triumph—a scintillating success, which sent the sub-normal temperatures soaring.

So outclassed were Southport that at times it seemed they were playing the game on roller skates. Athletic's soccer artistry, packed with pep and punch, left them skidding all over the place.

Just for the record, and for the benefit of those doubting fans who claimed that Southport must have been playing in studless boots, the sneakers were wearing regulation boots, studded equally as well as Athletic's.

Only left-winger Bill Perry decided on a second-half change of studs—but it didn't make any difference he didn't see anything of the ball.

No, it was Athletic's form and determination which led them to this unequalled triumph. The efforts of players like Lister, Colquhoun and Williams, who did not acknowledge any danger in playing on such a treacherous surface.

● A final coincidence note: Referee J. Mitchell, of Prescot, told apprehensive Athletic officials before the game, "I never see home teams win. Of the last eight games I have refereed, five have been away wins and the other three drawn."

ATHLETIC: Bollands, Branagan, Marshall; McCall, Williams, Scott; Ledger, Johnstone, Lister, Colquhoun, Whitaker.
SOUTHPORT: Harris, Cairns, Griffiths; Peat, Darvell, Rutherford; Spence, Fielding, Blore, Cooper, Perry.
Referee Mr J Mitchell (Prescot).
Attendance 15,942.

DIVISION FOUR

	P	W	D	L	F	A	Pts
ATHLETIC	24	14	7	3	51	27	35
Brentford	23	13	3	7	47	29	29
Mansfield T.	23	13	5	5	51	26	31
Gillingham	24	13	3	8	41	24	29
Crewe Alex.	23	10	8	5	40	33	28
Carlisle	22	10	5	7	36	26	25
ROCHDALE	22	10	5	7	36	26	25
Torquay	23	8	8	6	39	34	26
Workington	24	10	5	9	35	30	25
Aldershot	25	7	11	7	39	39	25
Darlington	24	10	5	9	39	46	25
Oxford Utd	25	8	8	9	44	51	24
Newport Co.	24	8	7	9	50	47	23
Lincoln City	24	9	5	10	43	41	23
Chesterfield	25	6	11	8	40	40	23
Stockport Co.	25	9	5	11	28	37	23
Doncaster Rov.	25	9	5	11	33	43	23
Tranmere Rov.	22	9	4	9	45	38	22
Chester	24	8	5	11	35	37	21
Southport	24	8	5	11	45	75	20
Workington	24	6	7	11	35	38	19
Bradford City	24	7	4	14	38	47	18
Exeter City	25	4	9	12	27	39	17
York City	24	5	6	14	26	48	16
Hartlepools U.	24	5	4	15	33	53	14

New boss Les McDowall opened the 1963-64 season with the motto "Give the fans a winning team and they'll turn up."

And Athletic certainly lived up to their part of the bargain.

By October they were top of the table with 17 points — a role even the most ardent fans could not have foreseen for a club so fresh out of the Fourth Division.

Athletic were top or second until January 25, when they lost at Crewe to start a remarkable fall from grace.

They picked up only six points from 12 games — losing seven times at home — and ended the season 12 points adrift, in ninth place, of promoted Coventry and Crystal Palace.

The decline didn't end there for at the start of the following season, Athletic were hammered 5-1 by relegated Grimsby and 5-0 by Peterborough.

It was October before Athletic pulled themselves together with 12 points from seven games but they had slipped back to fifth from bottom by Easter when a win over Q.P.R. and draws against Barnsley and Q.P.R. ensured their safety for another season.

It was a similar struggle in 1965-66 with Gordon Hurst now manager. Half-way through the campaign he stepped down to assistant to Jimmy McIlroy but 37 points and 20th place was the best Athletic could manage.

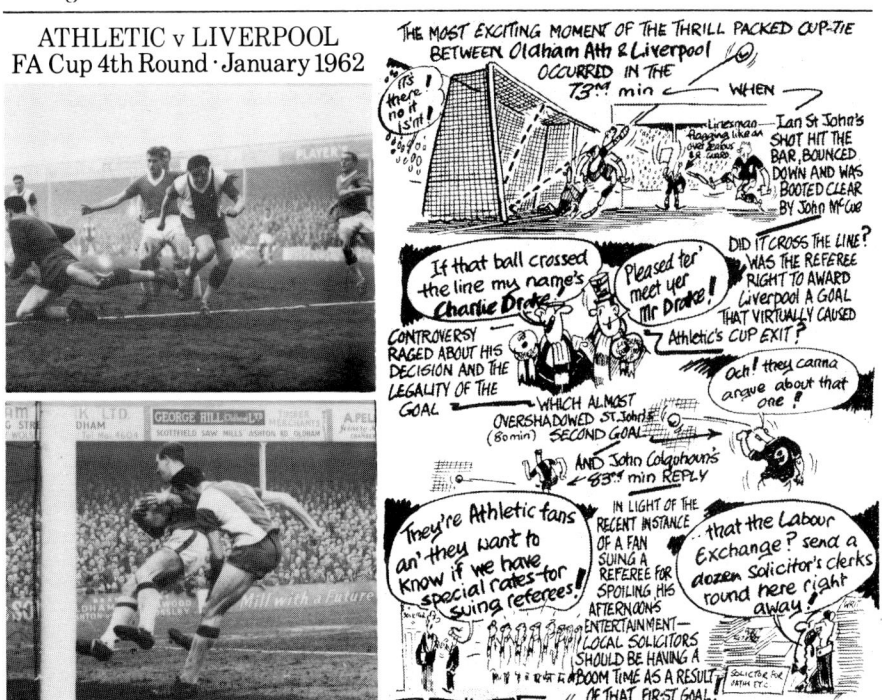

ATHLETIC v LIVERPOOL
FA Cup 4th Round · January 1962

"THE TEAM FROM A TOWN OF CHIMNEYS"

Chairman Ken Bates set out his simple recipe for success for the new season:— The club's wages come from home gates; the club needs £75,000 a year — therefore attendances must average 15,000. The fans want victory or they don't turn up — therefore the team must win matches.

With the main stand re-seated and private boxes installed, increased prices didn't seem to deter the supporters and it wasn't a bad season with Athletic finishing 10th on 48 points.

The improvement — and a successful close-season tour of Rhodesia and Malawi — raised hopes for the 1967-68 season, but they didn't materialise after a poor start.

A late flourish, inspired by Jimmy Frizzell and Alan Lawson, saw the team take 17 points from 12 games to finish in 16th place.

If fans were reluctant to look back on that campaign, it was

OLDHAM ATHLETIC TEAM & OFFICIALS MEET A PRIME MINISTER
The then Prime Minister of Rhodesia, the Hon. Ian Douglas Smith, this day (4th July 1967) met the Oldham Athletic party, who had been on a two week, eleven match tour

downright painful to recall the 1968-69 season.

Athletic went from bad to worse and, by the end of November, Jack Rowley had returned as manager.

Under Jimmy Frizzell's coaching things bucked up a little, but a spate of injuries towards the end of the season finally killed off Athletic's hopes. They were relegated to the Fourth Division.

As if that wasn't bad enough, the following season developed on equally miserable lines until December 29, 1969, when manager Rowley was sacked.

Frizzell was appointed caretaker manager and, with the signing of striker Jim Fryatt for £8,000 from Blackburn Rovers, Athletic's fortunes improved.

Finishing in 19th place and so avoiding the embarrassment of applying for re-election, Athletic appointed Frizzell as manager on a two-year contract.

It was a move certainly to pay handsome dividends over the next decade.

"THE TEAM FROM A TOWN OF CHIMNEYS"

COLERAINE 0, ATHLETIC 4, PRE-SEASON FRIENDLY, 1966
Photo shows both teams

'A TUSSLE IN THE SNOW' — ATHLETIC V SHREWSBURY, JANUARY 1965

"THE TEAM FROM A TOWN OF CHIMNEYS"

ATHLETIC V WEST HAM UTD. F.A. CUP 3rd ROUND, JAN 1966
Athletic's goalkeeper Bollands allows a 90 yard clearance kick by West Ham's full-back Burnett, bounce over his head, and into the net to register West Ham's first goal.

ATHLETIC V GILLINGHAM, 7 MARCH 1965
'Tony Bartley signals a corner after Dearden had been tackled'

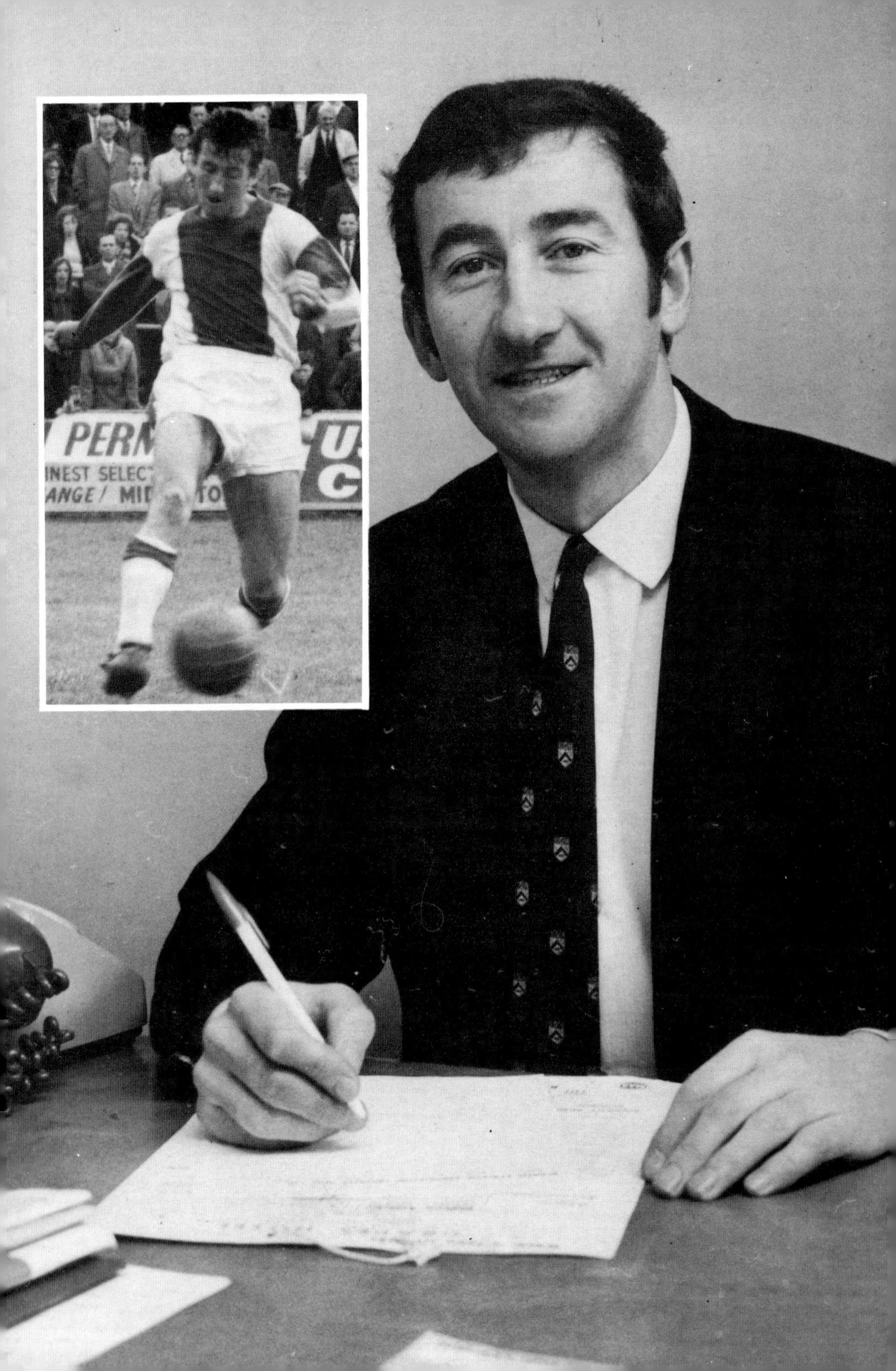

"THE TEAM FROM A TOWN OF CHIMNEYS"

Frizzell's Era

Season 1970-71 is arguably the one when all the years of frustration came right and Athletic played host to both cash and honours.

The cash came as the product of the Ford Sporting League scheme whereby teams earned points for goals scored and had them deducted for players being booked or sent off.

Athletic won the cash prize every month of the season and the end-of-season bonus to pick up £70,000. The effort is commemorated to this day by the club's Ford Stand.

The honours came in the shape of promotion to the Third Division, achieved with 59 points and third place.

FORD SPORTING LEAGUE WINNERS — 1970-71

In distant days to come when old men sit smugly in bars the conversation turns, as such conversations inevitably must, to talk of football and great football memories, there will be a special awe and reverence reserved for the events of season 1970-71 at Boundary Park.

For it was the season of the minor miracle; a season of startling achievement when cash and honours finally came knocking at the Boundary Park door.

The actual statistics of a marvellous and momentous season are now common knowledge. Everyone knows that Athletic, by finishing third in the Fourth Division with 59 points gained promotion, and that by scoring goals and keeping cool heads under pressure, won a grand total of £70,000 from Fords.

Everyone knows it now and regards the fact of promotion with a bland acceptance that does not do full justice to the amount of work and worry that went into the promotion drive.

For who, during the dark and depressing days of the previous season when it seemed that the club's very existence was in jeopardy, could have forecast such a change in fortunes?

It would have been a very brave man indeed who at the end of the previous season when Athletic had narrowly won a battle against the menacing claws of a re-election application, could have forecast such a dramatic rise.

PRE-SEASON VISIT TO R.A.F. VALLEY, ANGLESEY, 1972
CRANSTON . SHAW . SPENCE . DOWD . MULVANEY . BOWIE . McNEILL . WHITTLE
SWEENEY . ROBINS . WOOD . JONES . GARWOOD . CLEMENTS

But it is in this context that Athletic's achievement must be viewed. Never must it be forgotten that their springboard to glory was not only carefully planned, but born out of near disaster.

The crucial planning started when the club was lodged at the foot of the Fourth Division with apparently no hope of pulling off a dramatic escape.

And it was that inspired planning and the events of early 1970 which determined Athletic's mercurial rise this season.

Just look back at those hectic early months and you can see the vital part they were to play in Athletic's future.

Jimmy Frizzell became manager, first on a temporary basis and then, after distinguishing himself, on a two-year contract.

Jim Fryatt was signed for £8,000 from Blackburn Rovers and Tommy Bryceland for a nominal fee from Norwich City. Those two key signings, were to mean a tremendous amount to Athletic.

During the close season with board room optimism at a new high, the good work continued.

Maurice Short was picked up from Middlesbrough, Bill Cranston from Preston, Don Heath from Swindon and utility man Barry Hartle from Stockport County.

And so the scene was set. The players were ready and well rehearsed and the opening performance at Grimsby on August 14th was eagerly awaited.

But disaster! Athletic never found any sort of form at all and suffered a terrible 4-1 hammering at the hands of the Mariners. Jim Fryatt scored the only goal and after that defeat, there were grave doubts in the town about the team's actual potential.

The club and its players were bitterly disappointed at such a start but it is to their eternal credit that they shook off the misery and fought back with a grim tenacity that was soon to bring its own rewards.

Goals from Shaw, Fryatt and Bryceland swept Athletic to a shock 3-1 League Cup win over Bury at Gigg Lane and then Fryatt and Bryceland popped in two more as Exeter City were conquered in a League match at Boundary Park.

Despite a defeat at Cambridge — the League's newcomers — Athletic had now gained an appetite for success; an appetite that could only be satisfied by a feast of goals.

And on Tuesday, September 1st, the feast really started; the tables were set and the first course was served.

Athletic travelled to meet a Scunthorpe side that, at the time was doing quite well with a formidable home record. But Athletic were not afraid. They found their full, flowing flair and although Arthur Thompson was booked, turned on a majestic display of attacking football.

Two goals from Jim Fryatt and a third from Alan McNeill saw

Athletic home by the odd goal in five and really started the promotion ball rolling.

It was Brentford's unfortunate task to face rampant Athletic next... and how they were tortured in a brilliant 5-1 win. David Shaw, having probably his finest game of the season, slammed home four superb goals and Bryceland netted the fifth.

Now Athletic knew what they could do; knew that they were capable of scaling the peaks of attacking adventure to swoop down and slaughter any formidable foe.

Middlesbrough handed out a League Cup defeat but nothing could halt Athletic's momentum now! In the next couple of weeks they slammed four goals at Newport and then, in the finest match of the season, beat Aldershot 5-2 at Boundary Park.

JIMMY FRIZZELL RECEIVES 'BELLS MANAGER OF THE MONTH', FEBRUARY 1973

The Aldershot game was the highlight of the season. Athletic were absolutely superb, hitting perfection in a performance that was a credit to the Fourth Division.

Aldershot too looked an outstanding side and it is to their eternal credit that they matched Athletic stride for stride, attack for attack, most of the game. It was indeed a football feast . . . a real match to remember.

Between the two wins over Newport and Aldershot was a terrible home defeat by Workington when Athletic turned on probably their worst performance of the season.

But by now Athletic had already established the pattern. They topped the Ford League and were among the promotion contenders. For the remainder of the season they were to keep both positions.

Throughout October there was a pretty mixed bag of results but then, on October 30th, Athletic were involved in another high scoring thriller.

This time the opponents were Crewe — the only side capable of offering much of a challenge in the Ford League. Athletic with two goals from Fryatt and further scores by Bryceland, Hartle and McNeill won 5-3 but it had always been a match where their defensive vulnerability had been exposed and punished.

JIM FRYATT - floats like a butterfly, stings like a bee! 1970/71

DAVID SHAW
Shaw's 23 League goals contributed greatly to Athletic's success in the Ford Sporting League, 1970/71

Athletic won the next three matches — two of them at Chester and Hartlepool, away — but then took an F.A. Cup knock-out by Rochdale.

At the time that defeat was dreadfully disappointing but, like the rapid League Cup exit it can be seen in retrospect as a blessing in disguise.

Too heavy a commitment in either tournament might have taken the edge off Athletic's promotion hopes . . . and it was always a season where promotion was the top priority.

Southport caught Athletic on the rebound from their F.A. Cup defeat to win 4-2 at Boundary Park but then Athletic won their next five matches in regal style to reaffirm their Third Division aspirations.

Northampton and Exeter City were conquered away and Newport, Barrow and Peterborough were the victims at Boundary Park.

At this stage Athletic were firmly established in second place in the League table. Notts County headed the list with 39 points from 24 games; Athletic had 37 from 26, Northampton 36 from 25 and Bournemouth 31 from 24.

Fifth place Southport also had 31 points from 26 games which seemed, at the end of the first week of the year, to leave Athletic home and dry in the promotion race.

Despite a 5-0 hammering at Bournemouth, Athletic refused to be shaken out of their stride and came back strongly to whip Darlington 3-1 and Southport 4-1.

The win at Southport, one of the leading away performances of the season, was the last game before the twin pressures of chasing promotion and the Ford prize caught up with Athletic and threatened to crush them.

Despite a win at Crewe, Athletic lost to Notts County, Lincoln and Southend and dropped points at Northampton, Aldershot, York, Chester, Brentford and Barrow.

By this time, with only four games to go, the promotion issue was far from certain. Notts County with 63 points from 42 games were already home and dry. Bournemouth (55), were second; York (54), third and Athletic (53) fourth.

Chester were just two points behind in fifth place and Colchester, with two games in hand, were only three points down on Athletic.

Could they do it? Could they keep their nerve over the last four games and pick up the precious points that would finally take them out of the Fourth Division.

It was a real cliff-hanger finish; full of suspense of uncertainty as Athletic prepared for the final four games. Could any four matches ever have been more crucial?

The fears that Athletic might fail; might fall at the final hurdle; were dashed with one dazzling performance before a crowd of over 10,000 at Boundary Park.

Close rivals Colchester were hammered out of the hunt as Athletic turned on a spectacular show and bagged four fine goals. Keith Bebbington netted two of them, Shaw got a third and defender Hall helped out with an own goal.

And so to York for a match against one of the best sides in the division . . . a side unbeaten at home for months and months.

And so too to Athletic's finest hour . . . an hour in which they pressured and powered York to defeat and looked, for the first time in a couple of months, a side well worthy of a place in the Third Division.

York were just played off the park as Athletic set out to attack from the start and never allowed the home side to settle. All were heroes in a magnificent team effort but none were more heroic than full-back Maurice Whittle whose rifled shot gave Athletic victory and virtually assured them of promotion.

It needed only a point from a goalless draw at Workington to clinch Athletic's fantastic season.

The new season was one of consolidation, Athletic finishing a respectable and untroubled 11th.

And 1972-73 saw them make a strong bid for further promotion. However, despite finishing fourth in the table, Athletic found that supporters were disgruntled — surprisingly not satisfied with the teams apparent improvement.

Any dissenting voices on the Boundary Park terraces were to be silenced in 1973-74.

It took Athletic five games to record their first win, but they made steady progress from then on, losing only to Brighton and Huddersfield up to December 8.

Still, it looked as though Bristol Rovers and Bournemouth were set to monopolise the division.

Chasing League and cup honours seemed to take its toll on Athletic. League results were hit-and-miss for a while but new acquisition Tony Bailey from Derby County slotted in well in defence, Colin Garwood began to hit the net regularly in attack and manager Frizzell pulled off another master-stroke by signing brilliant winger Alan Groves from Bournemouth.

Easter arrived, traditionally make-or-break time for promotion and relegation, with Athletic firmly in contention.

And they made the most of it by thrashing Southport 6-0, Bristol Rovers 2-1 and Southport again, 2-0.

After beating Huddersfield 6-0 on April 20, Athletic were sure of promotion. Now the hunt was on for the championship.

It looked like being a typical Athletic anti-climax as they lost to Grimsby 2-1 and dropped a point to York in a 1-1 draw.

Still needing one point to make sure of the title, Athletic faced Charlton in front of an 18,000 crowd — and lost 2-0.

"THE TEAM FROM A TOWN OF CHIMNEYS"

PLYMOUTH V ATHLETIC, May 1974
A triumphant Athletic after clinching the Div. 3. Championship with a 0-0 Draw.

"THE TEAM FROM A TOWN OF CHIMNEYS"

So to the final match at Plymouth. Full-back Maurice Whittle cleared a goal-bound effort off the line, Athletic held on for a goalless draw and the championship came back to Boundary Park.

After a break of 20 years, Athletic were back in the Second Division — haunted by the memory of George Hardwick's 1950's team which had dropped straight back.

ATHLETIC v HEREFORD UNITED, March 1974, Division 3
Alan Groves' flying header spins wide in a 1-1 draw

BRISTOL ROVERS v ATHLETIC, April 1974, Division 3
Groves again, proving a handful for the Bristol defence in a 2-1 victory

ROCHDALE v ATHLETIC, May 1974, Friendly
Dick Mulvaney leads out the Champions!

"THE TEAM FROM A TOWN OF CHIMNEYS"

THE STORY OF HOW A TITLE WAS WON – 1973/74

Few people, if they were really honest, could claim to have believed the Latics were promotion, let alone championship material, when last season kicked off on Saturday, August 25th at the Shay. And the result of that match — a particularly uninspiring goal-less draw — can have done little to plant the idea in many minds.

And yet, less than nine months later, Athletic travelled to Plymouth needing yet another goal-less draw to wrap up the coveted trophy.

Dramatic days indeed. And will those of us who tuned into Piccadilly Radio for a commentary on the final minutes of that match ever forget it?

The seconds ticked away and, with the passing of each and every one, Latics went nearer to winning the championship.

And then, remember, Plymouth won a corner. A thousand hearts missed a beat as that corner kick, more than 300 miles away floated into the goalmouth. But it came to nothing and, as the ball was cleared up-field, the final whistle blew and Latics were champions of Division Three.

But all that was a long, long way away when the season started. Athletic, following their draw with Halifax were knocked out of the League Cup by Fourth Division Bury and did not pick up winning points until the fifth match of the season.

That came on September 8th when a goal from Ian Robins gave the side a 1-0 win over Watford. Wins over Southend (home), Brighton (away) and Plymouth (home) and drawn games against Wrexham (home) and Cambridge (away) followed before we were all brought back down to earth by a 1-0 home defeat by Brighton.

October 2nd was the date of the Brighton defeat and Athletic were destined not to lose again until December 8th when an injury to Dick Mulvaney depleted the side and set them up for a 2-1 reverse at Huddersfield.

At the time, Bristol Rovers, and Bournemouth looked set to monopolise the division and Athletic, despite their run of success, were making little impact.

It was at this time that the strain of chasing League and Cup honours really began to tell upon the side.

After knocking Halifax out of the F.A. Cup in the second round, Latics suffered three successive League defeats — to Blackburn, Watford and Port Vale — and there were many who wrote off their promotion prospects there and then.

A third round marathon with Cambridge United really captured everyone's imagination.

The two teams drew 2-2 at Cambridge and then 3-3 at Boundary Park in a replay that took place in the afternoon because of the power crisis but nevertheless attracted a 10,000 plus crowd.

Athletic's championship winning tea

icially received, Oldham Town Hall 1974.

"THE TEAM FROM A TOWN OF CHIMNEYS"

Finally, the tie went to Nottingham Forest's ground where goals from George Jones and Colin Garwood carried Latic's into the fourth round.

Although Bristol Rovers and now Chesterfield and York City were setting a pretty hectic pace at the top of the table, Athletic, plugged away brilliantly on the rails.

A brilliant 3-0 win at Bournemouth — Colin Garwood scored all Athletic's goals — put the Hampshire club out of the running and served notice to the front-runners that Athletic really meant business.

In all, the side rattled off ten successive League wins, scoring 26 goals and surrendering only six in the process.

By this time, Tony Bailey had joined the side from Derby County and Alan Groves, a brilliant winger with devastating control, had been picked up from Bournemouth.

These two players, added to an already competent and confident squad, tipped the promotion scales in the Latics favour.

A great chance to knock major rivals Chesterfield off their lofty perch presented itself on March 16 — but Athletic, who had taken a huge following to Derbyshire, lost 1-0.

But they bounced back to complete the double over Bournemouth in a 4-2 win at Boundary Park only to lose some of their momentum when they were held to a 1-1 draw by a rugged Hereford side.

A savage 4-1 mauling at Charlton eroded the fans' confidence and even a win over struggling Shrewsbury and another against bogey team Grimsby did not really restore it.

YORK CITY v ATHLETIC, April 1974, Division 3
Jones and Hicks celebrate a 'Whittle special' in a 1-1 draw.

And so to Easter the spell which, in many people's eyes, really earned Athletic the championship cup.

They started the holiday programme on a brilliant note when a hat-trick from Colin Garwood and further goals from Maurice Whittle (penalty), George Jones and Andy Lochhead gave them a 6-0 win over Southport.

But then came the big one. On the next day, Athletic travelled to Eastville to meet the all conquering Rovers and provided some of their best football of the season to thoroughly earn a 2-1 win.

A crowd of 18,629 saw that game and might have known then that they were hailing the future champions of Division Three.

Just to rub it in, Athletic completed their three-match Easter programme with a 2-0 win at Southport and then needed to beat Huddersfield on April 20 to be sure of promotion.

A crowd of more than 16,000 came along to Boundary Park in a mood of rare excitement and expectancy. And, for once, Athletic didn't let them down.

A brilliant 6-0 victory was rough justice to a Huddersfield side that looked to have a lot of talent but it was no day to feel sorry for the vanquished.

For Athletic had done it. They had booked their place in Division Two and the scenes that followed the match will live with us all forever.

The colour, the cheering and the chanting made it a most memorable and emotional moment that all those who are connected with Athletic must surely treasure.

And then came one of those anti-climaxes for which Athletic have, over the years, become famous.

They lost 2-1 at Grimsby, drew 1-1 at York City in a tight and tense match and came to Boundary Park needing to take a point from Charlton to make sure of the championship.

But they were back at their most frustrating and, despite the encouragement of an 18,000 crowd, lost their final home game of the season 2-0.

And so to Plymouth and that desperately frantic final match. Athletic scraped through — partly thanks to a goal-line clearance by Maurice Whittle and the championship came to Boundary Park.

After a break of 20 years, Athletic had won a place in Division Two and the town went mad.

It was a great season, punctuated with some brilliant team and individual performances. But, in the final analysis, it was the side's remarkable consistency over that ten match, twenty point run from January 12th to March 12th, which made it all possible.

Striker Colin Garwood was Latic's top marksman that season with 17 goals to his credit. And, remembering that Colin played in only 29 out of a possible 54 matches, that was quite some going.

In all, he scored 16 times in the League — just one fewer than a personal best-ever total of 17 goals he netted while with Peterborough.

Indeed, the new season did prove to be a desperate struggle and, in the end, Athletic survived with only three points to spare over the relegated clubs.

Despite toiling to hold on to Second Division status, Athletic began 1975-76 with no new players. However, they picked up 30 points from 26 matches to reach fifth place before disaster set in once more.

From the final 16 games they mustered only eight points to finish in 17th place.

Increased admission charges, coupled with the failure to sign new players, lopped almost 55,000 off home attendances for the season, the average dropping 3,000 to 10,191.

Obviously the side needed strengthening and manager Frizzell again proved to be a most shrewd transfer-market dealer, picking up Vic Halom for £25,000 from Sunderland, where he was a soccer hero, and John Hurst and David Irving, on free transfers from Everton.

In view of Hurst's contribution in defence over the next few seasons, he was, arguably one of Frizzell's best ever bargains.

Athletic began the season well enough and enjoyed a decent cup run until being put out by Liverpool 3-1 at Anfield on February 26.

From then on nothing went right. The last 19 games brought only three wins and 12 defeats in a row to push them perilously close to the relegation zone.

Athletic seemed to have come to terms with life in the Second Division by 1977-78. They put together a run of 12 League games without defeat, winning four out of six away.

MANCHESTER UNITED V ATHLETIC, March 31st 1975
Alan Young scores for Athletic with a flying header

LIVERPOOL V ATHLETIC, F.A. CUP 5TH RD. FEBRUARY 1977

A goalbound effort from Robins is saved by Clemence in the Liverpool goal. (inset): David Shaw scores Athletic's goal from a Groves' pass

"THE TEAM FROM A TOWN OF CHIMNEYS"

ALAN GROVES, OLDHAM ATHLETIC 1974-1977

Steve Taylor, who joined the club from Bolton in mid-October, scored 21 goals in 34 games, but two popular figures left Boundary Park -- striker David Shaw, forced to quit with a knee injury, and much-admired Alan Groves who joined Blackpool.

Injuries struck Athletic a devastating blow over the final 16 matches, of which only two brought success. A squad, already hard pressed to keep pace with the likes of Bolton and Tottenham was decimated.

Still, the season ended with Athletic in eighth place on 42 points — their best total in the Second Division since 1933-34.

The close season was overshadowed in June, 1978, by the dreadful news of the death of Alan Groves, the flying winger who had been such a hit with Boundary Park fans before his move to Blackpool.

Athletic manager Jimmy Frizzell summed up the feeling of many when he said:

"The loss of Alan Groves to the game of football is a tragedy that the game is ill-equipped to stand. He was a player with the rare gift of an entertainer. He had ability that was respected the length and breadth of the League."

ATHLETIC V BLACKPOOL, January 1978

Alan Groves (Blackpool) & Carl Valentine (Athletic) tussle for possession. This was Groves' last appearance at Boundary Park

ATHLETIC V WEST BROMWICH ALBION · 1976, Division 2
Athletic's David Shaw is tackled by Albion's Johnny Giles

"THE TEAM FROM A TOWN OF CHIMNEYS"

By November, 1978, Athletic were on course for a good season with a point-a-game start from 15 matches.

However, they went through an astonishing five-month spell without a home win before beating Blackburn 5-0 on April 13. It was, in fact, Blackburn who had earlier put Athletic on the road to recovery after 12 matches without a win, the Latics scoring a victory at Ewood Park.

From their last nine games Athletic took 14 points to stay in the Second Division.

On the cup front, they lost to Burnley in the two-legged final of the Anglo-Scottish Cup and performed creditably against eventual winners Nottingham Forest in the League Cup, holding them 0-0 at home before losing 4-2 in the replay. In the F.A. Cup, Athletic reached the fifth round before succumbing 1-0 at home to First Division Tottenham.

In mid-season Simon Stainrod joined the club for a then record £60,000 and soon became a popular, entertaining goal-scorer, but Les Chapman, another well-liked midfield character was given a free transfer to Stockport County.

By the end of season 1979-80, Athletic had improved their Second Division position to 11th but most of the action centred on the comings and goings of players.

Pre-season, Athletic appointed Bill Taylor as assistant manager and chief coach to long-serving boss Jimmy Frizzell. Taylor, coach with the England international squad under manager Ron Greenwood, had previously been with Manchester City and the board of directors saw his arrival as an ambitious step forward.

ATHLETIC v TOTTENHAM HOTSPUR, F.A. Cup 5th Rd., February 1979
Athletic's Paul Heaton powers a shot at the Spurs goal with Glenn Hoddle in attendance

However, problems of a new sort faced the club in the shape of a newly-agreed "freedom of contract" procedure adopted by the soccer authorities and the players union, the Professional Footballers Association.

This enabled a player at the end of an existing contract to become a "free agent" if he didn't want to accept the new terms offered by his club.

Striker Alan Young decided to join Leicester City and the clubs were locked in a row over the transfer fee which was eventually decided at £200,000, with £50,000 after 50 appearances, by a Football League tribunal.

Athletic valued Young at twice that much and his departure was a bitter disappointment.

So, too, for many fans was the transfer of winger Carl Valentine to North American League club Vancouver Whitecaps for £80,000.

SIMON STAINROD & RODGER WYLDE, ATHLETIC'S NEW STRIKING PARTNERSHIP, 1979/80

ALAN YOUNG, JOINED LEICESTER CITY UNDER THE 'FREEDOM OF CONTRACT' PROCEDURE FOR £200,000

"THE TEAM FROM A TOWN OF CHIMNEYS"

Athletic were determined to strengthen their squad and, in September 1979, paid out a club record £200,000 fee to Manchester City for defender Kenny Clements.

In December a further £12,000 went on bringing midfield player Ryszard Kowenicki from Widzew Lodz in Poland — the club's first overseas signing.

Vic Halom was sold to Rotherham but late season saw striker Rodger Wylde join Athletic from Sheffield Wednesday for £80,000.

On March 25, 1980, Jimmy Frizzell celebrated ten years as manager at Boundary Park, and Athletic saluted him by recovering from a poor start to finish the season with a best points total since promotion.

Athletic seemed to have invested money wisely on players and had groomed promising youngsters.

As season 1980-81 beckoned, the big question was, were they now ready for a push towards the First Division?

Athletic's Kenny Clements is put through his paces by the late Bill Taylor

ATHLETIC'S GED KEEGAN, SIMON STAINROD & VIC HALOM PICTURED PRE 1979/80 SEASON

ENGINEERS INSTALLING UNDERSOIL HEATING SYSTEM AT BOUNDARY PARK PRE 1980/81 SEASON

To the present

Hooliganism on the terraces, fighting between rival so-called supporters, undoubtedly contributed a great deal to the ever-dwindling attendance figures throughout the Football League during the 1970s.

In an effort to improve all aspects of safety at grounds the Football Grounds Improvement Trust was set up by the League with money being allocated to clubs to carry out such work as re-terracing old stands, new crush barriers, the erection of perimeter fences to keep supporters from invading the pitch, and to keep rival fans apart.

Club's themselves were called on to make a massive contribution to the cost of such improvements and, in Athletic's case, work worth something like £250,000 was commenced in the close season leading up to the 1980-81 campaign.

The club, with one of the highest grounds above sea level in the country, also decided to install a £60,000 undersoil heating system to help prevent the postponement of matches during the winter months.

BILL TAYLOR
(Athletic's assistant manager & England coach)

SIMON STAINROD SCORES V SHEFFIELD WEDNESDAY SEPTEMBER 6TH, 1980, RIOTS WOULD SOON HALT THE GAME

THE F.A. PROBE TEAM BEGIN THEIR INQUIRY AT ATHLETIC'S BOUNDARY PARK GROUND FOLLOWING THE RIOT MATCH V SHEFFIELD WEDNESDAY, SEPTEMBER 1980

However, it was the safety work which was to be put to the test first when season 80-81 opened.

On September 6, 1980 the home match against Sheffield Wednesday was marred by a crowd disturbance which forced the game to be held up for 29 minutes as a stupid, minority element among Sheffield supporters got onto the pitch.

The incident was sparked off by the sending-off of Sheffield's Terry Curran for kicking Athletic's Simon Stainrod as referee George Tyson was booking both players.

When Football's top officials came to Oldham on September 15 to hold an inquiry into the "riots" they came to the conclusion, after seven hours of talks, that Athletic should be exonerated from all blame.

The F.A. commission decided that Athletic's ground and safety improvements were more than adequate and that the blame must lay with Wednesday — being responsible for the actions of their supporters.

Sadly for a Sheffield club with such proud traditions, the actions of a small group of their supporters blemished their name. Stiff penalties — financial and temporary restriction on ticket sales to their fans — were imposed by the F.A.

Athletic had won that ill-fated match by 2-0 to record their 999th victory in the Football League.

Annoyingly for fans, they had to wait until November 11 for the 1,000th win — Jim Steel's only goal of the game, beating Blackburn Rovers at Boundary Park.

JIM STEEL 1981

ATHLETIC V
Stainrod (on ground) watches his dow.

AUGUST 1980
...der bounce over the Ranger's crossbar

Generally, it was a bitterly disappointing season. Beginning with tremendous promise, it ended in another desperate struggle to avoid relegation — despite the team losing only once in their last 11 matches.

A two-legged League Cup defeat by lowly Portsmouth and a home, F.A. Cup replay beating by Fourth Division Wimbledon, all served to deepen the gloom and see Athletic's attendance figures dwindle even further.

The sale, for £275,000 to Queens Park Rangers, of popular striker Simon Stainrod, didn't seem to help the cause.

Athletic's home record, for so long their saviour in the Second Division, was poor — though their away record picked up — and there were complaints, as at many clubs, about the entertainment value of soccer.

There were also the usual calls made for new players to be signed, the squad to be strengthened. The response from the directors was dramatic — and somewhat surprising at the time.

As Athletic just escaped relegation, seven players were released on free transfers, including experienced defenders John Hurst and Ronnie Blair. Only one new signing was made — a 17 year-old reserve goalkeeper, Andy Goram.

The board of directors had decided that in times of financial difficulties, not just in football, but throughout the country as a whole, the only sensible way forward for Athletic was to bank on the club's thriving youth policy, so ably run in previous seasons by chief scout Colin McDonald.

Once again in the club's topsy-turvy history, it was make-or-break time.

Season 1981-82 started with Athletic having a squad of 22 professionals. Basically there was a squad of 15 recognised first-teamers and their average age was just 22.

The fan in the street wanted to know if a squad of experienced players had struggled the previous season, what hope was their for these fresh-faced youngsters?

The opening eight games of the campaign provided a clue. Athletic beat Bolton 5-4 on aggregate in a thrilling two-legged League Cup-tie and, after six matches, were the only unbeaten team in the Second Division.

RONNIE BLAIR - A fine professional

WEST HAM UNITED V ATHLETIC, MARCH 1981
Rodger Wylde scoring Athletic's goal in a 1-1 draw

RYSZARD KOWENICKI
At £12,000, Athletic's first overseas signing

They were the last team in the League to lose their unbeaten record in their tenth match — a 3-1 defeat at Charlton — but home support remained surprisingly poor.

League Cup hopes ended in a 3-0 replay defeat at Fulham after an earlier two-legged success over Newport County.

And the club had to bear the terrible shock of the death of assistant manager Bill Taylor at the end of November, after a long illness.

However, League form continued to be highly encouraging and a run of three wins, at Wrexham and over Grimsby and Orient, thrust Athletic into second place in the Second Division — their highest League placing for more than 50 years.

By Christmas they were the only Second Division team still with an unbeaten home record.

The New Year — and the First Division — beckoned invitingly . . .

ATHLETIC V CARDIFF CITY, 1981/82, Division 2
Paul Futcher heads over the Cardiff crossbar

ATHLETIC v BOLTON WANDERERS, September 1980, Division 2
Stainrod celebrates his equalising goal in a 1-1 draw

ATHLETIC v CARDIFF CITY, August 1981, Division 2
A header from Kenny Clements (hidden) registers Athletic's first goal of the 1981/82 season

"THE TEAM FROM A TOWN OF CHIMNEYS"

However, Athletic took the generous spirit of Christmas too far.

They were due to travel to Lancashire rivals Blackburn Rovers on Boxing Day but the Ewood Park pitch was frozen — in common with many other grounds in a sharp winter freeze-up.

The match was switched to Latics — with disastrous results for them. Blackburn romped to a 3-0 win and, when Athletic could only scrape a 1-1 home draw with Leicester City a couple of days later, the chance of going top of the table, above the inactive Luton Town, had passed.

The undersoil heating at Boundary Park meant Athletic could carry on playing home games while other clubs were hit by postponments. However, the Latics failed to make the most of it.

After unluckily going out of the F.A. Cup, 2-1 at Gillingham at the first hurdle, Athletic dropped another two home points in a 1-1 draw with promotion rivals Watford, redeemed themselves by winning 1-0 at Cardiff, but then lost by the same score at Derby, were held 1-1 at home by lowly Bolton and lost at Shrewsbury.

A 2-0 home win over Norwich City renewed hopes and that was followed by an exciting goalless draw at Cambridge.

Despite their indifferent form in the new year, Athletic had managed to hang on to third place as most of their leading rivals also turned in hit-and-miss efforts when catching up on their games in hand.

A 2-0 defeat at leaders Luton Town allowed several clubs to close within striking distance of Athletic, but as they turned into the final third of the season, they were still in contention — though deeply worried by the possible effects of injuries and suspensions on a small first-team squad.

ROTHERHAM UNITED v ATHLETIC, October 1981, Division 2
Rodger Wylde celebrates a goal for Athletic in a 2-1 victory

Jimmy Frizzell clears his desk for the last time – June 1982

Athletic needed strength in depth – and were found lacking.

Their supply of goals dried up (only 11 in 18 matches from Boxing Day to April 17 when they slumped 4-0 at Crystal Palace) and only 13 points were collected from a possible 63.

As fast as promotion hopes receded, so did the level of support.

Although Athletic lost only three times at Boundary Park another 18 points slipped by in home draws. Had they turned five of those stalemates into victories they would have been promoted.

Jimmy Frizzell reckoned he could exploit the free-transfer market during the summer to give Athletic the strength in depth they needed to sustain a promotion challenge the following season.

However, on June 15, 1982, Athletic dropped a bombshell by dispensing with Frizzell's services after 22 years as player and manager.

It seemed to the average fan quite incidental that the same day saw the end of the Falklands conflict.

Protests poured in and demonstrations were held in the town, amid calls for a boardroom takeover.

Many names were bandied about as possible successors but, on July 14, 1982, Athletic's new manager arrived at Boundary Park – on the back of a lorry!

Former Everton and England forward Joe Royle, on his way to the ground to meet local and national Press men, had to hitch a lift after his car broke down on the M62 motorway.

"My first job as manager will be to get a reliable car," quipped Royle, with a sense of humour to stand him in good stead for the future.

On a more serious note, the new manager noted: "Athletic are not a fashionable club, but success makes you fashionable – and that's what we are aiming for."

"THE TEAM FROM A TOWN OF CHIMNEYS"

WEST HAM UNITED V ATHLETIC, MARCH 1981
West Ham's Trevor Brooking tussles with Athletic's Keegan in a 1-1 draw

"THE TEAM FROM A TOWN OF CHIMNEYS"

Royle's Reign

JOE ROYLE soon realised he had inherited the need for another recognised goalscorer and an experienced midfield man if Athletic were to make a genuine promotion push.

However, Athletic's financial position was far from healthy and the pressure was on to sell players while searching the bargain basement for replacements.

Royle's first match in charge was at home to Shrewsbury when an own goal gave Athletic a 1-0 win in front of a crowd of only 3,731.

Joe Royle, appointed Manager on 14th July 1982

"THE TEAM FROM A TOWN OF CHIMNEYS"

Events off the field took centre stage during the early 80's. A countrywide recession saw 17% unemployment figures in Oldham, and business in general, including the majority of Football League Clubs, were feeling the pinch. Athletic were no different, striving to survive, and finding means to keep afloat. Chairman, Harry Wilde commissioned a local firm of Chartered Accountants to make economic recommendations, which came to no avail, culminating in Mr. Wilde's resignation on September 23rd, 1982, after 8 years as Chairman, and 13 years as Director.

Mr. Ian Stott, a Director since 1974, took over as Chairman, with Mr. David Brierley as the Deputy, and the size of their task soon became apparent.

Fortunately, help was at hand from the Club's major shareholders and long time associates, J.W. Lees Brewery.

A package deal involved the Brewery buying the Boundary Club and Sports Hall Complex and discharging the Club's bank overdraft, loans and other debts.

Altogether the rescue deal was worth over £500,000, for which the Brewery had a five year sponsorship package for ground, programme and shirt advertising, and Athletic had time to reorganise and settle the debt.

"Toast to Success" – J.W. Lees Brewery Chairman, Mr. Richard Lees Jones (left), and Athletic Chairman, Mr. Ian Stott, hold aloft the package deal contract on Friday, 12th November 1982

"THE TEAM FROM A TOWN OF CHIMNEYS"

Mr. Harry Wilde – Athletic Chairman 1974 – 1982

The team celebrated by whacking Wolves 4-1, in front of the television cameras, the day after the November 12 deal had been announced. Had the club's fortunes at last changed for the better?

Well, season 82-83 turned out to be their most successful in the Second Division since promotion was achieved in 73-74.

It could have been better but for the old curse of too many home draws (ten). However, they recorded their highest finishing position (7th), most goals (64), best points total (61) and fewest defeats (nine).

Joe Royle could feel justifiably proud of his first-season achievements but, with average crowds down to 6,961 and the club still deeply in debt, he was to see the other side of the managerial coin in 1983-84.

Having already sold influential defender Paul Futcher to Derby County for a six-figure sum, Athletic were further hit by the sales of John Ryan (£235,00 to Newcastle), Paul Atkinson (£175,000 to Watford) and marksman Rodger Wylde (£30,000 to Sporting Lisbon).

Newcomers Derrick Parker (£40,000 from Barnsley), and Joe McBride (£45,000 from Rotherham) struggled to blend in, while injuries also took a devastating toll.

The away form suffered in particular with only three wins and two draws in 21 attempts as Athletic used four different goalkeepers and 12 other players in various defensive combinations – producing a dreadful goals-against total of 73.

There were bright spots, in the £55,000 signing of aggressive striker Mike Quinn, from Stockport County, action-packed little midfielder Mark Ward (£9,500 from non-league Northwich Victoria) and the short-term addition of experience in Manchester United's former Scotland captain Martin Buchan and much-travelled striker David Cross.

A 'backs to the wall' season predicted – 1984-85

ATHLETIC v MIDDLESBROUGH *February 1983 – Division 2 Boro' keeper O'Hanlon is beaten by John Ryan's superb free kick for Latics second goal in a 3-0 victory*

It was a long, hard slog, but Athletic successfully fought off the threat of relegation, with teenager Andy Hodkinson's goal beating Grimsby in the last home game to secure safety.

Not surprisingly, the bookmakers had Athletic as favourites for relegation when the 1984-85 season opened with only one new face – that of vastly experienced defender or midfielder Willie Donachie on a "free" from Burnley.

Athletic managed only 17 points from their first 21 league games but mid-season signings Mick McGuire, from Barnsley, and Brendan O'Callaghan, from Stoke, gave the team valuable experience and cohesion, especially when they switched to a sweeper-style defence.

Only 14 goals were conceded in the final 14 games – and five of those came at champions Oxford United as Athletic finished comfortably in mid-table.

Once again, there was hardly any income from cup football. An F.A. Cup home win over Brentford was followed by a 5-1 thrashing at Sheffield Wednesday, while Athletic went out of the Milk (League) Cup 6-5 on aggregate to Bolton.

With average attendances in the league tumbling to 4,725, Athletic needed another major cash-flow boost and got an unexpected one in January 1985 when Liverpool paid £250,000 for talented teenage striker Wayne Harrison after only five first-team appearances.

Joe Royle welcomes new signing Martin Buchan (left), with Kenny Clements, Roger Palmer and Tony Henry – August 1983

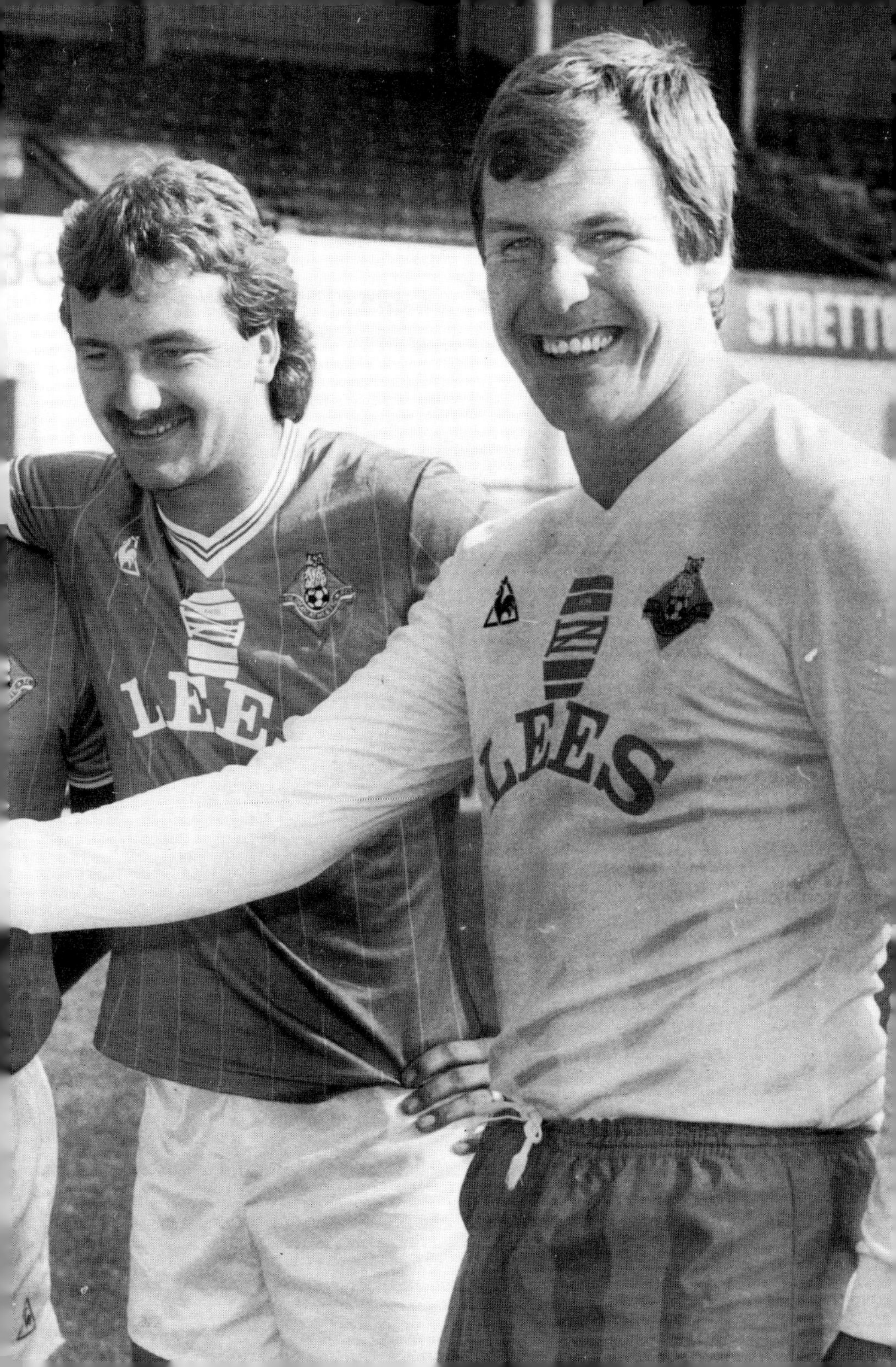
LEES
LEES

Boundary Park groundsman Harry Wood watches as Athletic's pitch is removed, as the first phase of work to instal the £385,000 plastic carpet in June 1986

During the close season English clubs faced an indefinite ban from playing in European competitions following the Hysel Stadium disaster in Brussels. Athletic were one of 14 First and Second Division clubs to seek permission from the Football League for a new knock-out cup competition, the Full Members Cup, with a Wembley final, as an alternative to a Super Cup for those qualified to play in Europe but prevented by F.I.F.A's ban.

Athletic also introduced a Members Card scheme to extend their existing segregation and safety arrangements.

Despite the problems facing football – its image tarnished by the hooligans latching on to the sport – Athletic chairman Ian Stott believed the club was winning its fight to strike a balance between improving the team, boosting commercial activities and upgrading spectator facilities.

In the summer of 1985, Athletic signed experienced striker Ron Futcher (£15,000 from Barnsley) and brought back Paul Atkinson (£30,000 from Watford) plus signing former Liverpool "super sub" David Fairclough for a short spell. However, the popular Mark Ward went to West Ham for £250,000 on the eve of the new season . . . a move only slightly tempered by the re-signing of John Ryan, a £25,000 capture from Sheffield Wednesday.

Athletic's first pre-season game was of double significance. Liverpool's visit to Boundary Park was their first fixture since the tragic European Cup final against Juventus at Hysel – and it marked Kenny Dalglish's first match as Anfield boss.

The 1-0 win for Athletic heralded the start of a 1985-86 season which was to go from the sublime to the ridiculous – and back again.

It began and ended with promise but, sandwiched in between was one of the worst spells of form since the club gained promotion.

From being second in the table going into November they slumped to fifth from bottom by the turn of the year, taking only one point from a possible 30.

Considering that disastrous spell it was quite an achievement for Athletic to finish the season with a flourish in eighth place – the signing of centre-back Andy Linighan (Leeds £55,000) being a significant turning point in January of 1986.

During the summer, Joe Royle signed a three-year contract, saying he would like to finish the job he had started – namely, aiming Athletic towards the top flight.

There was a major development at the ground – the installation of an artificial pitch, with the help of grants and Oldham Council backing, to provide consistent year-round training and playing facilities not only for the club, but also for the general public.

It was a race against time for the contractors to complete the installation ready for the first home game against Barnsley – and surprising to learn that the plastic needed watering to help it bed in.

Athletic's artificial surface takes shape – August 1986

Another significant development for the club's long-term future was the setting up of a Football Association-approved Centre of Excellence for boys aged 12 and over, under the guidance of qualified coaches, including Athletic's Willie Donachie and Billy Urmson. This replaced the club's "Search for a Star" scheme which in its first year produced local lad Mike Flynn, who progressed through the junior ranks to first-team status.

Pre-season, Athletic recruited defender Denis Irwin on a free transfer from Leeds and, shortly afterwards, raided Elland Road again to sign winger Tommy Wright for £80,000.

An absentee from part of the pre-season build-up was goalkeeper Andy Goram, who had spent the summer with Scotland's World Cup squad in Mexico. The campaign opened brightly with a fine 1-0 win at Derby County.

It was a taste of things to come in the first season of a new promotion play-off formula which meant the top two clubs automatically going up with the next three joining the First Division's bottom side in an end-of-season knock-out.

Andy Goram proudly shows his Scottish International call-up papers prior to the Mexico World Cup in 1986

ATHLETIC v LEEDS UNITED
(Play-Off 2nd Leg) May 1987
Athletic's Gary Williams scores for Athletic (top), Michele Cecere celebrates putting Athletic into an aggregate lead with 90 seconds left

Athletic provided some superb football as control and passing skills were improved on the new pitch and carried through into away games.

Never out of the top three all season, Athletic had to settle for a play-off place when, in any other year, they would have been promoted automatically. Unfortunately, they fell at the first hurdle, beaten in two dramatic matches by old rivals Leeds – a result which reduced grown men to tears at the apparent injustice of it all.

Still, Athletic's average attendance showed a healthy increase to 6,883 – and the rest of the Second Division knew that the "little" team from Boundary Park was now a force to be reckoned with.

Athletic had gambled financially on winning promotion and, to recoup some of the money, sold Ron Futcher to Bradford City and Kevin Moore to Southampton for £125,000. Money was spent on the team, as defender Glenn Keeley (£15,000 from Blackburn) and striker Andy Ritchie (£50,000 from Leeds) signed in the summer for fees set by independent tribunals.

However, the disappointment of the play-offs rubbed off on early-season displays in 1987-88 and it needed the £90,000 signing of striker Frank Bunn in December to put Athletic back on the rails.

Bunn and Ritchie formed a formidable partnership and Athletic struck form with a vengeance to lose only four of their last 25 games and show enormous potential.

Tommy Wright – an £80,000 signing from Leeds – 1986

Tycoon Robert Maxwell flies into Boundary Park to finalise a sponsorship deal with Maxwell Communications in July 1987

Roger Palmer collects an inscribed Silver Salver from Chairman Ian Stott in recognition of scoring 100 goals in the Football League

Former Athletic record goalscorer Eric Gemmell presents Roger Palmer with a Bro[nze?] Gemmell scored 110 goals in 195 appearan[ces]

ATHLETIC v IPSWICH TOWN *April 1989 – Division 2*
Roger Palmer breaks the Club's all time goal scoring record.
His first goal against Ipswich being his 111th for Athletic in a 4-1 victory

uette to commemorate his achievement of becoming the 'new' record holder.
Athletic in the late 40's and early 50's

Boundary Park from the air – August 1989

Some spectacular attacking displays were measured by the fact that the club had two strikers reaching 20 goals apiece for the first time since 1970-71. Ritchie and long-serving Roger Palmer netted 20 each.

Royle was understandably optimistic that a First Division place was within their grasp if Athletic could show more consistent form throughout the season. He was not entirely joking when he said: "I have had to remind the players that the season starts in August, not December."

Athletic faced the problem of replacing star 'keeper Andy Goram (£325,000 to Hibs) and Linighan (£350,000 to Norwich) by recruiting Andy Rhodes (£55,000 from Doncaster) and Ian Marshall (£100,000 from Everton).

Hopes for consistency in 1988-89 were, however, dashed by injury troubles which saw Athletic use no fewer than 31 players. Once again, it was only in the second half of the campaign that Athletic showed their true worth, being beaten only twice in the final 20 matches.

There were highlights, such as Roger Palmer smashing the club's all-time record for league goals. The first of his two in a 4-0 win over Ipswich on April 4 took his tally to 111 to beat the 35-year-old record set by Eric Gemmell.

Goals flowed for and against with 162 in 51 league and cup outings. There was certainly no shortage of entertainment and Athletic closed with a similar record to 1985-86 – a prelude to going close to promotion the following season.

Royle was now pinning his faith in 'keeper Jon Hallworth (£125,000 from Ipswich), Ian Marshall and Andy Holden (£140,000 from Wigan) providing a similar firm base as the likes of Goram, Moore and Linighan had done in the past.

Athletic certainly seemed to have the makings of their strongest squad for many years as they prepared for the 1989-90 season.

AND WHAT A SEASON THAT WAS TO BE!

The 'Pinch me' Season

IF anyone had said that Athletic would go to Wembley for the first time; would appear in the F.A. Cup semi-finals for the first time in 77 years, **AND** mount a promotion challenge all in one season, they would not have been believed.

Those are the dreams of any club in England and normally only within the grasp of the wealthy elite – not a so-called small-town team like Athletic, whose major concern for so long had been survival.

Yet it all came true, gloriously true, in the never-to-be-forgotten 1989-90 season.

It began in familiar fashion with a top player sold – Tommy Wright to Leicester for £300,000 – but the money was reinvested in Neil Adams (£100,000 from Everton) and tricky winger Rick Holden (£165,000 from Watford).

The new electronic scoreboard at Boundary Park, built to withstand the strongest gales that the Pennines could muster, blew down in the first fresh Easterly wind of the season – but it was to take centre stage on many a memorable day, beaming out the scorers to an ever growing number of fans as Athletic's cup exploits smacked of fantasy.

In the Littlewoods Cup, the old foe, Leeds United, were beaten over two legs before Athletic really hit the headlines by thrashing Scarborough 7-0 at Boundary Park, where Frank Bunn created a record for the competition by scoring six times.

When reigning First Division champions Arsenal were beaten 3-1 and another top-flight side Southampton were dispatched after a replay, Athletic found themselves in the semi-finals and the focus of national attention.

For, alongside their Littlewoods success, Athletic were also launching a bid for F.A. Cup glory. Wins over Birmingham and Brighton set up a fascinating contest against Joe Royle's old club, Everton.

"THE TEAM FROM A TOWN OF CHIMNEYS"

TUESDAY 19TH SEPTEMBER 1989

Gritty Latics hit back for slender cup lead

HOLDEN, RITCHIE STRIKE VITAL BLOWS

ATHLETIC 2
LEEDS UNITED 1

ATHLETIC face a test of endurance at Elland Road in two weeks time if they are to complete the task of knocking Leeds out of the Littlewoods Cup for the third time in four seasons.

They will travel to Yorkshire armed with a slender advantage from last night's second round, first leg. Crash helmets and body armour may be more appropriate since they will undoubtedly need to withstand a physical bombardment.

New-look Leeds, after their multi-million pound refit under manager Howard Wilkinson, have the Wimbledon-style combination of strength, aggression and organisation which hardly makes them the prettiest sight.

Effective they certainly are though, and for 27 minutes they managed to frustrate all Athletic's attempts at getting the ball on the floor to play football.

Then they broke the monotony by dashing into the lead — courtesy of former Manchester United and Scotland star Gordon Strachan.

Typically, the danger came from a set-piece at which Leeds apply considerable pressure.

Mel Sterland's throw in from the right was only partly cleared on the edge of Athletic's area and Vinny Jones made his only major contribution of the night by back-heeling the ball into the penalty box.

STRACHAN, the best Leeds player on view, pounced to drive a low, right-foot shot past 'keeper Andy Rhodes.

Athletic refused to buckle or be intimidated and bounced back to take the lead before the interval with two smartly-taken goals.

The first came from ex-Leeds man ANDY RITCHIE who hammered a cracking right-foot volley past Mervyn Day after Frank Bunn had neatly turned a pass inside

DENIED

from Andy Barlow's throw in.

Then, five minutes before the break, came an astonishing solo effort from Rick Ritchie at the far post. However, Ritchie powered his header narrowly off target.

HOLDEN latched onto the loose ball in midfield and, surging through tackles on a 25-yard run, he was tripped by Noel Blake just inside the area. Stumbling forward, Holden somehow managed to snake out his right foot to flick a shot past the advancing Day for his fourth goal of the season.

Athletic should have rounded off their fightback with another goal a few minutes later while Leeds were going through a bad patch after losing defender Chris Fairclough with an ankle injury.

Ian Marshall threaded a pass through down the left flank for Holden whose inch-perfect cross picked out Ritchie at the far post. However, Ritchie powered his header narrowly off target.

Leeds were stunned by Athletic's burst of form before the break and suffered another blow soon after the restart when striker Bobby Davison was injured.

Davison, travelling at top speed in a chase with Earl Barrett, was unable to stop in time and crashed head first into the perimeter fencing at the Chaddy End.

Although there was great concern about his well-being and he went off on a stretcher, Davison escaped with only cuts around an eye.

Despite that setback, Leeds applied the pressure in search

Report by .... BOB YOUNG
Pictures by .... GRAHAM COLLIN

of an equaliser, as for a time, Athletic again found themselves drawn into the visitors' style of play.

Rhodes made a fine save to touch over a dipping header from Sterland from a corner kick.

And, from a partly-cleared free kick, Strachan lobbed a neat pass into the area only for full-back Mike Whitlow to be denied an excellent opportunity as Rhodes got down well to block the close-range effort.

Strachan and substitute Andy Williams both slammed shots wide and there were one or two other hair-raising moments before Athletic began to settle down and play again.

SPIRIT

If fact, Holden almost grabbed the extra goal to give Athletic more breathing space. When the ball broke into space for him at the end of a Bunn-Ritchie-Palmer link-up, Holden sent an almost nonchalant 30-yard shot dipping over Day and against the bar.

As it is, Athletic will go to Elland Road with only a one-goal advantage but, if they can show the same spirit and resolution — as typified by the outstanding Barrett — then that could be enough to book a place in the third round.

This finely-balanced tie could yet turn out to be a re-run of 1986 when Athletic came from 2—0 down to lead 3—2 after the first leg, then went to Elland Road and won 1—0.

The ability to do so is there but, more than anything, the return match will be an enormous test of character.

ATHLETIC: Rhodes, Irwin, Barlow, Henry, Marshall, Barrett, Palmer, Ritchie, Bunn, Milligan, R. Holden. Subs: Williams, Wachorst.
LEEDS UNITED: Day, Sterland, Whitlow, Jones, Fairclough (Blake 30), Haddock, Strachan, Batty, Baird, Davison (Williams 67), Bundtle.
Referee: Mr. R. Hart (Darlington).
Attendance: 7,416.

Rick Holden celebrates (right) after stumbling into the penalty area (top) but managing to see his shot give Athletic the lead.

BLISSETT BACK TO HAUNT CITY

BRENTFORD 2
MAN CITY 1

THE ghost called Gary Blissett returned to haunt Manchester City — the club he supported as a child — at Griffin Park last night.

In January on the same ground, Blissett struck twice as Third Division Brentford flushed City out of the FA Cup fourth round.

And last night, Blissett, who had opened his goalscoring account against Brighton in the last round, scored the second of Brentford's goals to ensure that the Bees will travel to Maine Road on October 4 with a fighting chance of reaching the Littlewoods Cup third round.

Had it not been for David Oldfield's goal, two minutes from time, the tie could have already been decided.

"I am happy to be just a goal down," said City manager Mel Machin afterwards. "It's certainly not the easiest place to come."

Neil McNab, City's outstanding player, agreed. "Brentford played some very attractive football and made life difficult for us. David's goal was crucial, and, believe me, the tie is far from over."

But it really should have been. Brentford belying their appalling league form dominated large chunks of the match and went ahead in the tenth minute.

That man Blissett weaved his way into the City area and crossed for giant centre half Terry Evans to head powerfully home at the far post.

Then, with eight minutes remaining, Roger Stanislaus

lofted a free kick onto Blissett's head. When the ball came back off a post Blissett kept his composure to poke home the rebound.

Bee's manager Steve Perryman later conceded that City would have been most unlucky to have left without a goal, and when Oldfield stabbed the ball home, via a deflection, from eight yards out, the complexion of the second leg was totally changed.

LUCK DESERTS SCHOOLS SIDE

Oldham schools under-11s were unlucky to lose 1—0 at home to Warrington in their opening game of the season.

Within a five minute second half spell Paul Hewitt hit the upright, Paul Jackson crashed a shot against the crossbar and a Warrington defender headed a shot from Mark Jablonski against his own crossbar as Oldham searched for an equaliser.

The only goal of the game came from a well struck shot by Joseph Monks 10 minutes before half-time.

Mitchell leads scoring charge

Sportsmans FC took their goal tally to 16 in three games following a 5—1 victory against Watt.

Shaun Mitchell bagged a hat-trick for Sportsmans whose other goals came from Andy Charnley and John MacAlister.

TAKE THAT... Andy Ritchie slams in Athletic's equaliser.

162

"THE TEAM FROM A TOWN OF CHIMNEYS"

TUESDAY 3RD OCTOBER 1989

Cup misery for Leeds as stylish Latics march on

LEEDS 1, ATHLETIC 2
(Athletic won 4—2 on aggregate)

ATHLETIC dumped Leeds out of the Littlewoods Cup for the third time in four seasons, with a performance of grit and polish at Elland Road last night.

Already leading 2–1 from the first leg, Athletic virtually wrapped up a fascinating second-round tie with a superb first-half display, to stretch their advantage to 2–0 on the night and 4–1 on aggregate.

Although Leeds mounted a storming second-half fightback they could only score once as Athletic battled through to a deserved third-round place.

Leeds manager Howard Wilkinson's protestations that both Athletic's goals were offside and that his side had had 19 attempts at goal, compared to Athletic's seven, smacked of sour grapes.

It is true there was an element of doubt — particularly about the first goal — and equally true that Leeds missed chances. But even the partisan home fans recognised the quality of Athletic's first-half effort.

As Athletic defended stoutly and stroked the ball around with quality, accuracy and assurance, the Leeds faithful were prompted to chant "What the hell is going on?"

And by the time Athletic had grabbed two goals inside four minutes late in the first period the answer was clear. Leeds were going out of the cup

Report by: BOB YOUNG
Pictures by: GRAHAM COLLIN and VINCENT BROWN

STUNNED

After Vinny Jones made a mess of an attempted lob-shot and Gordon Strachan had been deprived of a shooting chance by the alert Denis Irwin, Athletic took over.

Rick Holden's teasing cross was driven back into the area by Roger Palmer and, in the ensuing goalmouth scramble, Andy Ritchie poked a shot against the base of a post before Jones hacked the ball to safety.

Leeds were ripped open in defence again when the impressive Mike Milligan sent Palmer sprinting through. Goalkeeper Mervyn Day blocked the shot but the ball came out to Holden who steered it towards an empty net from eight yards, only for Mel Sterland to make a lunging goalline clearance.

Athletic 'keeper Jon Hallworth had not had a real save to make by the time he set up the opening goal in the 36th minute.

Hallworth launched a mighty kick downfield and, with Leeds rushing out, it certainly looked as if Athletic had been caught offside. However, there was no signal from the linesman and Milligan gave chase to nod the ball over the advancing Day towards goal. FRANK BUNN galloped through with Peter Haddock in attendance and beat the defender to prod the ball into an unguarded net.

If that silenced the home crowd, they were absolutely stunned four minutes later when Athletic scored again. Earl Barrett — giving another inspired display in defence — won the ball just inside his own half and his neat through pass again sprang the Leeds offside trap. RITCHIE won the race with Haddock and, as Day came out to narrow the angle, the former Leeds striker rifled a low, right-foot shot between the 'keeper and his near post, for his seventh goal in as many games.

Bunn came within a whisker of rubbing salt in the wounds when he powered a header inches wide, from Holden's left-wing corner. But, when half-time arrived, Athletic knew that barring a catastrophe, they were on their way to victory.

Leeds really had no option but to make changes and gamble after the interval.

Jones and Noel Blake were taken off and substitutes Gary Speed and Chris Fairclough introduced.

With Athletic content to sit on their impressive lead, there was more room for Leeds to build attacks from the back and through midfield, which had previously been domina- ted by Milligan and Nick Henry.

As the talented duo of David Batty and Gordon Strachan saw more of the ball so Leeds were able to be more creative and, for the opening 20 minutes of the new half, Athletic were under siege.

DAMAGE

Striker Bobby Davison squandered several good opportunities — first by volleying tamely at Hallworth, then with the keeper way out of his goal, dragging a cross back too close to Barrett, who gratefully booted clear.

Hallworth blocked another Davison effort with his legs and pounced on a mis-hit shot from Sterland, before making a fine save to hold Davison's diving header from Strachan's cross.

Leeds finally made the breakthrough in the 59th minute when Henry played the attack on-side, allowing Batty to cross from the left. FAIRCLOUGH beat a hesitant Hallworth to the loose ball to poke his shot past the 'keeper.

That stung Athletic back into action and the defensive unit of Irwin, Warhurst, Barrett and Barlow — who all had a fine game — began to settle down again.

Barlow and Milligan blotted their copybooks by being booked, but those indiscretions apart, Athletic were poised and professional, to restrict Leeds to only one more genuine goal attempt — a rasping 30-yard shot from Sterland which was smothered by Hallworth.

In fact, Athletic might have inflicted further damage when Holden charged through on the left, cut into the area and went round Fairclough, only to have his close-range shot saved as Palmer waited unmarked in front of goal.

Manager Joe Royle had a special pat on the back for Earl Barrett at the end, but this was a prodigious all-round team effort — one which Athletic must now reproduce consistently in the league programme, if they are to establish themselves as genuine promotion contenders.

Leeds are fancied by many people to make it to the top flight, but Athletic again proved they are as good as anybody in the division — and that even without Ian Marshall and Andy Holden, who are regarded as the first-choice centre-backs.

Leeds United: Day, Sterland, Whitlow, Jones (Speed 45), Blake (Fairclough 45), Haddock, Strachan, Batty, Baird, Davison, Williams.
Athletic: Hallworth, Irwin, Barlow, Henry, Warhurst, Barrett, Palmer, Ritchie, Bunn, Milligan, R Holden. Subs: Adams and Donachie
Referee: Mr H King (Merthyr Tydfil)
Attendance 18,029

PRIEST INJURED IN CAR CRASH

Phil Priest Shrewsbury's former Chelsea midfielder, will be out of action for two weeks after a car crash.

Priest (22), was taken to hospital with shock and whiplash injuries after colliding with another car on the M54 as he was driving to Gay Meadow to catch the team coach for last night's Littlewood's Cup match at Swindon.

Shrewsbury's 38-year-old coach, Asa Hartford, deputised as the Third Division side went down 3—1.

"THE TEAM FROM A TOWN OF CHIMNEYS"

WEDNESDAY 25TH OCTOBER 1989

SIX-SHOOTER!

ATHLETIC 7, SCARBOROUGH 0

STRIKER Frank Bunn shattered sad Scarborough's dreams of Littlewoods Cup glory with an astonishing performance which earned him a place in the record books.

Bunn's six-goal personal tally was the best in one match in the 29-year history of the competition in its various guises.

And it certainly silenced the critics who reckoned that Bunn had lost his old sparkle this season. Try telling that to the poor Scarborough defenders who spent the night chasing shadows.

The fact is that Bunn has, by his own admission, made a slow start to the campaign after missing the pre-season build-up as he recovered from injury.

But his contribution to the team's well-being can never be underestimated. His unselfish work, on and off the ball, creates room and opportunities for other people.

This time it was big Frank's turn to bask in the limelight as Athletic produced the powerful, professional performance that manager Joe Royle had demanded.

Little Scarborough are no mugs, as they showed with a battling win over First Division Chelsea in the last round.

However, the Fourth Division outfit were simply swept aside last night as, for all the heart in the world, they just did not have the technical prowess to stop Athletic's march into the last 16 for only the second time in the history of the competition.

Any lingering doubts that supporters had about Athletic blowing their big chance in front of the television cameras were dismissed by a Bunn hat-trick inside 20 minutes.

Bunn in record spree

Bunn's one-man demolition job went like this:

16 minutes: Rick Holden curled in a wicked cross from the left that produced confusion between defender Steve Richards and 'keeper Ian Ironside. When the 'keeper failed to hold the ball the alert Bunn prodded it into an empty net.

18 minutes: Neil Adams, a late replacement for injured Roger Palmer, swung over a deep corner and Bunn came in from beyond the far post to head home his second.

20 minutes: Andy Ritchie burst through but Ironside made a fine save. Holden quickly knocked the loose ball back into the box and Bunn swooped with a peach of a left-foot, first-time drive to make it 3—0.

EAGER

Shell-shocked Scarborough were all over the place in defence — beaten for pace and quality by an Athletic side which has threatened so often in recent years to really punish a visiting side.

Ritchie had a header saved by the 'keeper from another teasing Holden cross and the tireless Nick Henry wasted another chance when he took the ball a fraction too far in the area, allowing Ironside to save at his feet.

Bunn, though, hadn't finished his remarkable contribution. Scarborough's tale of woe continued.

35 minutes: The visitors lost possession on half-way and the eager Mike Milligan threaded a pass through for Bunn to sprint clear. Ignoring Ritchie to his right, Bunn calmly slotted his shot past the advancing keeper 4—0.

42 minutes: Another sweeping, incisive move as Adams fed Denis Irwin on the overlap. Irwin's tantalising early cross caught Scarborough flat-footed again as Bunn stole in at the near post to complete an amazing naphand of first-half goals.

That had the scribes reaching for the record books in a half-time break that must have come as an enormous relief to sorry Scarborough.

Knowing that Bunn had already equalled the competition record, it came almost as a disappointment that someone else should score Athletic's sixth — but he couldn't resist playing a part in that.

53 minutes: Andy Rhodes launched a big kick forward, Bunn flicked it on and Ritchie lashed home a superb, dipping volley from 20 yards.

Although Scarborough grafted away bravely they only really threatened once when Rhodes dived to his right to hold a header from Richards.

Otherwise, Irwin, Barlow, Paul Warhurst and Earl Barrett were in command.

PERFECT

Athletic were relentless as Ritchie squandered a chance by shooting wide, an Irwin piledriver was superbly saved by Ironside and the 'keeper also pushed aside a swerving effort from Holden.

Bunn's moment of glory almost arrived in the 82nd minute when Ian Bennyworth's careless back pass let in the striker. However, Ironside managed to divert Bunn's shot for a corner.

Milligan and Bunn combined to carve out a half chance for Henry to toe-poke wide and we had to wait until the last minute for the record-breaking goal.

89 minutes: Andy Barlow's storming run down the left ended with a cross which eluded everyone and reached Bunn, lurking beyond the far post. Then, whack — a perfect low, right-foot volley zipped past Ironside.

Bunn's joy and Scarborough's misery was complete.

ATHLETIC: Rhodes, Irwin, Barlow, Henry, Warhurst, Barrett, Adams, Ritchie, Bunn, Milligan, Holden. Subs: Williams and Donachie.
SCARBOROUGH: Ironside, Kamar, Clarke, Short (Olsson 45), Richards, Bennyworth, Brook, Graham, Norr (Saunders 45), Robinson, Russell.
Referee: Mr J Martin (Alton).
Attendance: 7,712.

Bunn opens his account (above, left) as he prepares to tap the ball into an empty net. And he heads home number two (above).

The score goes to four and Bunn strikes again.

Report by .... BOB YOUNG
Pictures by .... MARTIN SMITH

It's five for Frank as he strokes in a Denis Irwin cross.

THE DRAW

LITTLEWOODS Cup giantkillers Tranmere were today looking forward to entertaining Tottenham in a dream fourth-round tie.

John King's Third Division side have already beaten Second Division Ipswich and First Division Millwall in the competition.

Now they must overcome Terry Venables' in-form team next month, if they are to progress to the fifth round of the tournament for the first time.

Spurs, who beat Manchester United 3—0 last night to earn a place in the last 16, will not relish the trip to Prenton Park.

They only just scraped through a second round tie against Southend and were beaten by Second Division sides in the Littlewoods and FA Cups last season.

The full draw is: Derby County v West Bromwich Albion, Manchester City v Coventry, Aston Villa v West Ham v Middlesbrough, Wimbledon, ATHLETIC v Arsenal, Tranmere Rovers v Tottenham, Swindon v Bolton v Southampton, Barrie v Sunderland v APC Bournemouth, Crystal Palace v Nottingham Forest v Everton.

Ties to be played week starting November 20.

ATHLETIC v SCARBOROUGH
(Littlewoods Cup 3rd Round) October 1989
Frank Bunn scores his sixth and record breaking goal

Frank Bunn proudly displays the match ball

"THE TEAM FROM A TOWN OF CHIMNEYS"

WEDNESDAY 22ND NOVEMBER 1989

LITTLEWOODS CUP SPECIAL

Gunners blasted out on Latics glory night

ATHLETIC 3, ARSENAL 1

AS a famous former Oldham MP might have said . . . this was their finest hour and a half. Mighty Arsenal, league champions and First Division leaders, were not edged out of the Littlewoods Cup fourth round by any fluke. They were simply dumped out on merit on the night.

Athletic swarmed all over their illustrious rivals in their best all-round team performance for many a year. And Arsenal boss George Graham was first to recognise the fact.

Graham, who has clearly not forgotten the art of humility in victory and graciousness in defeat, said: "That performance was totally unacceptable from an Arsenal team, but I take nothing away from Oldham.

'It would have been an injustice if we had gone in level at half time and although their 'keeper made three great saves early in the second half, there was only one team in it.

"The plastic pitch is no excuse. We trained on a similar surface for two days. The fact is that Oldham were by far the better team."

The honest Arsenal boss was right. Straight from the start, it was obvious that Athletic were in the mood to cause a major cup upset and earn a quarter-final place for the first time ever.

From No 1 Andy Rhodes through to No 11 Rick Holden there was an air of determination about Joe Royle's team.

A determination not to be over-awed by the big occasion; a determination to impose themselves on an Arsenal side packed with experienced internationals and Wembley finalists in this competition in two of the last three seasons.

Arsenal were simply never allowed to feel comfortable as Athletic refused to let them dwell on the ball. The yard dogs were back, hunting as a hungry pack — snapping at the heels of the Highbury aristocracy.

Nobody typified the spirit better in the first half than marauding left-back Andy Barlow who seemed to be involved in everything.

It was probably Barlow's best performance for his home-town club for not only did he shut out the threat of England winger David Rocastle, he also found time to storm forward to set up the first of three top quality goals.

We were 30 seconds into stoppage time at the end of the first half when Barlow swung over a deep cross from the left.

ANDY RITCHIE, lurking beyond the far post, chested the ball down past Nigel Winterburn and unleashed a rasping right-foot drive past 'keeper John Lukic from a narrow angle.

It was no more than Ath-

letic deserved for their skill and endeavour.

They felt they should have had a penalty when Frank Bunn went down in a Tony Adams tackle; Nick Henry fired a couple of shots wide; makeshift striker Ian Marshall slammed another one at Lukic and the 'keeper made an excellent save from a 30-yard piledriver by Denis Irwin.

Arsenal's great escape came in the 42nd minute when inspirational skipper Mike Milligan darted through on the left and his hard driven cross bounced off Winterburn towards goal only for David O'Leary to hack the ball off the line.

PRIDE

The Gunners simply could not get going as all the finer quality they undoubtedly possess was swamped beneath a tidal wave of Athletic enthusiasm.

Arsenal forced only one corner in the first half and the only thing 'keeper Andy Rhodes had to do was deal with a cross-cum-shot from Winterburn.

It was a different story for ten minutes after the restart, though, as Arsenal set about trying to restore their pride.

That is when Rhodes really earned his money and changed the course of the match.

Three stunning saves in quick succession — rapidly followed by Athletic's second goal — effectively broke Arsenal's spirit.

When Michael Thomas burst through into the area it looked like a re-run of his dramatic title-clincher at Anfield in May, but Rhodes dashed off his line to make an excellent block at the midfielder's feet.

From the resulting corner kick, the ball was cleared out to full-back Lee Dixon just outside the area and when he crashed in a shot, the unsighted Rhodes reacted instinctively to push it aside.

Rhodes was tested to the full once more when Thomas crossed from the right and Niaj Quinn got in a twisting, diving header which was heading for the top corner until the 'keeper beat it away.

After that it was business as normal with Athletic making all the running.

MAULING

Milligan's 64th minute run was checked just outside the box by an O'Leary foul which earned the defender a booking. However, justice was done.

Arsenal managed to clear the free kick but only as far as HENRY, who sent a fierce 30-yard right-foot shot hurtling through a crowd of players and just inside Lukic's right-hand post.

What a way to score your first senior goal — and what better a time to do it. The dynamic 20-year-old Liverpudlian was left sporting a grin as wide as the Mersey — and no wonder.

Henry's midfield partner Milligan almost made it 3—0 after linking up with Ritchie but he dragged his shot inches wide.

Athletic would not be denied, though, and the killer

Report by . . . BOB YOUNG
Pictures by . . . VINCENT BROWN and GRAHAM COLLIN

third goal rounded off a superb 74th minute move.

Ritchie started it on half way, Irwin took over on the overlap and crossed perfectly for RITCHIE to arrive unattended in the area to plant a glorious header past Lukic from eight yards.

"We want seven" roared the terraces started long before the ecstatic home supporters — a reference to the 7—0 mauling of Scarborough in the previous round.

Well, they might have had five. Marshall put a shot straight at Lukic when

everyone was expecting referee Rodger Gifford to stop play for a foul on Holden.

Then when Henry and Marshall combined, the unmarked Holden drove a shot over from 12 yards.

The celebrations on the terraces started long before the end and hundreds of dejected Arsenal supporters making their way out of the ground probably didn't even see QUINN volley home a consolation goal when Athletic's concentration lapsed

for the only time in the dying seconds.

That gave the scoreline a rather flattering appearance for Arsenal, but it could not detract from a memorable night for Athletic — one of the best in post war history

ATHLETIC: Rhodes, Irwin, Barlow, Henry, Barrett, Warhurst, Marshall, Ritchie, Bunn, Milligan, Holden. Subs: Palmer and Williams
ARSENAL: Lukic, Dixon, Winterburn, Thomas, O'Leary, Adams, Rocastle, Richardson, Smith, Quinn, Jonsson (Groves 66). Sub: Caesar
Referee: Mr R. Gifford (Mid Glamorgan)
Attendance 14,224

ATHLETIC v ARSENAL
(Littlewoods Cup 4th Round) November 1989
Athletic's goalkeeper Andy Rhodes clears from Arsenal's Quinn

THE ROYLE AIR FORCE

Another Royle command performance!

WHO CAN OLDHAM?

GLORY BOY IAN MARSHALL, who scored the winner on Saturday against Everton, signals his delight as Oldham clinch an FA Cup semi-final against Manchester United

Oldham 3, Aston Villa 0

HANDY ANDY OLDHAM hero Andy Ritchie nods home his second and his side's third to see off champions Arsenal
Picture: JOHN DAWES

Joe's Wembley double dream still alive

Red-hot Ritch pops Gunners

3-0 Oldham told 'em

magical plastic carpet from under champions cup upsets
● FA Cup Special
—Pages 34, 35, 36

ARSENAL BOSS HAILS ROYLE'S ACES

Latics tipped for the top!

Latics win cup war of attrition!

Heroes' salute ... Latics' hot men Andy Ritchie and ...

6-0 Hammers just can't hold 'em

Oldham the chan

QUOTES

Ritchie leads the slaughter

By JOHN BEAN Oldham

A DEVASTATED Lou Macari stood ashen-faced in the West Ham dressing-room after a defeat that could put his job in jeopardy and admitted: "It was a one-sided it was unbelievable."

He couldn't handle Oldham from the start. We had trained for three weeks on that surface but it wouldn't have made any difference tonight."

Oldham goal hero Andy Ritchie said: "I feel very sorry for Lou. He's had his problems this week and that performance just compounded it. But I'm sure he

Super Oldham Wembley bound

The West Ham manager this week lost the services of striker Jim Parkes, admitted: "I'm shell-shocked. Everything they tried tonight ..."

THAT'S ANDY!

ANDY RITCHIE was the toast of Oldham last night after his two goals put Arsenal out of the Littlewoods.
By ALBERT COOPER

The Royle Ascent!

ARSENAL'S PLASTIC BULLET

RAGS TO RITCHIE'S

ANDY RITCHIE dumped Arsenal out of the Littlewoods Cup last night — and Gunners boss George Graham blew his top.

Graham was furious with his team after two-goal Ritchie booked his Oldham a place in the quarter finals for the first time in the club's history.

Graham snapped: "It was a totally abject and wretched performance by an Arsenal team

Graham blasts beaten champs

6-0 OH WHAT A ROYLE RAVE-UP

OLDHAM 6 WEST HAM 0

ANDY RITCHIE ripped the heart out of his old Manchester United buddy Lou Macari last night — then said sorry.

Ritchie sends Lou down pan

SIX MANIAC Neil Adams wheels away in triumph after his goal opened the floodgates against West Ham last night and guaranteed a Littlewoods Cup final spot for Joe Royle's Oldham side
Picture: ROGER PARKER

Littlewoods Cup special

ROY CU ST S

LATICS' BOSS SALUTES HIS BATTERED HEROES

Pride of Royle's lions

Royle artillery

Super Latics fire a Final 6-gun salute!

EVEN Lou Macari
By Paul Hince

By David Meek

FA CUP heroes Oldham today counted the cost of last night's brave display at Everton.

The Latics battled to a draw, earning a second replay at Boundary Park next Wednesday.

Manager Joe Royle

IN PLASTIC PANIC AS RITCHIE STRIKES AT THE DOUBLE

soccer special + Starsport soccer

JOE'S GEMS

By PAUL WALKER

JOE ROYLE'S marvels blasted their way within sight of Wembley last night.

Oldham sting sorry Saints

LAST NIGHT'S SOCCER

Arsenal plunge to plastic oblivion against Oldham

By William Johnson

Oldham Athletic........ 3 Arsenal........ 1

OLDHAM, unbeaten at Boundary Park in 23 matches since January, made excellent use of the considerable advantage that their artificial pitch provided to wreck the powerful Littlewoods Cup hopes of League champions Arsenal last night.

Andy Ritchie, averaging more than a goal every two games since his £50,000 arrival from Leeds two years ago, led the way for the Second Division promotion hopefuls.

He produced two clinical pieces of finishing, taking his...

Quarter-final draw
Swindon or Southampton v Oldham, West Ham v Derby, Exeter or Sunderland v Coventry, Nottingham Forest v Tottenham

A RIGHT ROYLE RAVE-UP!

Littlewoods Cup special

Right Royle party

Oldham glory boys earn boss birthday bonanza

By JOHN WRAGG Oldham 3 Aston Villa 0

JOE ROYLE got the best birthday present of his life last night — an FA Cup semi-final with Manchester United.

Royle's rampant Oldham Athletic team thrashed First Division leaders Aston Villa to set up the possibility of an incredible Wembley double...

6-0

YLE DO!

Oldham on Ritchie route to Wembley

IT IS Oldham take their remarkable season all the way to a Wembley cup final they should write protest and send Andy Ritchie up to the royal box...

Dell boys spiked by Milligan

By JOHN BEAN

SPORTLINE
Quickfire Lewis crushes Quaress
By TONY BOSLEY

Ritchie sees Arsenal overdrawn on plastic

By DEREK HODGSON at Boundary Park

FA Cup, sixth round: Oldham Athletic 3, Aston Villa 0

Conquering Oldham know no boundary

By Stephen Bierley

ARSENAL, Southampton, Everton and now Aston Villa. Boundary Park has become a First Division cup hell hole this season as Oldham...

GOLDHAM!

Joe gems slam Villa

JOE ROYLE saluted his astonishing Cup specialists last night as his rampant First Division...

6-0

THE ST VALENTINE'S DAY MASSACRE

By PAUL GRIFFIN

JUBILANT Joe Royle last night hailed his team of heroes after the greatest night in Oldham's history.

FAIRYTALE

CRAZY ATHLETIC M ON TO SEMIS

you at Wembley!

Everton can't Oldham!

EVERTON reject Ian Marshall fired fairytale Oldham into the next phase of their incredible quest for a Wembley cup final...

REJECT IAN IS HERO

Oldham Ath 3, Aston Villa 0

Big match special

IAN'S DREAM
Oldham fans mob their latest Cup hero Ian Marshall, who scored the half-time penalty against Everton, his former club — that gave The Latics a 2-1 victory yesterday.

Picture: HOWARD WALKER

We're on our way!

Royle marvels

"THE TEAM FROM A TOWN OF CHIMNEYS"

SATURDAY 6TH JANUARY 1990

Bunn ends drought to earn Latics second chance

BIRMINGHAM C. 1, ATHLETIC 1

FRANK BUNN rediscovered his goal touch to earn Athletic an FA Cup replay against Birmingham. And with another home match awaiting the winners of this tie in the fourth round, it could be every bit as valuable as the half-dozen he slammed past Scarborough.

Those sizzling six in the Littlewoods Cup back in October marked Bunn's last appearance on the scoresheet.

Saturday's equaliser may not have been so spectacular, but it was just reward for Bunn and his teammates, who slogged their way through the St. Andrew's quagmire to give themselves an excellent chance of making progress in the competition.

Underfoot conditions for Wednesday's rematch will be vastly different to the weekend and Athletic ought to be able to make home advantage count.

Birmingham cannot be dismissed lightly, however, as they showed in Saturday's robust, rugged encounter.

The Third Division side have plenty of experience and spirit about them and gave Athletic a good test in the gruelling conditions.

Athletic passed that test with another purposeful, determined performance.

Goalkeeper Jon Hallworth had no chance with Birmingham's 32nd minute goal from Nigel Gleghorn, but otherwise did not have a save to make until the final few seconds of the match.

PRESSURE

Solid defence was the platform on which Athletic built their display. But making sure they were not beaten was certainly not the limit of their ambitions.

Birmingham's Martin Thomas was by far the busier of the two 'keepers and, especially in the last quarter of the game, Athletic pressed strongly for victory on the day.

If anything, Birmingham seemed the more inhibited at times as they spent much of the game with Ian Atkins playing as sweeper, yet still failed to push full-backs Ian Clarkson and John Frain forward enough, often enough.

Wingers Neil Adams and Rick Holden did their job well, tracking back to help out when needed but always looking for the opportunity to probe the home defence on the flanks – something that Birmingham couldn't match.

In central midfield, Mike Milligan and Nick Henry were again outstanding as grafters and competitors – and needed to be against a side intent on taking no prisoners.

The midfield battle was a good, hard contest in difficult conditions, but the one area in which Birmingham didn't really seem to have the weapons to hurt Athletic was in the forward line.

Apart from the busy Simon Sturridge there was no one to really ruffle a defence in which Ian Marshall and Earl Barrett were commanding and had excellent support from Denis Irwin and Andy Barlow.

Once Athletic had repelled Birmingham's early pressure they might have established a first-half lead.

Adams warmed Thomas's hands with a fierce 20-yard drive, Bunn should have had a penalty when he was hacked down between two defenders and, in the end, Thomas twice rescued his team when sloppy back passes threatened to let in Roger Palmer.

Birmingham's best opening came from their former Manchester City pair, Kevin Langley drove in a free-kick from the left and Gleghorn powered a header narrowly wide.

Gleghorn had his revenge seven minutes into the second half when Birmingham broke the deadlock.

Frain sent in a deep cross from the left and it was nodded down into the six-yard box from beyond the far post. Athletic failed to clear the danger and Sturridge laid the ball back for GLEGHORN to slam home a rasping, rising drive.

That setback really stung Athletic into action as they gambled on pushing Marshall forward, leaving three in defence.

Irwin brought a fine save from Thomas with a powerful 25-yard free-kick, then played a major part in the 65th minute equaliser.

It was typical Irwin as a precision long pass picked out BUNN who advanced a few paces into the area and, although he failed to make a clean contact on his right-foot shot, it was enough to beat the wrong-footed 'keeper.

Bunn went close again within a minute when he collected the ball just outside the area and let fly with a right-foot shot which was aiming for the top corner of the net until Thomas made an excellent save.

After that it was almost all Athletic. Palmer planted a header at the 'keeper from Irwin's cross and Barrett lashed a shot just wide after Adams had nodded down a cross from Holden.

CHANCE

Holden also had a shooting chance, set up by Palmer, but fired his left-foot drive narrowly off target.

Birmingham's frustration showed in bookings for Frain and Trevor Matthewson, but they might have snatched a dramatic victory in the last minute.

Milligan seemed to win the ball fairly in a challenge 25 yards from his own goal but was penalised. When Langley drove his free kick through the defensive "wall", Hallworth got down low to his left to make his only save of the game.

BIRMINGHAM C: Thomas, Clarkson, Frain, Atkins, Overson, Matthewson, Bell (Hopkins 78), Bailey, Sturridge, Gleghorn, Langley Sub Yates.

ATHLETIC: Hallworth, Irwin, Barlow, Henry, Barrett, Marshall, Adams, Palmer, Bunn, Milligan, R Holden Subs Williams and Hoenline.

Referee: Mr. K Cooper (Pontypridd). Attendance: 13,131.

ROYLE'S MEN BATTLE FOR CUP REPLAY

Frank Bunn slides in Athletic's equaliser and sets off to celebrate (below).

Mossley pay for early mistakes

MOSSLEY 1
COLNE DYNAMOES 3

LANKY striker Dave Lancaster scored two early goals for Colne Dynamoes to kill off Mossley's hopes of victory at Seel Park on Saturday.

Lancaster was on target twice in the opening 18 minutes to take his season's tally to 14 in the HFS Loans League premier division.

The victory extended the runaway league leader's advantage over second-placed Witton Albion to 12 points. Mossley, by contrast, dropped two places to next to bottom.

The full-time professionals from Colne must have been delighted by the charity of the Mossley defence as Lancaster scored twice, through a well-struck shot on the turn and a header.

Question marks were raised about goalkeeper Phil Jackson who got a hand to the first goal and failed to come for a corner which led to the second.

Stewart Anderson, the former Chadderton player, ought to have added a third when he blazed wide after bursting through.

Mossley were restricted to a couple of long-range efforts from Carl Gleave and Paul Buckley as they found Colne's five-man back line dominant on the glue-pot pitch.

Jackson saved well from Andy Lee's free kick before the visitors netted their third goal midway through the second half.

Paul Showier stabbed the ball home at the far post after excellent work on the right by Mike Carter.

Mossley hit back immediately through a Paul Bowler penalty after he had been tripped by Steve McNellis.

The last 20 minutes saw Mossley come alive, but they had left themselves too much to do.

Player-manager Mark Hilton said. "We showed them too much respect in the first 20 minutes, and by then we were two down.

"We sorted things out and had them pinned back for much of the second half. The only edge they had was in terms of fitness and organisational skills, but overall we were as good as them."

One boost for Mossley was the season's best crowd of 839.

Report by . . . BOB YOUNG
Pictures by . . . GRAHAM COLLIN

Frank Bunn fires in a shot but 'keeper Martin Thomas makes a flying save (left).

"THE TEAM FROM A TOWN OF CHIMNEYS"

WEDNESDAY 10TH JANUARY 1990

Birmingham's Martin Thomas makes another fine save to keep out a shot from Denis Irwin.

Athletic's winning goal is captured in our action sequence, as Rick Holden surges past Birmingham defenders and manages to regain his balance to slide his shot past 'keeper Martin Thomas.

Holden's gem earns Latics cup ticket

ATHLETIC................. 1
BIRMINGHAM CITY..... 0

by BOB YOUNG

RICK HOLDEN'S moment of magic steered Athletic into the fourth round of the FA Cup for the first time in five years and earned a home tie with Brighton on January 27.

It needed a splendid piece of individual flair from Joe Royle's record £165,000 signing to end the gallant rearguard action of Third Division Birmingham City in last night's tense third-round replay at Boundary Park.

Extra time was looming large on the horizon when HOLDEN collected the ball just outside the Birmingham penalty area and darted into the box, stumbling and bustling through three challenges before poking his match-winning shot past 'keeper Martin Thomas.

LURKING

It was reminiscent of his Littlewoods Cup winner against Leeds United back in September — and it needed a flash of brilliance to settle this robust, competitive cup clash.

Athletic knew that this was going to be no easy assignment without the likes of Frank Bunn, Andy Ritchie and Paul Warhurst against Birmingham's well-organised and uncompromising sweeper-defence system.

The visitors put up a sterling fight and might even have shocked Athletic to the core after only 90 seconds when left-back John Frain fired in a shot that 'keeper Jon Hallworth had to push away for a corner.

Once Athletic settled down they enjoyed the lion's share of possession but, despite the surging runs from the back by the impressive Ian Marshall, they had to wait 25 minutes for a strike at goal.

Busy midfielder Nick Henry fired a low, 25-yard drive narrowly wide with a "Chaddy End", having visions of another Arsenal game special from the young Liverpudlian.

Goalkeeper Thomas was called into serious action for the first time in the 29th minute — and how he earned his money to keep Birmingham's hopes alive.

Denis Irwin hammered a long-range free-kick through the defensive "wall" and it was travelling like a guided missile towards the bottom corner of the net when Thomas launched himself low to his right to touch the ball aside.

Thomas also grabbed a shot from Roger Palmer to end a powerful run and cross from Andy Barlow and Athletic's all-time record scorer went desperately close with a cheeky back-heel flick into the sidenetting from Holden's centre.

Birmingham battled well, happy to surrender space and get men back behind the ball, then counter-attacking in lively fashion through Denis Bailey and Simon Sturridge.

However, Athletic almost broke the deadlock in the last few minutes of the first half.

Thomas produced another tremendous save when Scott McGarvey played a short free-kick for Irwin to send in another 25-yard thunderbolt.

Then big defender Vince Overson just got a toe in to whip the ball away from the lurking McGarvey as a Neil Adams cross skidded across the six-yard box.

McGarvey did quite well in attack considering that this was his first major match for Athletic and he was unfortunate not to score after 50 minutes with a cracking long-range drive that beat Thomas and cannoned out off the underside of the bar.

Athletic kept up the pressure with Earl Barrett heading over from Holden's corner and McGarvey missing the target with a header at the far post from one of several fine crosses from Irwin.

APPEALS

Birmingham, though, almost caused an upset when, despite looking offside, Bailey was allowed to chase after Overson's through pass. Hallworth had to make a vital block tackle outside his area.

The game was heading towards an extra 30 minutes when Holden came up with his superb goal. But the tie was far from dead.

Athletic had been about to send on Gary Williams as substitute to pep up the attack when Barlow went down injured. Holden's strike forced a quick re-think as Royle opted for safety first and gave Wayne Heseltine his first taste of senior action as a straight swop at left back.

Birmingham abandoned their defensive posture and roared on to the attack for the closing ten minutes.

Hallworth made an astonishing save with his legs as Sturridge seemed certain to score with a close-range right-foot shot.

Then Bailey burst free in the area and toe-poked a shot past Hallworth but inches wide of a post.

In the dying moments goal-hero Holden showed the other important side of his game. When an attack broke down and Sturridge darted away on the right, Holden was the first to get back and put in a vital tackle Birmingham thought it was a foul but referee Keith Cooper quite rightly waved away penalty appeals based on desperation more than reality.

Even so, you had to feel some sympathy with Birmingham's belief that they were worth a second replay. They were far from disgraced throughout the two matches.

It is to Athletic's credit, though, that there is obviously a tremendous team spirit which carried them through a difficult tie at a time when injuries are robbing them of key players.

ATHLETIC: Hallworth, Irwin, Barlow (Heseltine 76), Henry, Barrett, Marshall, Adams, Palmer, McGarvey, Milligan, R Holden, Sub: Williams.
BIRMINGHAM: Thomas, Clarkson, Frain, Atkins, Overson, Matthewson, Bell (Yates 80), Bailey, Sturridge, Gleghorn, Langley Sub: Peer
Referee Mr. K Cooper (Pontypridd)
Attendance 9,925.

PICTURES BY . . . VINCENT BROWN

"THE TEAM FROM A TOWN OF CHIMNEYS"

WEDNESDAY 24TH JANUARY 1990

RITCHIE KEEPS THE CUP DREAM ALIVE

Last-gasp goal earns Athletic replay chance

SOUTHAMPTON 2, ATHLETIC 2

ANDY RITCHIE kept Athletic's Wembley dream alive with a dramatic injury-time equaliser at The Dell last night.

Southampton fans were already celebrating victory when highly-rated striker Matthew Le Tissier hit his second goal of the match, from the penalty spot, with only five minutes of normal time remaining.

However, Athletic refused to believe that their marvellous effort would go unrewarded in this, their first-ever Littlewoods Cup quarter-final tie.

When tricky Ricky Holden drilled over a low cross from the left four minutes into stoppage time, RITCHIE lunged at a near-post chance to force the ball home and send Joe Royle's blue and white army of supporters into ecstacy.

Referee Roger Milford played almost two minutes more of overtime — an agonising wait for Athletic's vociferous fans before they could erupt into a riot of colour, singing and dancing.

Sadly, a small gang of Southampton fans got on to the pitch and threatened to spoil the party by trying to get amongst the visitors.

Fortunately, the sensible majority managed to swallow their disappointment — and plenty were willing to admit that Athletic deserved their replay chance to rewrite the club's history books.

Report by BOB YOUNG

Pictures by VINCENT BROWN

Andy Ritchie (grounded, left) hits Athletic's equaliser and celebrates (below) with Roger Palmer to the anguish of ex-Latics man Kevin Moore.

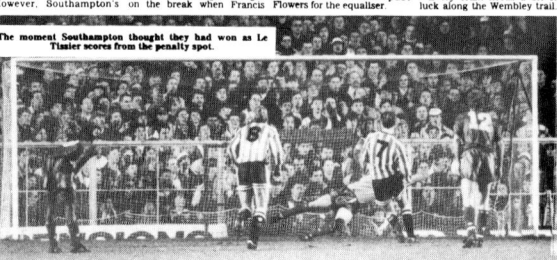

ANXIOUS

This was no fluke result. Athletic have already shown courage and quality in this competition by beating Leeds at home and away, demolishing Scarborough and toppling league champions Arsenal.

And Southampton discovered that Athletic don't just rely on their artificial pitch to create a favourable impression.

Here was an away performance when the impartial observer might have wondered for long periods which was the home team highly placed in the First Division.

The Saints were allowed only one shot on target in the opening 45 minutes — and that went into the net thanks to a deflection.

Athletic could have been in front in the first few minutes as they made their intentions clear — to carry the game to their hosts.

Ritchie hit a curling drive inches wide from the edge of the area and Holden's smart 18-yard volley was held by keeper Tim Flowers, diving low to his right.

However, Southampton's first attack, after eight minutes, saw them take the lead.

LE TISSIER, having temporarily swopped wings with Rod Wallace, cut in from the left and his shot from just outside the area deflected off Earl Barrett and flew inside Jon Hallworth's right-hand post.

The Saints didn't have another genuine goal attempt as the brilliant Barrett and his colleagues blotted out a much vaunted strike force.

Royle's raiders enjoyed most of the possession but, apart from a swerving left-foot effort from Holden which caused an anxious moment for Flowers, they lacked penetration in the last third of the field.

It seemed that Southampton would finish the job early in the second half when they began to find a few gaps in an otherwise solid defence.

Le Tissier caught them on the break when he galloped down the right flank and chipped a delightful pass over Paul Warhurst and Ian Marshall only for Hallworth to make a desperate save to divert Wallace's shot over the bar.

Within a minute the same combination carved out an opening down the left and Wallace drove an angled shot into the side-netting.

Athletic were again caught on the break when Francis Benali belted a long pass out of defence. Warhurst and Andy Barlow moved to cover but got in each other's way, allowing Barry Horne a clear sight of goal. However he managed to miss the target from six yards.

It could have been all over and done with but never-say-die Athletic settled down again and kept going forward.

As the game gathered momentum towards its amazing climax, Athletic introduced Scott McGarvey in place of Neil Adams in a bid to add punch to the front line.

McGarvey's flick-on let in Roger Palmer but Flowers did well to hold a curling right-foot shot. McGarvey headed over when well placed from Ritchie's cross while at the other end Hallworth made a magnificent one-handed stop to deny Paul Rideout.

The tie might have turned away from Athletic when they lost Warhurst, who twisted an ankle in a collision with an advertising hoarding around the perimeter fencing.

They would have none of it, though, and Flowers had to make an excellent save to keep out McGarvey's header, then one from Milligan, as Holden began to weave his magic spell on the left flank.

It was no more than Athletic deserved when, ten minutes from the end, midfield dynamo Nick Henry clipped in a short cross from the right and RITCHIE launched a header past Flowers for the equaliser.

The joy turned to despair five minutes later when Horne went down in the area in a tangle of legs. Referee Milford pointed to the penalty spot, ignoring Athletic protests and LE TISSIER shot his side in front once more.

Southampton tried to kill the game off, but Milford repeatedly warned them for time wasting and deep into injury time RITCHIE poked home his 18th goal of the season despite Benali's attempted clearance on the line.

Every team needs a bit of luck along the Wembley trail. Perhaps Athletic had a slice last night with such a late leveller — but of such moments are cup triumphs made.

The replay, scheduled for next Wednesday, depending on FA Cup results, will be far from easy. But Athletic are halfway to the semi-finals.

SOUTHAMPTON: Flowers, Dodd, Benali, Case, Moore, Osman, Le Tissier, Cockerill, Rideout, Horne, Wallace. Subs: Ruddock and Shearer.

ATHLETIC: Hallworth, Barrett, Barlow, Henry, Marshall, Warhurst (Donachie 80), Adams (McGarvey 65), Ritchie, Palmer, Milligan, R Holden.

Referee: Mr R. Milford
Attendance: 21,026

The moment Southampton thought they had won as Le Tissier scores from the penalty spot.

Paul Warhurst outjumps the defence to get in a header.

"THE TEAM FROM A TOWN OF CHIMNEYS"

SATURDAY 27TH JANUARY 1990

Quick double keeps Latics on course for cup glory

ATHLETIC 2
BRIGHTON 1

SCOTT McGarvey and Andy Ritchie grabbed the goals to keep Athletic on course for a double date at Wembley.

Report by . . . **BOB YOUNG**
Pictures by . . . **KEDRICK WHITEHEAD**

But it was the now tried and trusted tactical switch of Ian Marshall from defence to attack which held the key to a place in the FA Cup fifth round for only the second time in 11 years.

Athletic were facing the prospect of a shock exit against their struggling Second Division rivals when Mark Barham sent the Seagulls' spirits soaring by scoring with their first and only on-target shot after 51 minutes.

Taking the lead was possibly the worst thing Brighton could have done, for it stung Athletic into action.

Marshall was unleashed from his defensive duties, leaving three men at the back, while orthodox winger Neil Adams replaced recent signing Neil Redfearn on the right of midfield.

The strength and deceptive speed of Marshall created room for McGarvey and Ritchie, while the wing play of Adams and Rick Holden began to stretch Brighton to the limit.

It was almost a throw-back to the good old days of five forwards — and it certainly did the trick.

When midfield man Robert Codner failed to cut out a low cross from Holden, McGARVEY sneaked in behind the defence to drill home a left-foot shot for a 66th minute equaliser.

MISSED

Two minutes later, Athletic were in front and on their way to the next round when Holden's perfect centre was met some ten yards out by RITCHIE whose powerful header flew just inside 'keeper John Keeley's right-hand post.

Not for the first time, the gamble of pushing Marshall forward as an extra attacker paid dividends and, in view of the defensive attitude of many teams visiting Boundary Park, Athletic could be tempted to try the ploy from the outset some time.

Athletic certainly needed something to liven them up after a rather lethargic opening on Saturday.

The exertions, both physical and mental, of the midweek Littlewoods cup draw at Southampton seemed to take their toll.

Athletic were the better side, but lacked that bit of verve and sparkle to really stamp their authority on the contest.

They still did enough to make a hero of 'keeper Keeley for the second time in under three months.

The former taxi driver threatened to drive Athletic to despair, as he had done when Brighton escaped from Boundary Park with a league point.

When defender Keith Dublin missed a cross from Redfearn, McGarvey brought it under control and tried to chip a shot past the advancing 'keeper only for Keeley to make a splendid save.

McGarvey set up a chance when he unselfishly headed down a Holden centre for Ritchie to fire in a rasping right-foot volley which brought an astonishing block from the keeper. Steve Gatting scrambled McGarvey's follow-up effort away from goal.

TENACITY

And Keeley defied Athletic again shortly before the interval with a tremendous instinctive save to keep out Ritchie's point-blank header from Redfearn's cross.

It was a game of limited opportunities, however, as several Athletic players — with the notable exception of the tireless Nick Henry — struggled to find their best form.

Brighton, with only two wins in 15 matches, had little other than a few breakaway attacks by Narnham and a 20-yard shot from Codner which was charged down by a wall of defenders.

It came as a surprise when, from only their second corner kick of the game, Brighton went ahead as Redfearn miscued his clearance, Dublin lobbed a neat pass over an advancing defence and BARHAM cut in from the left to beat Jon Hallworth with a low, right-foot shot.

Athletic's tenacity showed through, as it has done so often recently, and their quick double goal strike was enough to polish off Brighton.

In fact, Keeley had to make another fine save to deflect Mike Milligan's low, left-foot drive and another excellent cross from Holden forced Dublin into a desperate headed clearance that almost produced an own goal.

Victory extended Athletic's remarkable unbeaten home record to 29 games and, although it was not particularly convincing, it keeps the pot simmering nicely.

For the first time ever, Athletic are in the last 16 of the FA Cup and have a good chance of reaching the Littlewoods Cup semi-finals, all in one season.

Promotion has to be the top priority but, judging by the ever increasing attendances at Boundary Park, the cup runs are becoming an attractive and lucrative sideline.

ATHLETIC: Hallworth, Irwin, Barlow, Henry, Barrett, Marshall, Redfearn (Adams 41), Ritchie (Palmer 85), McGarvey, Milligan, R.Holden.
BRIGHTON: Keeley, Chivers, Chapman, Curbishley, Gatting, Dublin, Nelson, Barham, Barnham (Cowan 73), Codner, Wilkins Sub: Crumplin
Referee: Mr M Bodenham (Cornwall)
Attendance 11,034.

Scott McGarvey (above) fires in Athletic's equaliser and that was quickly followed by Andy Ritchie's headed winner which flew past 'keeper John Keeley (below).

BRING ON EVERTON

EVERTON at home in round five of the FA Cup. It was almost inevitable wasn't it?

If it is not Leeds United then it is the Merseyside men who seem to stand in Athletic's way to cup glory.

The Boundary Park boys have already disposed of Leeds in this season's Littlewoods Cup. Now they have the chance to avenge two defeats by Everton in that competition when they tackle the Goodison Park outfit on the weekend of February 17-18.

Athletic will meet the First Division outfit in cup action for the third season in a row.

Last season Everton won 2—1 at Boundary Park with two goals from Tony Cottee in the last six minutes after Athletic had earned a 1—1 draw at Goodison in the Littlewoods third round.

The previous season it looked on 86th minute goal from Neil Adams — now with Athletic — to give Everton a 2—1 home win in the fourth round.

This year's cup clash promises to be a cracker as in-form Athletic take on last season's beaten FA Cup finalists.

The game will be especially significant for manager Joe Royle and Ian Marshall and Neil Adams — all former Everton players.

Everton, looking for a record 12th cup final appearance and their fifth in seven years, earned their fifth round place by winning 2—1 at Sheffield Wednesday yesterday.

Former Manchester United man Norman Whiteside scored both goals, taking his tally to six in seven games, and Wednesday boss Ron Atkinson — a close friend of Royle — reckons that big Norman has the Wembley scent in his nostrils.

THE DRAW

C Palace v Rochdale
Reading or Newcastle v Manchester Utd.
Blackpool v Arsenal or QPR
ATHLETIC v EVERTON
Bristol City v Millwall or Cambridge Utd.
WBA v Aston Villa
Sheffield Utd. or Watford v Barnsley
Norwich or Liverpool v Southampton

Ties to be played on February 17-18.

"THE TEAM FROM A TOWN OF CHIMNEYS"

WEDNESDAY 31ST JANUARY 1990

RECORDS TUMBLE AS ATHLETIC MARCH ON

ATHLETIC 2, SOUTHAMPTON 0

ANDY RITCHIE'S love affair with the Littlewoods Cup goes on as Athletic continue their march towards Wembley and chapters of the club record book are rewritten after almost every round.

Ritchie's early goal last night set Athletic on their way to a famous replay victory over First Division Southampton and maintained his record of scoring in every Littlewoods match this season.

Urged on by a capacity crowd, Athletic completed the task they had begun so dramatically by grabbing an injury time equaliser at The Dell last week.

Mike Milligan's superbly worked second goal shortly after the interval guaranteed Joe Royle's men not only a semi-final place against West Ham, but a slice of club history.

The 30-match unbeaten home sequence Athletic have now set up beats the club's all-time record set in 1923-24. And you have to go back even further — to 1913 — to find the one and only other time that the boys from Boundary Park were in the semi-final of a major cup competition.

There have been two World Wars since Athletic last had a cup final in their sights. And last night's action was a war of a different kind.

It was a war of wills and nerves — and Athletic proved they have the determination and drive to succeed.

Hundreds of disappointed fans were locked out of the big match and, while they did not miss a classic of flowing football, they did miss a most memorable momentous occasion.

Southampton might have rewritten the script had striker Paul Rideout not fluffed an early chance — hitting a shot straight at 'keeper Jon Hallworth who well placed.

Hot-shot Ritchie sparks famous victory

Report by: BOB YOUNG
Pictures by: MARTIN SMITH and VINCENT BROWN

But Athletic's dreams of glory were a step closer to reality after only nine minutes — thanks to that man Ritchie.

Ian Marshall sprayed a long pass out of defence, Rick Holden cleverly "dummied" the ball and allowed left-back Andy Barlow to gallop away down the wing. The local lad chipped in a precise cross and RITCHIE glanced a header past 'keeper Tim Flowers and in off a post.

BATTLED

The roar of approval from the crowd must have shaken the foundations of an old stadium which has undergone many changes but which has seldom witnessed such dramatic events.

Athletic pressed forward for another goal but the blustery wind made it difficult to produce the sort of controlled display they had shown at The Dell.

Scott McGarvey was unlucky when he initiated an attack and met the return cross from Holden only for his goalbound header to hit the unwitting Neil Ruddock and bounce to safety.

Ritchie then hit a low 20-yard shot wide with Holden unmarked out to his left.

However, Southampton battled to restore their pride and find the goal touch which has made them a potent First Division force.

Substitute Alan Shearer — on for the injured Rod Wallace — forced his way past Earl Barrett inside the area but the defender managed to get a toe in to divert the shot for a corner.

Barry Horne then burst through in the inside-right slot but Hallworth made a vital save to push aside an angled right-foot shot.

Athletic thought they had settled the issue just before the break when Ritchie had the ball in the net again only for the grounded McGarvey to be ruled offside. What referee George Courtney had not spotted was McGarvey being thrown to the ground by Ruddock.

Justice was done, though, five minutes after the interval when Athletic scored an excellent second goal.

GAMBLE

Milligan began the move by slotting a pass out to Ritchie on the left flank. Ritchie darted into the area and cut back a low cross, McGarvey's run to the near post distracted the defence and MILLIGAN arrived to stroke the ball home from close range to crown a fine performance.

Athletic must have sensed that it was their night when Matthew Le Tissier swung over a corner kick and the ball skidded through a crowded six-yard box without any one of a host of Southampton players able to apply the finishing touch.

In desperation, the Saints took off right-back Jason Dodd and left three defenders back as substitute Neil Maddison joined the search for goals.

The gamble almost paid off as Barrett slipped and let in Rideout for a thumping 20-yard strike which flew just off target.

And, from another Le Tissier corner, Rideout powered in a header which hit Nick Henry, standing on the goalline. Appeals for handball were rejected.

Athletic were in no mood, though, to let glory slip from their grasp — even when Ritchie stunned the crowd with a bizarre long-range back pass which nearly let Saints in.

It seems Ritchie can do no wrong at the moment, though. He leads the Littlewoods Cup scoring charts with eight goals, has scored five times in the last four matches and, with half a season to go at, has a grand total of 20 to his credit.

Athletic's march towards honours has not been a one-man show by any means, though.

Milligan and Henry were again outstanding in central midfield, Denis Irwin oozed quality, while back-four colleagues Ian Marshall, Earl Barrett and Andy Barlow grew in stature as the game wore on.

Saints manager Chris Nicholl swallowed his disappointment to generously concede: "We have no complaints. We had the chances to win it at The Dell but Oldham deserved a draw there and they deserved their win tonight.

"Oldham are a good side and have given us as many problems as some First Division teams. Good luck to them."

ATHLETIC: Hallworth, Irwin, Barlow, Henry, Marshall, Barrett, Adams, Ritchie, McGarvey, Milligan, R. Holden. Subs Palmer and Donachie.
SOUTHAMPTON: Flowers, Dodd (Maddison 68), Benali, Case, Ruddock, Osman, Le Tissier, Cockerill, Rideout, Horne, Wallace (Shearer 20).
Referee: Mr G. Courtney (Spennymoor).
Attendance: 18,862

CONFIDENT HAMMERS

WEST HAM are convinced they can survive their ordeal by plastic at Boundary Park to reach Wembley for the first time in 10 years.

After beating Derby's novices 2—1 at the third time of asking to reach the Littlewoods Cup last four for the second consecutive season, match-winner Kevin Keen insists the artificial surface will not be a major stumbling block.

Keen said: "Going there first gives us a great advantage, because we know our crowd will lift us when it matters down here.

"Whatever the score up there, whether it's 1—0 or even 3—0, we think our fans will pull us through in the second leg."

Manager Lou Macari had no doubt they played the major role against Derby last night, saying: "They had a belief beyond belief that we were going to win".

Andy Ritchie heads home Athletic's opening goal (above) and is surrounded by delighted teammates joining in the celebration (below).

Mike Milligan slots in the vital second goal (below) to the delight of striker Scott McGarvey (above).

174

"THE TEAM FROM A TOWN OF CHIMNEYS"

WEDNESDAY 14TH FEBRUARY 1990

RAMPANT LATICS NAIL HAMMERS

Wembley beckons as Royle's men turn on six-hit super show

ATHLETIC 6, WEST HAM 0

ATHLETIC are halfway up Wembley Way after a devastating Littlewoods Cup semi-final first leg display against West Ham last night.

Unless the Hammers produce one of the biggest fightbacks in football history in a fortnight's time — and I wouldn't put Lou Macari's money on that, let alone my own — then Athletic will make their first major cup final appearance on April 29.

In doing so they will have rewritten not only the club's 95-year-old record books, but also the coaching manual.

Did anyone tell them that semi-finals are supposed to be close-fought, tense affairs? Did anyone mention that you don't usually play the first half of these occasions with five forwards?

Obviously not, for after taking five minutes to look at West Ham's ultra-cautious "sweeper" line-up, Athletic threw defender Ian Marshall forward as the fifth attacker and proceeded to rip them apart with a superbly confident display of skilful, attacking football.

To a man they were faster, more determined, more adventurous than their illustrious London rivals, who seemed to leave their hearts and minds behind on the team coach.

TOP GEAR

West Ham came to shut up shop and subdue Athletic any way they could. Full-back Stewart Robson, who at £700,000 cost more than the entire Athletic team put together, set the tone when he was booked after only eight minutes for his second crunching late tackle on the elusive Rick Holden.

However, fortune was to favour the posse, not the cynical, and West Ham were reduced to a shambles as Athletic's goal machine rolled into top gear with an all-round performance not matched since that epic 3–1 home win over league champions Arsenal back in November.

The floodgates began to open after only 11 minutes when Athletic got the early breakthrough they needed.

Marshall's unexpected presence in attack caused havoc and he threaded a crossfield pass to the darting Neil Adams. In turn, Adams knocked the ball forward to Andy Ritchie and, when the striker slipped an almost nonchalant return pass into his path, ADAMS arrived to slam home a superb 20-yard left-foot drive in off the base of the post.

by BOB YOUNG

Athletic were in danger of throwing away the advantage within a minute when keeper Jon Hallworth raced out to clear from George Parris. The loose ball fell for Stuart Slater to chip towards an empty net, but his shot dropped inches wide.

The plucky Slater was often left alone in attack and was just about the only Hammer to emerge with credit for his never-say-die approach.

In stark contrast, Athletic were bristling with attacking menace as fluid, fluent moves tore West Ham to shreds.

With 19 minutes gone, the magnificent Nick Henry stopped a West Ham attack in its tracks deep in his own half by winning the ball off Liam Brady.

RITCHIE took up the running and raced into West Ham territory. With defenders backing off he let fly with a low right-foot shot from 20 yards and the ball took a deflection past keeper Phil Parkes to make it 2–0.

West Ham were forced to come out of their defensive shell and, at times, showed some neat skill and approach play. But it floundered on a rock-solid defence or was strangled in midfield by the astonishing work-rate of those terriers Henry and Mike Milligan.

The Hammers were lashed by torrential rain and by the rampant Latics.

The mercurial Holden laid on the third goal when his corner kick was partly cleared. Holden swung the ball back in. Roger Palmer nodded it down and EARL BARRETT forced his way through between defenders to poke the ball past Parkes.

SHATTERED

It could have been worse for the bewildered Hammers but for a brilliant save by Parkes. Another teasing Holden cross was met by Marshall but Parkes flung himself to his right to make a superb one-handed save from a powerful, close-range header.

If West Ham entertained any thoughts of sneaking back into the contest in the second-half they were rudely shattered only 30 seconds after the interval.

Milligan nodded the ball down for Adams whose pass sent Denis Irwin galloping away on the overlap. Irwin's deep cross cleared the defence to the far post where HOLDEN had time to bring the ball under control before lashing home a left-foot drive.

West Ham abandoned their sweeper system by replacing centre-back Gary Strodder with midfield man Alan Devonshire. But Athletic had already stiffened up the defence at the break by dropping the mighty Marshall back.

There was a glimmer of hope for the Hammers when Robson netted, but referee Lester Shapter had already blown his whistle for a foul. And, in the 69th minute, Athletic drove another nail into the Hammers coffin.

Marshall flicked on Holden's corner kick and PALMER forced the ball over the line in a close-range scramble.

Many West Ham fans had already left the ground when Athletic, roared on by a capacity crowd, added their sixth, 12 minutes from the end.

Holden drifted past Robson out on the left and sent over another inch-perfect cross for RITCHIE to dart in front of two defenders and head home his 24th goal of the season.

The fans were baying for another goal to match the 7–0 third-round mauling of Scarborough — and they almost got their wish.

Henry surged through into the penalty area and calmly waited for support before pulling the ball back for Palmer to stab in a close-range shot. It beat Parkes, but Julian Dicks managed to clear off the line and give the ball to his keeper.

At the other end, Hallworth, who had spent virtually the whole of the match admiring his team-mates' work, was suddenly called into action to smother a deceptive cross from Devonshire that deflected off Barrett's boot.

PRIDE

However, it was a rare moment of alarm as Athletic completed one of the most convincing victories you are ever likely to see in a major cup semi-final.

West Ham's pride will have been badly hurt and they will want some measure of revenge at Upton Park. But Athletic will surely now end all those years of waiting by striding out on to the famous Wembley turf.

ATHLETIC: Hallworth, Irwin, Barlow, Henry, Marshall, Barrett, Adams, Ritchie, Palmer, Milligan, R Holden. Sub: McGarvey and Donachie.

WEST HAM: Parkes, Robson, Dicks, Parris, Martin, Gale, Brady, Slater, Strodder (Devonshire 50), Kelly, Keen. Sub: McQueen.

Referee Mr. L. Shapter (Torquay)
Attendance 19,263.

Pictures by:
VINCENT BROWN
and TONY MILLER

175

Cheers... champagne heroes Andy Ritchie and Rick Holden following Athletic's Littlewoods Cup Semi Final

"THE TEAM FROM A TOWN OF CHIMNEYS"

SATURDAY 17TH FEBRUARY 1990

JOE'S CUP BATTLERS EARN REPLAY CHANCE

ATHLETIC 2, EVERTON 2

EVERTON must be favourites for a place in the FA Cup quarter finals now that they have wrested home advantage away from Athletic. But don't write off the Boundary Park boys for Wednesday's replay.

Joe Royle's cup battlers showed tremendous spirit to claw their way back from two goals down against First Division opposition as formidable and experienced as Everton.

The men from Goodison Park were a vastly different proposition to West Ham, who were crushed by Athletic in the midweek Littlewoods Cup semi final first leg.

Everton had more than a touch of Northern grit, were willing to attack, and were obviously determined to protect their record as one of the best FA Cup teams of modern times.

Four of the last six Wembley finals have featured Everton — and they must have thought they were well on the way to the last eight again when Graeme Sharp and Tony Cottee scored in quick succession.

They reckoned without a storming second-half fightback from Athletic, which not only earned a replay but very nearly made one unnecessary.

From seeming set to lose their tag as the only team in the country still in both major cup competitions, Athletic dragged themselves back in contention.

They needed a slice of luck before reducing the arrears in the 60th minute.

Roger Palmer and Nick Henry chased a loose ball across the area, keeper Neville Southall, diving at their feet to try to another, missed Henry but, rather unfortunately, caught Palmer with his legs.

PRESSURE

Referee Tony Ward had no hesitation in awarding a penalty, much to the annoyance of the Everton players. Stuart McCall's protests made him the fourth Everton man to be booked, following Neil McDonald, Kevin Sheedy and Sharp.

The spot kick was entrusted to ANDY RITCHIE and he fired in his 10th goal in eight matches and his 25th of the season.

Roared on by another capacity Boundary Park crowd, Athletic suddenly had their tails up.

Mike Milligan's neat pass sent Palmer scampering clear on the right and, when he crossed the ball in low, Southall had to make a brave block at the feet of Ian Marshall.

Athletic were level, though, in the 66th minute — and in familiar fashion.

Rick Holden loped down the left flank and a perfect deep cross picked out PALMER, who headed home his fourth goal in as many games.

That set up a rousing finish to a cracking cup-tie which defied the wet and windy conditions.

Both sides had the ball in the net but had the efforts ruled out for infringements. And it was Athletic who came closest to snatching victory as they piled on the pressure in the closing stages.

When Marshall nodded down Ritchie's cross, Palmer just beat Southall to the ball but poked it wide.

Then Marshall's goalbound effort was charged down by Dave Watson before Ritchie's low shot from 18 yards forced Southall to save, diving full-length to his right.

It was a tremendous effort by Athletic to put themselves in a position where they had a chance of winning.

Everton had earlier punished them for two lapses in defence and are a notoriously difficult side to peg back.

Athletic started reasonably well, although some of the zest was missing and the quality of the final pass was below par.

Watson cleared off the Everton line when Marshall flicked on Holden's corner kick and, when Palmer nipped in ahead of Southall to reach Ian Snodin's weak back pass, Holden crossed the ball back in and McDonald had to hack it clear.

Sheedy somehow blocked a point-black effort from Neil Adams at the far post after a Holden corner had been helped on.

APPEALS

But it was far from being one way traffic as Everton knocked the ball around with confidence.

The visitors made the breakthrough in the 22nd minute when McCall drove in a low cross from the right. Earl Barrett sliced his attempted clearance straight to SHARP and, although keeper Jon Hallworth got a hand to his powerful shot he could only help it on its way into the net.

Four minutes later it was 2–0. Athletic's marking let them down and, as Sharp ran through into the area, Marshall tried to tackle him from behind. As Everton appealed for a penalty, the loose ball bobbled past the advancing Hallworth and COTTEE rifled it into an empty net.

It was then that Athletic decided to take off winger Adams, put substitute Paul Warhurst in defence and send Marshall forward to add more height and strength to the attack.

The move almost paid immediate dividends as Marshall broke away down the left. When he crossed to the far post. Sheedy appeared to push Ritchie out of the way, but penalty appeals were rejected.

Marshall also fired a shot past Southall only to be pulled back for a close offside decision.

The turning point, though, came when Cottee again found room in the area and slammed in a fierce low shot which brought a brilliant save from Hallworth.

A third goal would surely have killed off Athletic, but they emerged for the new half in determined fashion.

They lacked the sparkle of the champagne performance against West Ham, but showed battling qualities which will stand them in good stead in the replay at Goodison. The Wembley double dream is still alive

ATHLETIC: Hallworth, Irwin, Barlow, Henry, Marshall, Barrett, Adams (Warhurst 30), Ritchie, Palmer, Milligan, R Holden. Sub: Redfearn.
EVERTON: Southall, Snodin, McDonald, Ratcliffe, Watson, Whiteside, Ebbrell, McCall, Sharp, Cottee, Sheedy. Sub: Newell, Keown.
Referee: Mr A Ward (London)
Attendance 19,320.

Roger Palmer takes a tumble (top) as Everton 'keeper Neville Southall dives out to try and prevent Nick Henry from reaching the ball. Despite Everton protests that Palmer had merely fallen over the 'keeper's legs, referee Tony Ward gave a penalty which Andy Ritchie (above) slotted in for his 10th goal in eight matches, and his 25th of the season.

by BOB YOUNG

Pictures by: GRAHAM COLLIN and MARTIN SMITH

Athletic's Ian Marshall is denied by a brave save from his former Everton colleague Neville Southall.

Ex-Evertonian Neil Adams sees a close-range effort blocked on the line by Kevin Sheedy.

177

"THE TEAM FROM A TOWN OF CHIMNEYS"

WEDNESDAY 21ST FEBRUARY 1990

WHITESIDE OFF IN CUP STORM

Everton 1, Athletic 1
(after extra time)

THIS is not just a cup-tie anymore — it is a war of attrition. And, if it goes on much longer, it could end up with neither club having enough players to field a side.

Athletic's dogged cup battlers could be too bruised and battered, too physically drained, to pull on a shirt, while Everton are in danger of having everyone suspended.

There seems to be a bitterness creeping into this fifth round FA Cup clash which referee Tony Ward may have a job controlling in next week's second replay at Boundary Park.

And I would lay the blame firmly at the door of the First Division club.

In the two games to date they have displayed a mean streak which goes beyond the bounds of competitiveness. And they have shown a disturbing petulance and level of dissent which does not befit their status as one of the country's leading clubs.

Mr. Ward clearly will not stand for it.

He booked four Everton players on Saturday — three for speaking out of turn — and he incensed the Goodison Park fans last night with five more cautions and the sending off of Norman Whiteside early in the second half.

Whiteside, booked after 19 minutes for a tackle on Nick Henry, got his marching orders for a waist high challenge on Mike Milligan after 49 minutes.

Whether it was malicious or just downright clumsy is debateable, but the fact is that Mr. Ward had already warned Whiteside twice after the first booking.

And Everton ought to count themselves lucky that more players didn't go the same way.

Substitute Mike Newell's first contribution was another late, high challenge on Denis

Latics take credit in bruising battle

Irwin which earned only a booking, while skipper Kevin Ratcliffe spoiled an immaculate display by wrestling Roger Palmer to the ground, punching and trampling on him.

In fact, Everton should be grateful that Mr. Ward amazingly did not give Athletic a penalty when Nick Henry was tackled chest high by Ian Snodin, and that he ignored his linesman's signal for a penalty when Neville Southall pushed Ian Marshall out of the way at a corner kick.

I have never seen Athletic's physio Ian Liversedge called on to the field so often. Almost every player needed treatment at some stage.

Everton may not like Mr. Ward for handing Athletic a dubious penalty on Saturday, but their attitude towards him and their sheer aggressive malevolence was a disgrace.

Much of it is, I suspect, born out of frustration for, apart from the opening 45 minutes at Boundary Park at the weekend, Athletic have enjoyed much more of the possession and have, for long spells, looked a more controlled, composed side.

In the absence of Andy Ritchie last night — rested with a slight thigh strain — Athletic's attack did not really turn that possession into clear opportunities, even when Everton were reduced to ten men.

Athletic stroked the ball around smartly enough — Milligan being outstandingly good in midfield — but chances were limited.

'Keeper Neville Southall was forced to make a superb one-handed save to touch aside Andy Barlow's low, 20-yard skidding shot.

And Ian Marshall had a headed effort disallowed for challenging Southall with an arm raised. Marshall also blazed a right-foot effort off target when the ball fell loose in the penalty area.

Everton had the clearer openings but Kevin Sheedy blasted a close range chance way over the bar and Graeme Sharp hit a tame volley at 'keeper Jon Hallworth.

A pulsating tie really came to life in the closing moments of normal time and then again in the extra 30 minutes.

Sheedy threaded a powerful free kick through the defensive wall but it hit the base of a post. Then, from a Sharp flick-on, Sheedy fired in a shot which was well saved by Hallworth.

The game really exploded in extra time, however, when, 10 minutes into the first period, Athletic snatched the lead.

The overlapping Irwin drove over a cross which eluded everyone to reach the classy Rick Holden out on the left. When Holden clipped over a cross, MARSHALL nodded home the goal against his old club to send Athletic's army of supporters into raptures.

Within a minute, Sharp missed the chance to level when he hurriedly hit a rising drive off target.

In the second period of additional time, though, Athletic could have wrapped up a famous victory.

Adams floated over a cross from the right and Palmer's diving header brought an excellent save from Southall.

Athletic's leg-weary, battle-scarred troops were within five minutes of completing a memorable success when disaster struck.

Paul Warhurst, feeling the effects of a Sheedy tackle in his first full game for a month, failed to cut out a through ball. Sharp bustled into the box, hooked the ball away from Hallworth and collided with the 'keeper.

Referee Ward, who upset Everton with Saturday's penalty decision, redressed the balance by awarding a spot kick which SHEEDY smashed home to save their cup lives.

Evertons: Southall, Snodin, McDonald (Kevin 109), Ratcliffe, Watson, Whiteside, Atteveld (Newell 100), McCall, Sharp, Cottee, Sheedy.
Athletic: Hallworth, Irwin, Barlow, Henry (Redfearn 80), Warhurst, Barrett, Adams, Palmer, Marshall, Milligan, R Holden, Sub: McGarvey.
Referee: Mr T Ward (London).
Attendance: 36,663.

Ian Marshall, partly hidden by the post, beats the Everton defence to reach Rick Holden's cross and head home Athletic's goal against his former club. It was the makeshift striker's first goal for 15 months, and set up a rousing finish to last night's cup battle.

Not this time . . . Marshall beats Neville Southall (above) but the effort was disallowed for a foul on the 'keeper. Penalty! Jon Hallworth and Graeme Sharp go down in a tangle and Everton were given an FA Cup lifeline.

Flashpoint . . . Mike Milligan and Graeme Sharp come face to face.

Report by .... BOB YOUNG
Pictures by .... MARTIN SMITH and VINCENT BROWN

"THE TEAM FROM A TOWN OF CHIMNEYS"

SATURDAY 10TH MARCH 1990

SPOT-ON MARSHALL SETTLES CUP SAGA

ATHLETIC IN LAST EIGHT FOR FIRST TIME IN 77 YEARS

ATHLETIC 2, EVERTON 1
(after extra time)

EVERTON old boy Ian Marshall fired Athletic into the FA Cup quarter finals for the first time in 77 years. And few could deny that Athletic's remarkable knock-out heroes deserved to win a marathon fifth-round battle.

Goodison reject Marshall — a £100,000 signing two years ago — settled this second replay with an extra time penalty.

It was just reward for his efforts in the three cracking meetings between the clubs for the versatile Liverpudlian — at home in attack or defence — has caused all sorts of problems for his former club in his role as stand-in forward.

Four times he has had the ball in the net, but two potential match winners have been disallowed. This time there was no doubt — and no way back for an Everton side which disintegrated surprisingly in the strength-sapping extra period.

SUBDUED

Athletic are the busiest team in the country as they fight for honours on three fronts. But they still had too much in reserve for Everton in terms of sheer determination and guts.

Marshall, for example, could hardly raise a walk, let alone a gallop, in extra time, but might still have helped himself to a hat-trick.

The extent of his joy at grabbing the winner was matched at the other end of the spectrum by the misery of Everton left-back Neil McDonald.

McDonald was guilty of two horrendous blunders which presented Athletic with their historic victory.

Report by:
BOB YOUNG

Pictures by:
VINCENT BROWN
and
TONY MILLER

First he left 'keeper Neville Southall stranded with a terrible back pass. Athletic's all-time record marksman ROGER PALMER showed his awareness as he darted into force the ball past the 'keeper for a 33rd minute equaliser.

Everton had gone in front after 12 minutes when Athletic, playing with only three defenders, were punished for some sloppy marking. McDonald's precise pass let in TONY COTTEE who beat Jon Hallworth to the ball to chip a delightful shot over the diving 'keeper.

That was a rare moment of inspiration from Everton as Andy Barlow, Denis Irwin and the magnificent Earl Barrett largely kept the visitors in check.

Athletic came close when Neil Adams chested down a Barlow cross and fired a right-foot shot inches past the angle of bar and post, while Nick Henry was only just off target with a dipping 25-yard effort.

Everton's best efforts came when Raymond Atteveld's header bounced over the bar from Stuart McCall's cross and when Atteveld volleyed disappointingly wide from a McDonald centre.

Athletic could have snatched it in a strangely subdued second half.

Rick Holden's cross was blocked by Ian Snodin, the busy Neil Redfearn blazed a close-range volley over the top, and Southall had to make a fine save to tip over a thunderous 25-yard drive from Irwin.

Everton did have the ball in the net twice in a minute, both through Cottee, but one was disallowed for a foul on the 'keeper and the other for Sharp's foul on Barrett.

Redfearn brought a good save from Southall with a neat snap-shot, but the match drifted into extra time and looked good for a few more replays.

However, the decisive moment came two minutes into the additional period.

Marshall chased Palmer's pass across the corner of the penalty area and posed no immediate threat. McDonald, though, hauled him down from behind and, when referee Roger Milford awarded a penalty, MARSHALL whacked his shot past Southall.

PRESSURE

At the other end, Hallworth had to make an excellent one-handed save to keep out a Cottee effort but, once the tie turned into the second period of extra time, there was only one team in it... Athletic.

Palmer put a first-time shot over the top from eight yards after Irwin's penetrating run down the right; Southall saved desperately with his legs after Marshall had gone past Martin Keown, then Marshall's downward header clipped the bar from Holden's cross.

Southall also made a fine close-range save to keep out Redfearn's shot as Athletic piled on the pressure, forcing weary limbs to keep going while Everton wilted under the mental pressure of knowing that this was their last chance for glory this season.

Athletic, already guaranteed a Wembley appearance in the Littlewoods Cup, seemed more relaxed, though no less determined, and on the balance of the action in the three meetings with Everton they thoroughly deserved this success.

They face another enormous task in the quarter finals on Wednesday when they take on First Division leaders Aston Villa at Boundary Park. But, the way things are going, nothing is impossible.

Athletic: Hallworth, Irwin, Barlow, Henry, Redfearn, Barrett, Adams (Warhurst 90), Palmer, Marshall, Milligan, R Holden Sub McGarvey

Everton: Southall, Snodin, McDonald (Beagrie 100), Ratcliffe, Keown, Ebbrell, Atteveld (Newell 70), McCall, Sharp, Cottee, Sheedy

Referee Mr R. Milford (Bristol) Attendance 19,346

Villa confident

ASTON VILLA manager Graham Taylor, with his team re-established at the top of the First Division, insists that Athletic's feared plastic pitch holds no terrors for his side.

Villa visit on Wednesday in the delayed FA Cup sixth-round tie, with the prospect of a semi-final clash with Manchester United in their sights — but well aware of the power of Joe Royle's side.

Athletic continued their amazing cup season by knocking out Everton on Saturday to stretch their unbeaten run on the Boundary Park pitch to 35 matches.

"We won 1—0 there when we were in the Second Division, and we've won on Luton's plastic this season. These pitches have been about for quite a while, and all my players have experienced them," claimed Taylor.

Taylor added: "We all have an opinion about them — and I'm sure when Joe leaves Oldham he'll express his true feelings about theirs.

"They're doing extremely well, everything seems to be falling into place for them, and it proves that the difference between a good Second Division side and the majority in the first is minimal.

"But at least all these FA Cup delays mean we've had a chance to turn round our results."

Stuart Gray looks certain to continue as replacement for the injured Derek Mountfield for Villa, but Ian Ormondroyd — once on loan with Athletic — is likely to return on Wednesday after being dropped against Luton to give Gareth Williams a run.

Rick Holden's spectacular header is blocked by defender Ian Snodin.

Roger Palmer forces home Athletic's equaliser.

Neil Redfearn blasts his shot over the bar from close range.

"THE TEAM FROM A TOWN OF CHIMNEYS"

WEDNESDAY 7TH MARCH 1990

HAMMERS WIN THE BATTLE — ATHLETIC WIN THE WAR

DAVID KELLY (far left) sits and watches as his shot beats goalkeeper Jon Hallworth for West Ham's third goal.

ALVIN MARTIN swoops at the far post to head home West Ham's opening goal.

See you at Wembley!

THE DREAM COMES TRUE FOR LATICS

WEST HAM 3, ATHLETIC 0

WEMBLEY became a reality last night as Athletic reached the final of the Littlewoods Cup.

The greatest night in the club's history was not without some anxious moments, though, as West Ham staged a valiant fightback in the second leg of the semi-final.

West Ham's thoroughly-deserved 3–0 victory took some of the gloss off the celebrations, but over the two matches there was no denying that Athletic were the superior side.

David Kelly gave the Hammers a glimmer of hope when he netted the third goal after 65 minutes. Soon after defender Julian Dicks crashed a drive against the crossbar and suddenly the prospect of a remarkable turnabout was on.

Goalkeeper Jon Hallworth had to pull off a string of fine saves on a night on which Athletic had to put up a rearguard action throughout 90 anxious minutes.

But when referee Terry Holbrook blew his whistle for the final time, the 3–0 defeat was met with great celebration.

The below-par performance was disappointing, but understandable, considering Athletic went to the East End of London in such a commanding position.

COMPLACENT

Captain Mike Milligan summed up the feelings: "We are disappointed with the performance tonight, but delighted to have got to Wembley.

"I think we were complacent and rested on our laurels. We expected it to be hard, but not as tough as this."

West Ham were a different proposition to the side so comprehensively beaten at Boundary Park three weeks ago.

Had the Hammers displayed such pride and passion that night, the final outcome might have been different.

Since that defeat Lou Macari has resigned from the managerial position and the popular Billy Bonds has taken over the reins.

West Ham, without four cup-tied players and the injured Frank McAvennie, made light of those setbacks to subject Athletic to a torrid time.

It was hard to believe that this quick and inventive side was virtually the same one which was lacking in ideas at Boundary Park.

The Hammers had nothing to lose and certainly achieved

Big-match report by TONY BUGBY

Bonds's objective of restoring some pride after the first-leg trouncing.

Seldom of late has the Athletic defence been subjected to such a grilling, but despite some anxious moments they stood up to the test. Lesser sides might have folded completely under such an onslaught.

The return of striker Leroy Rosenior gave the Hammers an added aerial threat and the Athletic defence looked somewhat suspect in this department.

The speedy back four of Denis Irwin, Andy Barlow, Paul Warhurst and Earl Barrett also had to be on their toes to deal with the pace of Stuart Slater and David Kelly, who completed the strike force.

The speedy twosome were supplied with a stream of through balls from midfield which stretched the Athletic defence.

DRAMA

Athletic's midfield had to play second fiddle as the delightful touch play of Liam Brady and industry of Kevin Keen took centre stage.

Up front, 25-goal Andy Ritchie was sorely missed.

The tie should have been put beyond the Hammers reach shortly after half-time when Ian Marshall, now operating as a centre forward, jinked his way through the defence only to blaze wide with only goalkeeper Ludek Miklosko to beat.

Had the chance been accepted — at a time when West Ham were two ahead — then the suffering of the

vast travelling army of Athletic supporters would have been eased at a stroke.

Little of the drama in store was evident as Athletic made a spirited start, Marshall and Milligan both having cracks at goal in the opening two minutes.

The Hammers soon got into their stride, with Kelly sounding an ominous double warning with a fierce shot on the turn and then putting the ball into the net only for the goal to be ruled out for handball.

Hallworth was tested for the first time in the 12th minute when he brilliantly kept out Rosenior's diving header which followed a move involving Brady and Dicks.

TRIPPED

Barely two minutes later, ALVIN MARTIN put the home side ahead following a well-rehearsed corner kick routine.

Keen's kick was flicked on at the near post by Slater for Martin to steal in unmarked at the far post and nod home.

West Ham launched wave after wave of attacks which were repelled by the Athletic defence. Had Athletic conceded a second goal at this early stage, the nerves would have been jangling.

Athletic weathered the storm and play became increasingly hard-fought in midfield.

When Athletic left the field only one-goal down at half-time, they had reason to feel well satisfied with their efforts.

The second West Ham goal

ATHLETIC goalkeeper Jon Hallworth is beaten, but David Kelly's effort is ruled out for handball.

came only 90 seconds after the restart.

Hallworth ran from his line to meet Keen, who had raced onto a through ball which had split the Athletic defence. Referee Holbrook adjudged Hallworth had tripped the Hammers' striker and DICKS fired home from the spot to give his side renewed hope.

Marshall ought to have snuffed out that optimism when he burst through the home defence only to fire wide with the goal at his mercy.

Athletic's anxiety increased when KELLY hit the

Hammers' third goal after 66 minutes. Miklosko's long clearance was flicked on by Rosenior leaving Barrett and Warhurst stranded.

Kelly sprinted between the pair to coolly slide the ball past the advancing Hallworth.

The first hint of panic set in as Marshall was pulled back to complete a five-man defence. The home fans were by now in full voice, singing their famous "I'm for ever blowing bubbles" anthem.

West Ham also made a

change, bringing on Tommy McQueen for Brady, a move which enabled Martin to switch from the centre of defence to attack.

TESTED

Hallworth was tested twice, but showed superb handling skills to claim Keen's centre from the right and to take Rosenior's spectacular volley under the crossbar.

Athletic created only their second clear-cut chance after 76 minutes when Nick Henry and Milligan set up Irwin, whose rocket shot was well turned over by Miklosko. It was the Czech keeper's first save.

West Ham were still intent on finishing in a blaze of glory. Dicks rattled the crossbar and Hallworth was forced to block well at Rosenior's feet before turning away Keen's fierce angled drive as he cut in from the right.

As the seconds ticked away the Athletic fans started celebrating. It was clear the Wembley dream had been realised.

Marshall sank to his knees at the final whistle, indicating his relief that the ordeal was over.

The jubilant players jigged their way to the corner of the ground accommodating their fans.

It was a night on which Athletic made club history and, even though they were beaten, it was still a privilege to be there.

WEST HAM: Miklosko, Slater, Dicks, Parris, Martin, Gale, Brady, McQueen, 70, Allen, Rosenior, Kelly, Keen. Sub:

ATHLETIC: Hallworth, Irwin, Barlow, Henry, Barrett, Warhurst, Adams, Palmer, Marshall, Milligan, Holden. Sub: Donachie, Rhodes.

Referee: Mr T. Holbrook (Wolverhampton).

Attendance: 15,431.

A RARE attack by Athletic... Neil Adams's glancing header is wide of the target.

Pictures by Martin Smith and Vincent Brown

180

Champagne flows at 18,000 feet, as Athletic players celebrate reaching the Littlewoods Cup Final after their 2nd Leg Semi-Final v West Ham United, Wednesday March 7th 1990

"THE TEAM FROM A TOWN OF CHIMNEYS"

WEDNESDAY 14TH MARCH 1990

CUP CRAZY ATHLETIC STORM ON TO SEMIS

Villa flattened as Royle's boys keep Wembley double in sight

ATHLETIC 3, ASTON VILLA 0

HAS anyone out there got a book of soccer superlatives? I think I'm running out as Athletic's incredible cup exploits continue to grab the nation's attention.

"Put the champagne on ice, we're going to Wembley twice". If you had sung that at the start of this season you would have run the risk of being locked up.

Now, amazingly, Joe Royle's excellent young team is only one step away from achieving the impossible dream . . . and despite their great reputation, Manchester United will know they are in for a battle when the teams turn out at Maine Road on April 8 for the FA Cup semi-final.

In true "Boys Own" fashion, Athletic did not simply beat Aston Villa in last night's quarter final. They swept aside the First Division leaders with another remarkable attacking show.

And gracious Villa boss Graham Taylor was the first to concede that Athletic's success should not be attributed to the artificial pitch.

"That is a red herring," said Taylor. "It is the way Oldham play which causes teams problems. They are so direct. They get the ball into the box quickly — more than any First Division team we have met. They'll give any team in the land problems."

Ask the big-time Charlies like Leeds, Arsenal, Southampton and Everton, who have all fallen prey to goal-hungry Athletic this season in their surge to the Littlewoods Cup final and, now, to the brink of another Wembley appearance.

Villa were always going to the same way as the other so-called superior teams once winger RICK HOLDEN fired Athletic in front with a spectacular 38th minute strike.

Tricky Ricky stunned the visitors with a superbly struck left-foot drive from 20 yards which flew past 'keeper Nigel Spink and hit the net via the underside of the bar.

Athletic needed that goal to break the ice for Villa — and ex-Manchester United defender Paul McGrath in particular — had earlier been solid and well organised.

Once the breakthrough came, though, you could almost see the self confidence and belief slipping away from Villa as Athletic stepped up a gear.

STYLISH

Panic set in five minutes into the second half, when, following Holden's right-wing corner, the ball eventually came out to Paul Warhurst.

The impressive young defender threaded through a pass and full-back CHRIS PRICE, hounded by Ian Marshall, hurriedly slipped a back pass beyond the reach of

Report by:
BOB YOUNG

Neil Redfearn puts the issue beyond doubt as he scores his first goal for Athletic.

his advancing 'keeper to make it 2—0.

There was no way back for Villa as Athletic relentlessly surged forward.

Goalkeeper Jon Hallworth was virtually a spectator as Villa forced only one corner in the 90 minutes and brought the 'keeper into action only once to hold a low drive from Chadfordonian David Platt.

Full-backs Denis Irwin and Andy Barlow were in commanding form. Villa's potential star Tony Daley had no luck against Irwin, got no joy when he was switched across to Barlow's flank and was utterly disillusioned by the time he was substituted in the 58th minute.

Minutes later, the whole Villa camp was down in the dumps as Holden destroyed them again.

Cutting in from the left wing, Holden nudged the ball through Price's legs, darted into the area and fire in a low, right-foot shot. Spink could only knock it aside and the busy NEIL REDFEARN was on hand to tap home his first goal for the club since his £150,000 move from Watford.

If Villa entertained any thoughts of an astonishing comeback they were snuffed out by the gifted Warhurst and that brilliant tower of defensive strength known as Earl Barrett.

Athletic were staggeringly efficient and stylish as, after a slow start, the midfield duo of Nick Henry and Mike Milligan took command and strikers Roger Palmer and Marshall ran themselves ragged to create gaps in the Villa rear-guard.

Palmer, Marshall, Redfearn and Irwin all came close to improving Athletic's goals tally as another mighty all-round team performance sent them soaring into their first FA Cup final for 77 years.

Villa boss Taylor, reacting in typically honest fashion to his team's crushing defeat, commented: "Every Oldham player knows his job and they play with great confidence.

"Irrespective of the surface I am sure they will do well against any team wherever they play. They push up on you, the midfield squeeze you and there is nothing you can do about it. Consistently they get the ball into areas that hurt you.

"Now the impossible dream of Wembley twice is a whisker away from being a reality and,

if Athletic can apply their cup form to the remainder of their league programme, we might even be celebrating promotion as well.

Is this really happening to Oldham Athletic? I just hope I don't wake up some time in May to suddenly discover it has all been a dream.

As former Latics favourite David Holt said "It's believable. Holt, a nervous spectator last night, added: "It's just so difficult to take it all in — but what a team. They're incredible."

Athletic: Hallworth, Irwin, Barlow (Henry) Barrett, Warhurst, Redfearn, Palmer, Marshall, Milligan, R Holden Subs: Adams and McGarvey

Aston Villa: Spink, Price, Gage, (M) Platt, Olney, Cowans, Gallacher, McGrath, Gray, Nielsen, Daley (Mountfield), Bob Blake
Referee: Mr K Hackett (Sheffield)
Attendance 19,490

Heading for Wembley . . . Rick Holden keeps the Villa defence under pressure.

Jubilant Redfearn and skipper Mike Milligan celebrate the third goal.

182

ATHLETIC v ASTON VILLA
(F.A Cup 6th Round) March 1990
Rick Holden's stunning first half goal gave Athletic the lead in a 3-0 victory

"THE TEAM FROM A TOWN OF CHIMNEYS"

SUNDAY 8TH APRIL 1990

WEMBLEY DOUBLE IS STILL ON CARDS FOR BATTLING ATHLETIC

Palmer forces replay in cup thriller

ATHLETIC 3, MANCHESTER UNITED 3

WHO said that FA Cup semi-finals were boring, tense affairs? Not one of the 44,026 people who witnessed this gripping Maine Road encounter — that's for sure. Nor those who watched the contest on television in 26 countries.

Crystal Palace and Liverpool set the trend for drama and entertainment in their semi-final at Villa Park earlier in the day. And the all-North West battle more than lived up to that example.

From the moment that Earl Barrett broke the ice with an early goal, right through to a nerve-wracking 30 minutes of extra time, this was a cup-tie to savour not always because the football was of the highest quality, but for the sheer drive, determination, enthusiasm — and sportsmanship — of the teams.

It was a match which had more twists and turns than an Alpine track — and one in which Athletic's Second Division cup marvels hopefully laid to rest the myth that they can only play on their artificial pitch.

There was nothing artificial about the way Athletic set about the task of tackling one of the greatest clubs in football.

It may have been United's 18th appearance in an FA Cup semi-final and only Athletic's second in 77 years, but it was the Reds who were rocking anxiously when Joe Royle's upstarts had the audacity to snatch the initiative.

When former Old Trafford man Andy Ritchie galloped away down the right, his low cross caused confusion between 'keeper Jim Leighton and right-back Mike Phelan. Rick Holden almost took advantage but succeeded in winning Athletic's first corner of the game after six minutes.

Holden's flag-kick was cleared back out to him and, when he drilled in a low centre, Ritchie's presence disturbed Leighton, allowing the ball to run through to the unmarked BARRETT, who had a simple, close-range tap-in to put Athletic in front.

That did nothing to settle United's nerves and Athletic enjoyed a slight edge in a hectic, hundred-miles-an-hour first half.

Royle's side had a better pattern and flow as United struggled to settle the likes of England skipper Bryan Robson and international colleague Neil Webb back into the side after long injury lay-offs.

However, manager Alex Ferguson's bold decision to include them both from the start paid handsome dividends with a 29th minute equaliser.

CLEARED

Steve Bruce won a sliding tackle on Ritchie just inside Athletic's half, the ball flew through to Webb and his neat pass picked out Robson darting through a square defence. Keeper Jon Hallworth got his hand to ROBSON'S low, right-foot shot but could not prevent it from bouncing into the net.

Athletic might have restored their advantage before the interval as the magnificent Mike Milligan and his partner Nick Henry took a grip on midfield, despite being out-numbered as United often left only Mark Hughes up front.

The hard working Neil Redfearn and Ritchie worked an opening for Denis Irwin to cross but the well-placed Ian Marshall planted his header against defender Gary Pallister.

When Redfearn swung over the resulting corner kick, it was partly cleared out to Henry whose low, right-foot drive was cleared off the line by Paul Ince — United's best performer.

United had their moments as well, though, as this memorable battle gathered pace.

Robson's shot from Brian McClair's cross was blocked by Irwin and Hallworth held an angled left-foot shot from Hughes on just about the only occasion he escaped the attentions of the brilliant Barrett.

Leighton was almost surprised by a Marshall snap-shot which he managed to beat away, while United felt they might have had a penalty when Andy Barlow appeared to push Webb to the ground.

However, Webb had his revenge in the 71st minute when he put United ahead for the first time — although he probably didn't know much about it.

Danny Wallace had only been on the pitch for a minute as a replacement for the tiring Robson when he lobbed in a cross from the right. Colin Gibson nodded it into the area, Andy Holden challenged Webb, Hallworth came off his line late to join in and the ball hit WEBB'S head and dropped into an empty net.

Athletic would not believe that their dreams of a Wembley double were over and were level within four minutes.

Irwin combined with Redfearn on the right and the latter did well to whip in a cross which picked out MARSHALL for a cracking first-time right-foot volley which flew into the bottom corner of the net.

Either side could have matched victory in the dying minutes.

Webb's powerful shot was beaten away by Hallworth and Barrett blocked Hughes's follow-up volley, while, at the other end, Marshall galloped away from Pallister but fired his shot into the side-netting with Ritchie waiting unmarked in the middle.

Marshall was unlucky not to make amends in the first minute of extra time when his shot was blocked on the line.

However, it was United who again broke through when McClair's superb pass split Athletic's defence, allowing WALLACE to sprint clear and scuff a left-foot shot past the advancing Hallworth.

Marshall brought another save from Leighton when he sneaked through round the back of the defence but Athletic had to wait until the 107th minute before they again levelled this remarkable game.

Milligan's excellent pass set in Marshall on the left and, when he curled over a precise low cross substitute ROGER PALMER ghosted in at the far post to apply the finishing touch from point-blank range.

Athletic looked the stronger side as the game wore on and the likes of Marshall and Rick Holden began to really get going.

Even so, it could have gone either way — and what a fairytale finish it would have been had Oldham-born substitute Mark Robins won it for United with a fine header which brought a good save from Hallworth.

Rick Holden almost had the last word, though, when he cut in from the left flank and whacked in a fierce 20-yard drive which flew a whisker wide.

Nobody really deserved to lose on the day, though, and this finely-balanced, intriguing tie resumes at Maine Road on Wednesday, when only a brave man would dare to predict the outcome.

ATHLETIC: Hallworth, Irwin, Henry (Warhurst 82), Barrett, A. Holden, Barlow, Ritchie (Palmer 96), Marshall, Milligan, R. Holden.

MAN. UNITED: Leighton, Martin (Robins 108), Gibson, Bruce, Phelan, Pallister, Robson (Wallace 70), Ince, McClair, Hughes, Webb.

Referee: Mr. J. Worrall (Warrington)
Attendance: 44,026.

Report by
BOB YOUNG

Pictures by
VINCENT BROWN
and
TONY MILLER

Roger Palmer (above) pounces for the sixth and final goal in a tremendous semi-final.

Neil Webb puts United ahead.

Delighted Earl Barrett salutes the opening goal.

In the space of seven hectic days, Athletic virtually assured themselves of a Littlewoods Cup final place by a St. Valentine's day massacre of West Ham 6-0 in the home leg of the two-legged semi-final, and faced Everton in an F.A. Cup fifth round replay.

That was rapidly followed by a 3-0 defeat at West Ham – a disappointing result but one guaranteeing a first-ever Wembley visit; then an extra-time second replay success against Everton and a sixth-round win over Aston Villa.

In the league, though, the cracks were beginning to show as Athletic staggered from one big game to another with scarcely time to draw breath, and with a backlog of fixtures building up.

The feeling that perhaps Athletic were running out of steam, and luck, was compounded by the narrowest of defeats by Manchester United in the F.A. Cup semi-final replay after two epic encounters.

Few outside of Old Trafford felt that Athletic deserved to lose but, for many of the nation's football followers, the magic had died.

Not so in Oldham as the new club shop did a roaring trade in the build-up to the historic visit to Wembley for the Littlewoods Cup final against Nottingham Forest. Replica kit, scarves, rosettes, coffee mugs, pencils – you name it, the fans snapped it up as 30,000 prepared to journey down South for the biggest day in the club's history.

Oldham was virtually closed on Sunday April 29, 1990, but one goal from Nigel Jemson broke Athletic's heart and gave Forest the cup. Next day, Athletic returned to town for a Civic reception and Oldham saluted the brave boys in blue as an estimated 60,000 turned out to watch an open topped bus ride through the streets.

On the league front, Athletic finished within three points of securing a promotion play-off place. The 2-0 home defeat by Sheffield United on March 28, saw Athletic lose their club record of 38 unbeaten home matches, and was a major setback.

Athletic's skill, flair, entertainment value and sportsmanship of players, officials and supporters, won universal approval, but such attributes proved to be not enough in themselves to secure a trophy or promotion.

Athletic's injury problems, acute at times, were overlooked as a tidal wave of emotion and excitement swept them through the second half of the campaign ... the emotion heightened by the fervent wish that Joe Royle's loyalty would be rewarded.

The manager had declined the chance to talk to Manchester City about their vacant managerial post, believing it would have been unforgiveable to walk out on Athletic midway through such a season.

He admitted it had been a tough decision but the depth of feeling among Athletic fans persuaded him to stay. Supporters paid for messages on the scoreboard reading – "Please Joe, Don't Go" and, after the 3-0 home win over Blackburn on December 1, one fan stayed behind for hours in freezing conditions to make a personal plea to the boss.

ATHLETIC v BLACKBURN ROVERS *December 1989 – Division 2*
Athletic's scoreboard sends out a message – and Manager Joe Royle did not disappoint anxious supporters

Athletic supporters queue all night for Littlewoods Cup Final tickets

"THE TEAM FROM A TOWN OF CHIMNEYS"

Athletic players recording their Wembley record 'The Boys in Blue' with Shaw based comedian Bobby Ball

"THE TEAM FROM A TOWN OF CHIMNEYS"

WEDNESDAY 11TH APRIL 1990

ROBINS SHATTERS LATICS DREAM OF WEMBLEY DOUBLE

ATHLETIC 1, MANCHESTER UNITED 2
(after extra time)

ATHLETIC'S dreams of an amazing Wembley double were shattered at Maine Road last night — ironically by a Chadderton lad who played for Boundary Park Juniors.

Promising young striker Mark Robins (20), who has popped in a few vital goals for United this season, finally settled this epic FA Cup semi-final struggle by snatching a winner after 110 minutes of tension and drama.

But football was the real winner. BBC television probably cannot believe their luck after live showings of Sunday's goal-packed encounters between Crystal Palace and Liverpool, Athletic and United — and this replay.

Now soccer fans in 26 countries know that our game is in good shape when teams take to the park trying to play football the way it should be — with style and determination, but also in a good spirit.

Perhaps late had determined that Athletic were not destined to follow up their record-breaking achievement of reaching the Littlewoods Cup final with another Wembley date in the nation's most glamorous knock-out event.

But their attempts to pull off a remarkable double cannot be faulted.

In two splendid matches, it has been impossible for the impartial observer to say which was the First Division team.

Never at any stage has the multi-million pound team from Old Trafford been able to stifle the talents of Joe Royle's magnificent cup battlers.

And, there are plenty who will argue that, with a slice of luck, Athletic could so easily have been marching up Wembley Way.

With the benefit of a television monitor and hindsight, it is clear that Nick Henry's seventh minute shot did cross the goalline after bouncing off the underside of the bar.

Local lad is United hero in cup epic

by BOB YOUNG

Referee Joe Worrall did not have the action replay to turn to and no goal was given.

It is also true that Denis Irwin was desperately unlucky when his 63rd minute free kick deflected off the defensive wall, left keeper Jim Leighton utterly stranded and, almost in slow motion it seemed, clipped the outside of a post.

Leighton was the busier of the keepers as Athletic again adopted the only approach they know — go for it.

Makeshift striker Ian Marshall almost created a sensation in the opening minutes when he cut out Gary Pallister's back pass and, from the tightest of angles, hooked a left-foot shot just off target.

United, though, looked much sharper, more in tune with their game, than they had been in Sunday's first encounter.

Several times in the first half they found gaps through the inside right channel as first Neil Webb, then Mark Hughes, went through to test Jon Hallworth with fierce, angled shots.

Athletic carved out an opening in similar fashion and Andy Ritchie's right-foot drive flew across the face of goal and inches wide of the far post.

Ritchie had a 20-yard shot saved by Leighton while, at the other end, the sensational Mike Milligan cleared a Mike Phelan cross from in front of an open goal as the match gathered pace.

Perhaps one of the deciding factors came during the half-time interval when Athletic had to withdraw Marshall from the fray with a thigh muscle injury.

Substitute Paul Warhurst twice posed a threat early in the second period. Steve Bruce hacked one header clear and Bryan Robson whipped another off Ritchie's toes.

However, Athletic did miss Marshall's height and deception gave up front when they found themselves trailing to a 50th minute strike from Brian McClair.

GAMBLE

It was similar to Roger Palmer's extra-time equaliser on Sunday which forced this cracking tie to a replay.

Robson's persistence out on the left won possession, Danny Wallace fired in a low cross and it eluded everyone until reaching the far post, where McCLAIR had a simple tap-in.

United might have wrapped it up shortly afterwards when Mark Hughes escaped the attentions of the brilliant Earl Barrett for about the second time in four hours of combat. Hughes clipped over a cross but the unmarked Paul Ince just failed to direct a diving header on target.

The Reds were never allowed to feel comfortable with their slender advantage. Just as in the first game, whenever United scored, Athletic simply rolled up their sleeves and went straight back at them.

England skipper Robson was forced deeper and deeper to help out at the back and, when Athletic took the 57th minute gamble of taking off Andy Barlow and sending on a fifth forward in the shape of Roger Palmer, Robson ended up playing as a third centre-half — and very well he did too.

Athletic tried all sorts of tricks to claw their way back while, suddenly, Warhurst was pulled back to defence and big Andy Holden sent forward to try to cut down on Pallister's aerial dominance.

United, though, were stubborn and competitive, fiercely determined to hold on and hit Athletic on the counter-attack.

RELIEF

Leighton made a brilliant save to keep out Milligan's 18-yard volley but, just when it seemed that Athletic were doomed, Royle's never-say-die troops silenced the celebratory chants of United fans.

Only 10 minutes were left when Rick Holden popped up on the right flank and curled in a teasing cross which found RITCHIE unfettered six yards out to slot a first-time left-foot shot into the roof of the net.

And so, it was into extra time again as this fascinating battle raged on.

Most clubs would settle for another replay — but Athletic have this lovely, refreshing approach.

Unfortunately, they are liable to pay for it at times by being caught out at the back — and so it proved in the 110th minute.

Phelan, whose losing battle with Rick Holden cost him a booking, managed to overlap for only the second time in the game and, when he slipped a pass inside, ROBINS might have been offside but kept admirably calm to sneak a low right-foot shot past Hallworth.

Even then, United could not relax as Ritchie clipped in a cross-cum-shot that Leighton flicked away for a corner.

And, in the very last minute Ritchie broke away on the left and pulled back a low cross but the ball was slightly behind Palmer who could only scoop his left-foot shot off target.

The final whistle came as a massive relief to United and, in what has been a troubled season for them one way or another, they head for Wembley with an obvious chance of lifting the trophy.

Athletic simply have to lift their heads. There is no need for them to be bowed.

They came up against one of the greatest clubs in the world and a team costing ten times what they did. And they were not disgraced. Far from it.

The message that will go out from every Athletic supporter — indeed many soccer fans throughout the world is simple —

YOU DID US PROUD!

ATHLETIC: Hallworth, Irwin, Barlow (Palmer 57), Henry, Barrett, A. Holden, Redfearn, Ritchie, Marshall (Warhurst 45), Milligan, R. Holden.
MAN. UNITED: Leighton, Ince, Martin (Robins 106), Bruce, Phelan, Pallister, Robson, Webb (Gibson 80), McClair, Hughes, Wallace.
Referee Mr J Worrall (Warrington)
Attendance 35,005.

Pictures by VINCENT BROWN and ANTHONY MILLER

Andy Ritchie slots in Athletic's dramatic late equaliser (above) but Nick Henry (below) saw this shot hit the bar in the opening minutes of the match.

Two of the games most influential characters, Mike Milligan and Gary Pallister, in high-stepping action.

188

Joe Royle talks to his Athletic players at the end of 90 minutes in the Maine Road F.A. Cup Semi-Final v Manchester United

Athletic's ex-Manchester City contingent, Paul Moulden, Earl Barrett and Paul Warhurst – May 1990

SUNDAY 29TH APRIL 1990

"THE TEAM FROM A TOWN OF CHIMNEYS"

The goal that

NIGEL JEMSON beats Athletic's defence to get in a shot.

Royle's eyes still on the play-offs

by DAVID WHITE

ANOTHER chapter in Athletic's historic season may have ended, but manager Joe Royle believes that there could still be a happy ending to the Boundary Park club's dramatic campaign.

Yesterday's Wembley defeat by Nottingham Forest in the Littlewoods Cup final came 18 days after Athletic were beaten by Manchester United in their FA Cup semi-final replay at Maine Road.

The next week will decide whether Royle's team makes it into the semi-finals of the play-offs for a place in Division One next season.

Royle said: "We have played 61 games this season and it has been a lovely adventure. Unfortunately, the fairy tale did not come true against Forest, but there is still time.

"We have got four league games to play, including two against fellow promotion hopefuls Wolves and Sunderland. If we win all four, we will skate it into the play-offs and we could do it if we win three — if they are the right three."

Strains

Reflecting on the Littlewoods Cup final, Royle continued: "We feel we can play better. We did not play as we can.

"One or two of the players showed the strains of the 61st game of the season.

"We have not been caught out on ability, but by a timetable which would have even stretched Liverpool."

"They are tired, but they will come back in tomorrow for the game against Oxford. We have kept going and we arrived at the pinnacle in this game.

"At the end of the day, we have been beaten at the highest level. Consider the fact that an England 'international defender, Des Walker, has won the man of the match against a Second Division side."

From the Forest camp, there was praise for Athletic.

Forest's assistant manager Ronnie Fenton said: "It was a pity there had to be a loser — especially when it was Athletic.

"They have had a magnifi-

cent season, but there is a possibility they could finish with nothing and that would be a shame.

"Joe Royle is a young manager with a great future and we wish him well.

"I have been watching Athletic for a few months and they try to get the ball wide as quickly as they can and try and get their crosses in as soon as possible.

"Athletic stretched us to the limit and kept coming at us. Everyone, except Forest supporters, would have been hoping they would have won."

Style

Turning to Forest striker Nigel Jemson, whose 48th-minute goal gave the Nottingham club its fourth trophy in this competition, Fenton said: "He has shown great character.

"He thought he had arrived when we paid Preston £150,000 for him, but that when the hard work started He knows what he has to do, but it has taken a lot of time to convert him."

Describing his goal, Jemson said: "Nigel Clough played a great ball to me. Andy Rhodes narrowed the angle well and saved my first shot, but I got the angle right to tuck away the rebound.

"It has not sunk in yet and it won't for a while.

"It took time for me to settle into Forest's game of playing the ball to feet, but once I had adjusted to the style of play I started to enjoy it."

they have two of England's defence and midfield man Steve Hodge is now back in international plans."

While Walker became the first player to win with the Alan Hardaker Trophy as man of the match, he must have been run pretty close by Athletic central defender Earl Barrett.

"Earl was magnificent and we are taking his performance for granted," said Royle.

The Athletic boss also disclosed that right-back Denis Irwin played the second half with a groin strain.

Turning to the club's injury problems on the run up to the final, Royle said: "On Saturday, I thought Ian Marshall would be fit to play, but he felt the thigh strain and could not play.

"At the same time, I thought Nick Henry had no chance of playing with his hamstring injury, but he played the 90 minutes at Wembley . . . I don't know how. It is Nick's first full season in league football."

Royle added that Marshall could be fit to return to the side this week, but that central defender Andy Holden (hamstring) had no chance and midfield-man Neil Redfearn (knee ligaments) was doubtful.

AND ONE THAT GOT AWAY

ATHLETIC'S top goalscorer, Andy Ritchie, thought he had put them ahead with this powerful left-foot shot (above) but Forest goalkeeper Steve Sutton pulled off a superb first-half save to deny the Boundary Park boys.

Pictures by

MARTIN SMITH

and

VINCENT BROWN

"THE TEAM FROM A TOWN OF CHIMNEYS"

ended a dream

ANDY RHODES beats out Jemson's effort and tries to recover.

RHODES and Earl Barrett can only watch as Jemson gets to the rebound first to score the all-important goal.

We did not deserve to lose...

by TONY BUGBY

CAPTAIN Mike Milligan declared without hesitation: "That was definitely the proudest moment of my life as I led the team on to the field.

"To walk on to the pitch was a dream come true. The atmosphere was electrifying and we had unbelievable support.

"We gave a great account of ourselves and I do not think we deserved to lose. They soaked up our pressure, then sneaked the winning goal."

Local lad Andy Barlow appeared at Wembley as a youngster for Oldham Schools' Rugby League.

Afterwards he dispelled the theory from most players that the 90 minutes fly by.

"It seemed to take ages near the end. I can remember everything and every attack.

"We got behind their defence and got in crosses, but just could not get a goal. Their goalkeeper made a couple of good saves."

BUZZING

Goalkeeper Andy Rhodes was preferred to Jon Hallworth and responded to Joe Royle's faith by turning in a splendid display.

"What a poxy goal to lose the final. I made the initial save from Nigel Jemson, but, unfortunately, the ball fell to him. It could have gone anywhere.

"I made a couple of good saves early on which boosted my confidence. I was buzzing and did not think I would be beaten.

"I am cursing our luck. We did ourselves justice and had a taste of the good life and want more. Hopefully, we will be back in three weeks time in the play-offs.

"We are very disappointed because we thought we could beat them. I was pleased with my display. I have been in and out of the side recently, but never doubted my own ability. It was only the manager who had done so. I have always been confident."

Neil Adams was making his third Wembley appearance, having turned out for Everton in the Charity Shield and Mercantile Credit Centenary Classic.

Adams had not figured in first-team plans of late and did not learn he was playing until 1.30 p.m. after Ian Marshall failed a late fitness test.

"The feeling is as good as ever. You can never tire of a place like this.

"Everyone must be tremendously proud of what we have achieved as a second division club, although there is nothing on the mantelpiece yet. Hopefully, we can return in the play-offs.

"I came very close to getting a touch to Roger Palmer's header. It literally skimmed my foot by inches, and I ended up in the back of the net. Without doubt it should have been an equaliser.

"We created chances, but needed luck and did not get it today."

As Joe Royle stepped on to the Wembley turf he said: "I feel very proud and we have received a fantastic reception.

"God knows who is left in Oldham — there cannot be many people. We are very proud to be here and have come to enjoy the day.

"We used the build-up similar to any away game, spending minimal time in the hotel because we did not want to break our usual routine. Today is a big day and we are here to enjoy it."

Player-coach Willie Donachie said: "It is a brilliant occasion coming to Wembley and would still be fantastic if you came every month.

"It is different for me today.

Had I been playing I would be walking on cloud nine.

"As it is, I can be more objective and relaxed sitting on the sidelines."

Andy Ritchie, the leading scorer in the Littlewoods Cup campaign this season with 10 goals, was closely shackled by England defender Des Walker.

"Des is a good player. He played very well and we had a good tussle."

Paul Warhurst also faced an anxious wait before booking his place in the starting line. He received the nod when Andy Holden pulled out through a hamstring strain.

Playing at Wembley capped a remarkable rise in Warhurst's fortunes. Eighteen months ago he was playing second-team football at Manchester City before moving to Boundary Park for £10,000.

SADDEST

"This is my first full season in the first team and a lot has happened in the last 18 months.

"I am just hoping things go from strength to strength in the future.

The 20-year-old admitted: "I was very nervous before the start as I think everyone was. Once the first five minutes were over I settled and really enjoyed the day — apart from the goal.

"The heat was tremendous and when you made a run of around 40 yards it took your breath away.

"It was a fabulous experience and makes you want to come back again. Hopefully it can come true again."

Nick Henry faced an anxious wait after straining knee ligaments in the defeat at Portsmouth five days before the final.

The midfielder, who has a great partnership with Mike Milligan in midfield, said: "It was worrying, but I never gave up hope of playing.

"I received intensive treatment and the knee was getting better every day."

Andy Holden was the saddest man at Wembley, missing out through injury.

Holden has had eight operations in the past four years, but after playing at Portsmouth looked set for a triumphant finish to another injury-blighted season.

"I am at the lowest since I have been a professional footballer. It has been an awful week because the manager also pulled me out of the Wales squad as well."

Club chairman Mr. Ian Stott said: "It was a marvellous day for the fans, although I expect it was a few degrees too high for the players.

"The lads in no sense let down us or football. I feel very sorry for them, but at the same time proud of what we have achieved.

"I am a little disappointed Earl Barrett was not named man of the match. Des Walker was very good, but Earl was absolutely outstanding.

"Both sets of fans were excellent and, from what I have learned, this was probably the best atmosphere here for many Littlewoods Cup finals.

"I feel sorry, but at the same time proud. It will be a shame if we finish the season with nothing to show for our efforts."

August 1990 – England's new Manager Graham Taylor visits Boundary Park to supervise a pre-season training session

The fans were certainly touched by Royle's loyalty and by his team's magnificent exploits which kept them in with the chance of honours right up to the final week of a hectic and remarkable season.

Royle narrowly failed to beat Kenny Dalglish, of champions Liverpool, in the voting for the Barclays Bank Manager of the Year award, but collected a special award by way of recognition.

That wasn't the only thing Athletic collected, however, for interest in the club had now been clearly re-established. Season ticket and membership sales for the 1990-91 season were at record levels.

Cynics suggested that Athletic had won nothing and that the promising young team would be dismantled. They scoffed when Denis Irwin went to Manchester United for £625,000 and Mike Milligan joined Everton as Athletic's first ever £1M sale.

However, with the club's finances now more bouyant than perhaps at any time in history, Royle set about rebuilding – and not, for a change – by bargain-basement hunting.

The club's transfer record was broken three times in quick succession as £240,000 Brighton 'keeper John Keeley replaced Andy Rhodes (£100,000 to Dunfermline), David Currie cost £450,000 from Nottingham Forest, and Richard Jobson was bought for £460,000 from Hull City.

Athletic set out their stall to make 1990-91 the season when promotion was finally achieved and, despite a few signs of a hang-over from the amazing "Pinch Me" season, they opened, in front of bumper crowds, with another piece of history. By winning their first five games they equalled their best ever start to a league campaign, set in 1930.

Could **THIS** really be **THE** season?

To be continued

Miscellany

Complete playing record in the Football League: 1907-1990

F.A. Cup results & scorers: 1906-1990

Football League Cup results: 1960-1990

Miscellaneous Information

"THE TEAM FROM A TOWN OF CHIMNEYS"

COMPLETE PLAYING RECORD IN THE FOOTBALL LEAGUE: 1907*1990

F. HESHAM 1907

R. PALMER 1990

"THE TEAM FROM A TOWN OF CHIMNEYS"

DIVISION 2 — 1907-08

							H	A
Bradford C.	38	24	6	8	90:42	54	4—0	0—1
Leicester Fosse	38	21	10	7	72:47	52	1—1	1—4
OLDHAM	38	22	6	10	76:42	50	—	—
Fulham	38	22	5	11	82:49	49	3—3	2—1
West Bromwich	38	19	9	10	61:39	47	2—1	2—1
Derby	38	21	4	13	77:45	46	3—1	0—1
Burnley	38	20	6	12	67:50	46	1—1	1—2
Hull	38	21	4	13	73:62	46	3—0	2—3
Wolverhampton	38	15	7	16	50:45	37	2—0	1—2
Stoke	38	16	5	17	57:52	37	3—1	3—1
Gainsborough	38	14	7	17	47:71	35	4—1	1—1
Leeds C.	38	12	8	18	53:65	32	4—2	2—1
Stockport	38	12	8	18	48:67	32	5—0	3—2
Clapton Orient	38	11	10	17	40:65	32	4—1	0—2
Blackpool	38	11	9	18	51:58	31	3—2	0—1
Barnsley	38	12	6	20	54:68	30	1—0	1—2
Glossop	38	11	8	19	54:74	30	0—0	0—0
Grimsby	38	11	8	19	43:71	30	2—0	0—2
Chesterfield Town	38	6	11	21	46:92	23	4—0	2—1
Lincoln	38	9	3	26	46:83	21	4—0	2—0

APPEARANCES & GOALSCORERS

Bottomley W. 12
Brunton 1
Cook W. 2
Dodds W. 14
Fay J. 38
Hamilton J. 37
Hancock H. 27
Hesham F. 25

Hewitson R. 27
Hodson J. 36
Newton F. 37
Round 8
Shadbolt 22
Shufflebottom 1
Stafford J. 1
Swarbrick 3

Walders D. 26
Ward 15
Watts 7
Whaites A. 35
Wilson D. 38
Wolstenholme 3
Wright 3

Scorers:— Newton 25, Hancock 11, Hesham 10, Dodds 6, Whaites 8, Shadbolt 4, Fay 3, Wilson 3, Ward 2, Swarbrick 2, Walders 2.
Total: 76.

"THE TEAM FROM A TOWN OF CHIMNEYS"

DIVISION 2 — 1908-09

							H	A
Bolton	38	24	4	10	59:28	52	1—1	0—3
Tottenham	38	20	11	7	67:32	51	1—0	0—3
West Bromwich	38	19	13	6	56:27	51	2—0	0—1
Hull	38	19	6	13	63:39	44	2—2	0—1
Derby	38	16	11	11	55:41	43	1—1	0—1
OLDHAM	38	17	6	15	55:43	40	—	—
Wolverhampton	38	14	11	13	56:48	39	2—1	1—1
Glossop	38	15	8	15	57:53	38	2—1	1—2
Gainsborough	38	15	8	15	49:70	38	2—0	4—1
Fulham	38	13	11	14	58:48	37	1—0	2—3
Birmingham	38	14	9	15	58:61	37	2—0	0—2
Leeds C.	38	14	7	17	43:53	35	6—0	0—3
Grimsby	38	14	7	17	41:54	35	4—0	0—2
Burnley	38	13	7	18	51:58	33	4—1	0—1
Clapton Orient	38	12	9	17	37:49	33	2—0	0—2
Bradford P.A.	38	13	6	19	51:59	32	2—0	4—3
Barnsley	38	11	10	17	48:57	32	0—0	0—2
Stockport	38	14	3	21	39:71	31	0—1	3—1
Chesterfield Town	38	11	8	19	37:67	30	2—0	1—1
Blackpool	38	9	11	18	46:68	29	3—1	0—1

APPEARANCES & GOALSCORERS

Andrews W. 9	Hamilton J. 36	Speedie F. 15
Appleyard W. 4	Hesham F. 9	Stokes P. 2
Butterworth H. 2	Matthews W.H. 36	Shaw G. 10
Cook W. 11	Martin W. 4	Walders D. 27
Cope W. 3	Newton F. 34	Wilson D. 38
Dodds J.T. 8	Round E. 2	Whaites A. 6
Donnachie J. 31	Reid J. 1	Watts H.P. 3
Fay J. 38	Shadbolt J. 4	Wolstenholme A. ... 26
Griffiths A. 25	Shufflebottom J. ... 6	West J. 1
Hodson J. 26	Swarbrick J. 1	

Scorers:— Newton 14, Wolstenholme 10, Speedie 6, Donnachie 4, Griffiths 4, Fay 3, Andrews 3, Hamilton 3, Reid 2, Walders 2, Stokes, Hesham and Shaw each 1, O.G. 1.
Total 55.

F.NEWTON　　　　　　　　　　　　　　　　J.HAMILTON

"THE TEAM FROM A TOWN OF CHIMNEYS"

DIVISION 2 — 1909-10

							H	A
Manchester C.	38	23	8	7	81:40	54	1—0	2—0
OLDHAM	38	23	7	8	79:39	53	—	—
Hull	38	23	7	8	80:46	53	3—0	0—4
Derby	38	22	9	7	72:47	53	4—0	1—1
Leicester Fosse	38	20	4	14	79:58	44	2—1	0—3
Glossop	38	18	7	13	64:57	43	1—0	2—6
Fulham	38	14	13	11	51:43	41	0—1	1—1
Wolverhampton	38	17	6	15	64:63	40	3—0	0—1
Barnsley	38	16	7	15	62:59	39	5—0	1—2
Bradford P.A.	38	17	4	17	64:59	38	1—1	6—1
West Bromwich	38	16	5	17	58:56	37	1—2	1—1
Blackpool	38	14	8	16	50:52	36	2—0	3—1
Stockport	38	13	8	17	50:47	34	3—0	0—2
Burnley	38	14	6	18	62:61	34	1—0	2—1
Lincoln	38	10	11	17	42:69	31	6—1	2—0
Clapton Orient	38	12	6	20	37:60	30	5—0	2—1
Leeds C.	38	10	7	21	46:80	27	2—1	5—3
Gainsborough	38	10	6	22	33:75	26	2—0	2—0
Grimsby	38	9	6	23	50:77	24	4—1	0—0
Birmingham	38	8	7	23	42:78	23	1—1	2—2

APPEARANCES & GOALSCORERS

Broad T. 38	Hamilton J. 18	Newton F. 11
Butterworth H. 10	Hodson J. 32	Pennington T. 1
Carmichael R. 5	Martin W. 3	Reid J. 4
Cook W. 17	Matthews W.H. 37	Toward A. 21
Cope W. 9	Miller S. 27	Walders D. 27
Donnachie J. 18	Mitchell J. 4	Wilson D. 38
Downie A. 29	Montgomery W. 28	Wolstenholme A. 3
Fay J. 38		

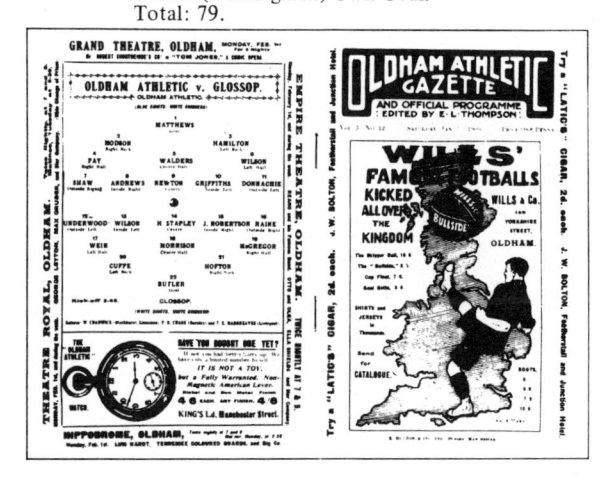

Scorers:— Fay 26, Montgomery 16, Toward 13, Broad 7, Newton 3, Cook 3, Donnachie 3, Walders 3, Wilson 2, Mitchell and Carmichael each 1.
Stokes (Birmingham) Own Goal.
Total: 79.

"THE TEAM FROM A TOWN OF CHIMNEYS"

DIVISION 1 — 1910-11

							H	A
Manchester U.	38	22	8	8	72:40	52	1—3	0—0
Aston Villa	38	22	7	9	69:41	51	1—1	1—1
Sunderland	38	15	15	8	67:48	45	2—1	1—2
Everton	38	19	7	12	50:36	45	2—0	0—1
Bradford C.	38	20	5	13	51:42	45	1—0	2—1
The Wednesday	38	17	8	13	47:48	42	1—0	0—2
OLDHAM	38	16	9	13	44:41	41	—	—
Newcastle	38	15	10	13	61:43	40	0—2	0—3
Sheffield U.	38	15	8	15	49:43	38	3—0	2—1
Woolwich Arsenal	38	13	12	13	41:49	38	3—0	0—0
Notts. Co.	38	14	10	14	37:45	38	2—1	0—1
Blackburn	38	13	11	14	62:54	37	2—0	0—1
Liverpool	38	15	7	16	53:53	37	3—1	0—1
Preston	38	12	11	15	40:49	35	2—1	1—1
Tottenham	38	13	6	19	52:63	32	2—0	0—2
Middlesbrough	38	11	10	17	49:63	32	1—1	2—1
Manchester C.	38	9	13	16	43:58	31	1—1	0—2
Bury	38	9	11	18	43:71	29	0—0	2—2
Bristol C.	38	11	5	22	43:66	27	1—0	2—3
Nottingham F.	38	9	7	22	55:75	25	2—0	1—4

APPEARANCES & GOALSCORERS

Broad T. 26	Hodson J. 24	Montgomery W. 18
Cook W. 17	Jones E. 14	Pilkington S.T. 5
Cope W. 19	Jones A. 1	Toward A. 23
Donnachie J. 38	McDonald H. 38	Walders D. 24
Downie A. 15	McTavish J.K. 10	Wilson D. 38
Fay J. 38	Miller S. 7	Woodger G. 26
Hamilton J. 15	Moffatt H. 22	

Scorers:— Toward 12, Jones 8, Fay 7, Montgomery 4, Woodger 4, Walders 3, Wilson 3, Broad, Cope and Donnachie each 1.
Total: 44.

DIVISION 1 — 1911-12

							H	A
Blackburn	38	20	9	9	60:43	49	0—1	0—1
Everton	38	20	6	12	46:42	46	3—0	1—1
Newcastle	38	18	8	12	64:50	44	2—4	1—1
Bolton	38	20	3	15	54:43	43	3—1	1—2
The Wednesday	38	16	9	13	69:49	41	1—0	0—1
Aston Villa	38	17	7	14	76:63	41	1—2	1—6
Middlesbrough	38	16	8	14	56:45	40	2—0	0—3
Sunderland	38	14	11	13	58:51	39	0—0	2—4
West Bromwich	38	15	9	14	43:47	39	3—1	0—0
Woolwich Arsenal	38	15	8	15	55:59	38	0—0	1—1
Bradford C.	38	15	8	15	46:50	38	3—0	0—0
Tottenham	38	14	9	15	53:53	37	2—1	0—4
Manchester U.	38	13	11	14	45:60	37	2—2	1—3
Sheffield U.	38	13	10	15	63:56	36	2—3	0—4
Manchester C.	38	13	9	16	56:58	35	4—1	1—3
Notts. Co.	38	14	7	17	46:63	35	1—2	1—1
Liverpool	38	12	10	16	49:55	34	0—1	0—1
OLDHAM	38	12	10	16	46:54	34	—	—
Preston	38	13	7	18	40:57	33	1—0	1—0
Bury	38	6	9	23	32:59	21	2—0	1—1

APPEARANCES & GOALSCORERS

Broad T. 36	Hodson J. 26	Marrison T. 17
Buxton S. 23	Hunter G.H. 17	Pilkington E. 1
Bradbury W. 7	Jones E. 34	Salley G. 3
Cook W. 17	Matthews W.H. 35	Toward A. 6
Cope W. 10	Moffatt H. 37	Wilson D. 34
Donnachie J. 34	Montgomery W. 25	Walders D. 10
Fay J. 2	McDonald H. 3	Woodger G. 27
Gee A. 1	Miller 2	Wilson C. 9
Hardman J.A. 2		

Scorers:— Jones 17, Montgomery 6, Woodger 5, Marrison 4, Moffatt 3, Bradbury 2, Cook 2, Donnachie 2, Wilson (D) 2, Broad, Hodson and Hunter each 1.
Total: 46.

T. BROAD & D. WALDERS, 1911-12

"THE TEAM FROM A TOWN OF CHIMNEYS"

DIVISION 1 — 1912-13 H A

Sunderland	38	25	4	9	86:43	54	3—0	1—1
Aston Villa	38	19	12	7	86:52	50	2—2	1—7
The Wednesday	38	21	7	10	75:55	49	2—0	0—5
Manchester U.	38	19	8	11	69:43	46	0—0	0—0
Blackburn	38	16	13	9	79:43	45	0—0	1—7
Manchester C.	38	18	8	12	53:37	44	2—1	0—2
Derby	38	17	8	13	69:66	42	2—2	2—1
Bolton	38	16	10	12	62:63	42	2—3	0—3
OLDHAM	38	14	14	10	50:55	42	—	—
West Bromwich	38	13	12	13	57:50	38	0—0	3—2
Everton	38	15	7	16	48:54	37	2—0	3—2
Liverpool	38	16	5	17	61:71	37	3—1	0—2
Bradford C.	38	12	11	15	50:60	35	0—0	0—0
Newcastle	38	13	8	17	47:47	34	1—0	1—4
Sheffield U.	38	14	6	18	56:70	34	2—0	1—1
Middlesbrough	38	11	10	17	55:69	32	1—0	2—2
Tottenham	38	12	6	20	45:72	30	4—1	0—1
Chelsea	38	11	6	21	51:73	28	3—2	1—1
Notts. Co.	38	7	9	22	28:56	23	4—0	1—2
Woolwich Arsenal	38	3	12	23	26:74	18	0—0	0—0

APPEARANCES & GOALSCORERS

Buxton S. 4	Hollis E. 2	Pilkington E. 6
Cook W. 16	Hunter G. 23	Taylor E. 1
Cope W. 17	Joynson G.E. 4	Toward A. 18
Davies D.W. 12	Kemp G. 18	Tummon O. 34
Donnachie J. 32	Lashbroke A.E. 1	Walters J. 29
Franks A. 1	Matthews W.H. 37	Wilson C. 12
Gee A. 15	Miller S. 1	Wilson D. 35
Hodson J. 34	Moffatt H. 34	Woodger G. 32

Scorers:— Walters 12, Woodger 8, Kemp 6, Gee 5, Tummon and Cook each 4, Davies and Toward each 3, Moffatt and Donnachie each 2.
Betts (Derby County) Own Goal.
Total: 50.

200

"THE TEAM FROM A TOWN OF CHIMNEYS"

DIVISION 1 — 1913-14

							H	A
Blackburn	38	20	11	7	78:42	51	1—1	1—2
Aston Villa	38	19	6	13	65:50	44	0—1	0—0
Middlesbrough	38	19	5	14	77:60	43	3—0	0—0
OLDHAM	38	17	9	12	55:45	43	—	—
West Bromwich	38	15	13	10	46:42	43	2—0	2—2
Bolton	38	16	10	12	65:52	42	2—0	2—6
Sunderland	38	17	6	15	63:52	40	2—1	0—2
Chelsea	38	16	7	15	46:55	39	3—2	1—2
Bradford C.	38	12	14	12	40:40	38	3—1	1—0
Sheffield U.	38	16	5	17	63:60	37	1—2	1—2
Newcastle	38	13	11	14	39:48	37	3—0	0—0
Burnley	38	12	12	14	61:53	36	1—1	0—2
Manchester C.	38	14	8	16	51:53	36	1—3	1—2
Manchester U.	38	15	6	17	52:62	36	2—2	1—4
Everton	38	12	11	15	46:55	35	2—0	2—0
Liverpool	38	14	7	17	46:62	35	2—2	3—0
Tottenham	38	12	10	16	50:62	34	3—0	1—3
The Wednesday	38	13	8	17	53:70	34	2—0	2—1
Preston	38	12	6	20	52:69	30	1—0	1—0
Derby	38	8	11	19	55:71	27	0—0	2—1

APPEARANCES & GOALSCORERS

Broad J. 10	Hodson J. 37	Taylor E. 7
Cook W. 26	Joynson G.E. 1	Toward A. 5
Cope W. 5	Kemp G. 9	Tummon O. 38
Dixon A. 20	Lawrence V. 1	Walters J. 28
Donnachie J. 36	Matthews W.H. 31	Wilson D. 38
Douglas J. 3	Moffatt H. 32	Woodger G. 29
Gee A. 24	Roberts C. 38	

Scorers:— Gee and Tummon each 10, Walters 9, Broad, Roberts and Woodger each 4, Cook, Donnachie and Toward each 3, Wilson 2, Douglas, Kemp and Moffatt each 1. Total: 55.

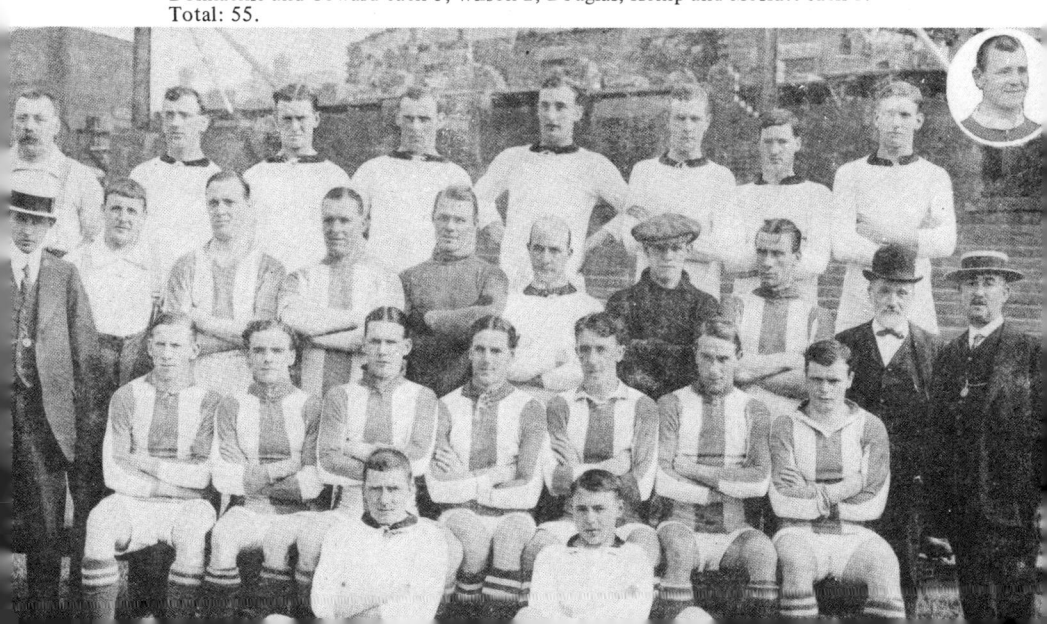

"THE TEAM FROM A TOWN OF CHIMNEYS"

DIVISION 1 — 1914-15

							H	A
Everton	38	19	8	11	76:47	46	1—1	4—3
OLDHAM	38	17	11	10	70:56	45	—	—
Blackburn	38	18	7	13	83:61	43	3—2	1—4
Burnley	38	18	7	13	61:47	43	1—2	3—2
Manchester C.	38	15	13	10	49:39	43	0—0	0—0
Sheffield U.	38	15	13	10	49:41	43	3—0	0—3
The Wednesday	38	15	13	10	61:54	43	5—2	2—2
Sunderland	38	18	5	15	81:72	41	4—5	2—1
Bradford P.A.	38	17	7	14	69:65	41	6—2	1—1
West Bromwich	38	15	10	13	51:43	40	1—1	0—0
Bradford C.	38	13	14	11	55:51	40	1—0	0—1
Middlesbrough	38	13	12	13	62:74	38	5—1	1—4
Liverpool	38	14	9	15	65:75	37	0—2	2—1
Aston Villa	38	13	11	14	62:72	37	3—3	0—0
Newcastle	38	11	10	17	46:48	32	1—0	2—1
Notts Co.	38	9	13	16	41:57	31	2—0	1—2
Bolton	38	11	8	19	68:84	30	5—3	0—2
Manchester U.	38	9	12	17	46:62	30	1—0	3—1
Chelsea	38	8	13	17	51:65	29	0—0	2—2
Tottenham	38	8	12	18	57:90	28	4—1	0—1

Middlesbrough v. Oldham was abandoned after 55 minutes, when an Oldham Full-back refused to leave the field after being ordered off by the referee. The Football League ordered the result to stand.

APPEARANCES & GOALSCORERS

Broad J. 5	Grundy H. 1	Pilkington E. 22
Cashmore A. 16	Hodson J. 37	Roberts C. 34
Cook W. 29	Kemp G. 37	Taylor E. 2
Dixon A. 9	Lester H. 1	Tummon O. 36
Donnachie J. 28	Matthews H. 36	Walters J. 23
Gee A. 23	Moffatt H. 37	Wilson D. 38
Goodwin W. 4		

Scorers:— Kemp 16, Gee 11, Walters 9, Cashmore 8, Tummon 6, Cook 4, Wilson 4, Moffatt 4, Pilkington 4, Donnachie 3, Broad 1.
Total: 70.

"THE TEAM FROM A TOWN OF CHIMNEYS"

DIVISION 1 — 1919-20

							H	A
West Bromwich	42	28	4	10	104:47	60	2—1	1—3
Burnley	42	21	9	12	65:59	51	1—0	1—2
Chelsea	42	22	5	15	56:51	49	1—0	0—1
Liverpool	42	19	10	13	59:44	48	1—1	2—2
Sunderland	42	22	4	16	72:59	48	2—1	0—3
Bolton	42	19	9	14	72:65	47	2—0	0—1
Manchester C.	42	18	9	15	71:62	45	1—3	1—3
Newcastle	42	17	9	16	44:39	43	1—0	1—0
Aston Villa	42	18	6	18	75:73	42	0—3	0—3
The Arsenal	42	15	12	15	56:58	42	3—0	2—3
Bradford P.A.	42	15	12	15	60:63	42	2—2	0—2
Manchester U.	42	13	14	15	54:50	40	0—3	1—1
Middlesbrough	42	15	10	17	61:65	40	1—2	0—1
Sheffield U.	42	16	8	18	59:69	40	4—0	0—1
Bradford C.	42	14	11	17	54:63	39	0—1	1—1
Everton	42	12	14	16	69:68	38	4—1	2—0
OLDHAM	42	15	8	19	49:52	38	—	—
Derby	42	13	12	17	47:57	38	3—0	1—1
Preston	42	14	10	18	57:73	38	4—1	1—2
Blackburn	42	13	11	18	64:77	37	0—0	1—0
Notts Co.	42	12	12	18	56:74	36	0—0	1—2
The Wednesday	42	7	9	26	28:64	23	1—0	0—1

APPEARANCES & GOALSCORERS

Bell P. 2	Goodwin W. 25	Smithhurst E. 2
Bradbury W. 38	Grundy H. 8	Stewart R. 22
Burrow G. 5	Halligan W. 18	Tatton J.H. 17
Carlisle R. 1	Hemsley C.J. 5	Taylor H. 23
Chadderton A. 1	Hooper D. 5	Thompson J. 2
Cook W. 20	Hooper J.W. 5	Wall G. 40
Cunliffe J. 2	Jones T. 9	Walters J. 31
Dolphin A. 16	Matthews W.H. 19	Wilson D. 42
Dougherty J. 15	Pilkington E. 37	Wolstenholme A. 22
Gee A. 30		

Scorers:— Gee 13, Halligan and Walters each 6, Dougherty 5, Wall 4, Bradbury 3, Jones and Wolstenholme each 2, Tatton, Burrows, Pilkington, Hemsley, J.W. Hooper, Broadhurst (P.N.E.) Gough (Sheffield United) Scott (Sunderland) each 1.

"THE TEAM FROM A TOWN OF CHIMNEYS"

DIVISION 1 — 1920-21   H   A

Burnley	42	23	13	6	79:36	59	2—2	1—7
Manchester C.	42	24	6	12	70:50	54	2—0	1—3
Bolton	42	19	14	9	77:53	52	0—0	1—1
Liverpool	42	18	15	9	63:35	51	0—0	2—5
Newcastle	42	20	10	12	66:45	50	0—0	2—1
Tottenham	42	19	9	14	70:48	47	2—5	1—5
Everton	42	17	13	12	66:55	47	0—1	2—5
Middlesbrough	42	17	12	13	53:53	46	3—3	2—1
The Arsenal	42	15	14	13	59:63	44	1—1	2—2
Aston Villa	42	18	7	17	63:70	43	1—1	0—3
Blackburn	42	13	15	14	57:59	41	1—0	1—5
Sunderland	42	14	13	15	57:60	41	2—1	1—1
Manchester U.	42	15	10	17	64:68	40	2—2	1—4
West Bromwich	42	13	14	15	54:58	40	0—3	0—0
Bradford C.	42	12	15	15	61:63	39	2—0	3—1
Preston	42	15	9	18	61:65	39	0—2	0—4
Huddersfield	42	15	9	18	42:49	39	1—2	1—3
Chelsea	42	13	13	16	48:58	39	1—2	1—1
OLDHAM	42	9	15	18	49:86	33	—	—
Sheffield U.	42	6	18	18	42:68	30	0—0	0—3
Derby	42	5	16	21	32:58	26	2—1	3—3
Bradford P.A.	42	8	8	26	43:76	24	1—0	1—2

APPEARANCES & GOALSCORERS

Bassindale I.B. 2	Edge 3	Marshall A.W. 7
Bell P. 1	Foweather V. 5	Nord J.G. 1
Bradbury W. 28	Freeman R.V. 20	Paterson A.A. 1
Braidwood E. 9	Gee A. 19	Pilkington E. 34
Broadbent W.H. 1	Goodwin W. 11	Stewart R. 12
Burrows G. 2	Grundy H. 17	Tatton J.H. 37
Butler R. 33	Halligan W. 10	Taylor E. 16
Byrom T. 5	Hemsley C.J. 2	Taylor W. 15
Charlton S. 6	Jones R. 16	Wall G. 34
Campbell A.F. 25	Matthews W.H. 25	Wilson D. 29
Carlisle R. 4	Marshall J.H. 32	

Scorers:— Butler 16, Wall 7, Campbell, J.H. Marshall each 6, Gee, and Halligan each 3, Pilkington and Wilson each 2, Braidwood, Foweather, Tatton, E. Scott (Liverpool) (own goal) each 1.
Total: 49.

"THE TEAM FROM A TOWN OF CHIMNEYS"

DIVISION 1 — 1921-22

							H	A
Liverpool	42	22	13	7	63:36	57	4—0	0—2
Tottenham	42	21	9	12	65:39	51	1—0	1—3
Burnley	42	22	5	15	72:54	49	0—1	1—0
Cardiff	42	19	10	13	61:53	48	2—1	1—0
Aston Villa	42	22	3	17	74:55	47	3—1	0—2
Bolton	42	20	7	15	68:59	47	0—0	1—5
Newcastle	42	18	10	14	59:45	46	0—0	1—1
Middlesbrough	42	16	14	12	79:69	46	0—1	1—1
Chelsea	42	17	12	13	40:43	46	0—3	0—1
Manchester C.	42	18	9	15	65:70	45	0—1	1—2
Sheffield U.	42	15	10	17	59:54	40	0—2	0—1
Sunderland	42	16	8	18	60:62	40	3—0	1—5
West Bromwich	42	15	10	17	51:63	40	1—0	1—0
Huddersfield	42	15	9	18	53:54	39	1—1	0—1
Blackburn	42	13	12	17	54:57	38	1—1	2—3
Preston	42	13	12	17	42:65	38	2—0	0—0
The Arsenal	42	15	7	20	47:56	37	2—1	1—0
Birmingham	42	15	7	20	48:60	37	0—1	0—3
OLDHAM	42	13	11	18	38:50	37	—	—
Everton	42	12	12	18	57:55	36	0—0	2—2
Bradford C.	42	11	10	21	48:72	32	0—0	0—3
Manchester U.	42	8	12	22	41:73	28	1—1	3—0

—— APPEARANCES & GOALSCORERS ——

Bassindale I.B. 3	Grundy H. 37	Tatton J.H. 13
Bell P. 15	Jones R. 9	Taylor E. 37
Broadbent F. 10	Marshall A. 37	Taylor W. 36
Broadbent W.H. 5	Marshall J.H. 29	Toms W. 20
Braidwood E. 1	Matthews W.H. 6	Wallace C.W. 34
Butler R. 29	Nord J.G. 2	Watson R.H. 24
Campbell A.F. 12	Parkinson H. 2	Wood W. 11
Carrick J. 5	Pilkington E. 38	Wynne S. 5
Freeman R.V. 42		

Scorers:— Butler 13, J.H. Marshall 6, Toms 5, F. Broadbent 4, Watson 3, Bell and Pilkington each 2, W. Broadbent, Wallace, Wood each 1.
Total: 38.

"THE TEAM FROM A TOWN OF CHIMNEYS"

DIVISION 1 — 1922—23

							H	A
Liverpool	42	26	8	8	70:31	60	0—2	1—2
Sunderland	42	22	10	10	72:54	54	0—0	0—2
Huddersfield	42	21	11	10	60:32	53	0—3	0—3
Newcastle	42	18	12	12	45:37	48	0—0	0—1
Everton	42	20	7	15	63:59	47	1—0	0—0
Aston Villa	42	18	10	14	64:51	46	0—2	0—3
West Bromwich	42	17	11	14	58:49	45	0—0	0—1
Manchester C.	42	17	11	14	50:49	45	0—3	2—3
Cardiff	42	18	7	17	73:59	43	3—1	0—2
Sheffield U.	42	16	10	16	68:64	42	0—2	2—2
The Arsenal	42	16	10	16	61:62	42	0—0	0—2
Tottenham	42	17	7	18	50:50	41	0—3	0—3
Bolton	42	14	12	16	50:58	40	3—1	1—3
Blackburn	42	14	12	16	47:62	40	1—0	0—1
Burnley	42	16	6	20	58:59	38	1—1	1—1
Preston	42	13	11	18	60:64	37	2—1	1—5
Birmingham	42	13	11	18	41:57	37	2—0	3—2
Middlesbrough	42	13	10	19	57:63	36	0—0	1—2
Chelsea	42	9	18	15	45:53	36	2—0	0—4
Nottingham F.	42	13	8	21	41:70	34	2—0	0—1
Stoke	42	10	10	22	47:67	30	4—1	2—2
OLDHAM	42	10	10	22	35:65	30	—	—

APPEARANCES & GOALSCORERS

Adlam L.W. 3	Freeman R.V. 40	Pilkington E. 41
Bassindale I.B. 13	Grundy H. 35	Spence D. 4
Blair F.E. 4	Hibbert W. 17	Staniforth O. 19
Broadbent W.H. 3	Horrocks H. 15	Taylor W. 34
Broadbent F. 3	Jones C. 9	Waddell G. 1
Butler R. 15	King 4	Wallace C.W. 13
Carrick J. 1	Marshall A. 22	Watson R.H. 26
Cooper A. 9	Marshall J.H. 20	Wood W. 18
Douglas G.H. 30	Matthews H. 33	Wynne S. 8
Fergusson W. 4	Naylor J. 19	Yarwood J. 4

Scorers:— J.H. Marshall 6, Hibbert 4, Butler, A. Marshall, Staniforth and Watson each 3, Horrocks, Naylor, Wallace and Wood each 2, Blair, Douglas, Fergusson, King and Taylor each 1.
Total: 35.

"THE TEAM FROM A TOWN OF CHIMNEYS"

DIVISION 2 — 1923-24

					H	A
Leeds	42	21	12	9	61:35	54	2—2	0—5
Bury	42	21	9	12	63:35	51	0—0	2—2
Derby	42	21	9	12	75:42	51	2—0	1—2
Blackpool	42	18	13	11	72:47	49	1—1	2—2
Southampton	42	17	14	11	52:31	48	1—3	1—3
Stoke	42	14	18	10	44:42	46	0—0	1—1
OLDHAM	42	14	17	11	45:52	45	—	—
The Wednesday	42	16	12	14	54:51	44	2—0	2—1
South Shields	42	17	10	15	49:50	44	1—0	0—2
Clapton Orient	42	14	15	13	40:36	43	1—0	2—1
Barnsley	42	16	11	15	57:61	43	1—1	1—4
Leicester	42	17	8	17	64:54	42	0—0	1—1
Stockport	42	13	16	13	44:52	42	3—1	1—0
Manchester U.	42	13	14	15	52:44	40	3—2	0—2
Crystal Palace	42	13	13	16	53:65	39	1—0	3—2
Port Vale	42	13	12	17	50:66	38	2—0	0—3
Hull	42	10	17	15	46:51	37	0—0	0—0
Bradford C.	42	11	15	16	35:48	37	0—0	1—2
Coventry	42	11	13	18	52:68	35	1—1	2—5
Fulham	42	10	14	13	45:56	34	2—1	0—0
Nelson	42	10	13	19	40:74	33	1—0	1—2
Bristol C.	42	7	15	20	32:65	29	0—0	0—0

APPEARANCES & GOALSCORERS

Adlam L.W. 4
Bassindale I.B. 26
Blair J.E. 17
Campbell A.F. 4
Douglas G.H. 32
Fergusson W. 1
Fleetwood T. 5
Gray A. 2
Grundy H. 41

Hargreaves F. 33
Heaton T. 6
Horrocks H. 8
Howson W. 21
Jones C. 13
Longmuir A. 22
Matthews W.H. 40
Middleton H. 7

Naylor J. 41
Pilkington E. 37
Staniforth C. 17
Taylor W. 18
Watson R.H. 25
Wilkinson H. 1
Wynne S. 35
Yarwood J. 6

Scorers:— Blair 14, Watson 8, Howson 5, Longmuir and Staniforth each 4, Hargreaves and Wynne each 3, Campbell 2, Heaton and Naylor each 1.
Total: 45.

Fulham v Athletic at Craven Cottage, a 0-0 draw.

"THE TEAM FROM A TOWN OF CHIMNEYS"

DIVISION 2 — 1924-25

						H	A
Leicester	42	24	11	7	90:32	59	0—1	0—3
Manchester U.	42	23	11	8	57:23	57	0—3	1—0
Derby	42	22	11	9	71:36	55	0—1	0—1
Portsmouth	42	15	18	9	58:50	48	0—2	2—2
Chelsea	42	16	15	11	51:37	47	0—5	1—4
Wolverhampton	42	20	6	16	55:51	46	2—0	0—2
Southampton	42	13	18	11	40:36	44	1—1	0—0
Port Vale	42	17	8	17	48:56	42	2—0	0—1
South Shields	42	12	17	13	42:38	41	1—0	0—0
Hull	42	15	11	16	50:49	41	1—0	0—1
Clapton Orient	42	14	12	16	42:42	40	2—1	1—5
Fulham	42	15	10	17	41:56	40	0—0	0—1
Middlesbrough	42	10	19	13	36:44	39	0—0	0—0
The Wednesday	42	15	8	19	50:56	38	1—1	0—1
Barnsley	42	13	12	17	46:59	38	2—0	0—0
Bradford C.	42	13	12	17	37:50	38	1—3	1—1
Blackpool	42	14	9	19	65:61	37	4—1	2—1
OLDHAM	42	13	11	18	35:51	37	—	—
Stockport	42	13	11	18	37:57	37	0—0	0—2
Stoke	42	12	11	19	34:46	35	2—0	1—0
Crystal Palace	42	12	10	20	38:54	34	0—2	1—0
Coventry	42	11	9	22	45:84	31	5—0	1—5

SCORERS:—Jones 6, Gillespie and Pilkington each 5, Keedwell 4, Watson and Wynne each 3, Carroll, Heaton and G. Taylor each 2, Blair, Douglas and Ivill each 1. Total: 35.

APPEARANCES

Adlam L.W.	3
Bassindale I.B.	
Blair J.E.	4
Broome A.H.	
Carroll J.E.	
Douglas G.H.	3
Gillespie R.	2
Glennie J.	
Gray A.	3
Grundy H.	4
Heaton T.	2
Ivill F.	1
Jones C.	3
Keedwell J.H.	1
Matthews W.H.	
Middleton H.	
Naylor J.	3
Pilkington E.	4
Scholes R.	
Taylor G.	
Taylor W.	
Watson R.H.	2
White C.	
Wilkinson H.	
Wynne S.	4

DIVISION 2 — 1925-26

							H	A
The Wednesday	42	27	6	9	88:48	60	1—1	1—5
Derby	42	25	7	10	77:42	57	2—0	0—1
Chelsea	42	19	14	9	76:49	52	1—1	0—3
Wolverhampton	42	21	7	14	84:60	49	1—2	1—2
Swansea	42	19	11	12	77:57	49	0—0	3—3
Blackpool	42	17	11	14	76:69	45	3—2	1—2
OLDHAM	42	18	8	16	74:62	44	—	—
Port Vale	42	19	6	17	79:69	44	3—2	0—3
Middlesbrough	42	21	2	19	77:68	44	4—1	1—2
South Shields	42	18	8	16	74:65	44	2—1	0—0
Portsmouth	42	17	10	15	79:74	44	1—3	2—0
Preston	42	18	7	17	71:84	43	3—2	1—2
Hull	42	16	9	17	63:61	41	2—1	2—1
Southampton	42	15	8	19	63:63	38	1—0	1—3
Darlington	42	14	10	18	72:77	38	0—1	0—1
Bradford C.	42	13	10	19	47:66	36	3—0	1—1
Nottingham F.	42	14	8	20	51:73	36	8—3	1—1
Barnsley	42	12	12	18	58:84	36	2—1	4—3
Fulham	42	11	12	19	46:77	34	4—0	1—2
Clapton Orient	42	12	9	21	50:65	33	1—1	2—1
Stoke	42	12	8	22	54:77	32	7—2	0—1
Stockport	42	8	9	25	51:97	25	3—0	0—1

SCORERS:—Ormston 21, Watson and Pynegar each 13, Barnes 10, Douglas 6, Hargreaves 5, Wynne and Kirkpatrick each 3.
Total: 74.

APPEARANCES
Adlam L.W. . . . 41
Barnes H. 21
Bassindale I.B. . 2
Colman E. 2
Douglas G.H. . . 33
Goodier E. . . . 1
Goodwin W. . . . 2
Gray A. 38
Grundy H. 36
Hargreaves F. . . 10
Heaton T. 21
Ivill E. 7
Kirkpatrick E. . 13
Matthews W.H. . 2
Middleton H. . . 9
M'Cue J.W. . . . 1
Naylor J. 42
Ormston A. . . . 33
Pilkington E. . . 14
Pynegar A. . . . 40
Schofield J. . . . 1
Seddon R. 1
Walker G. 2
Watson R.H. . 41
White C. 2
Wilkinson H. . . 8
Wynne S. . . . 39

"THE TEAM FROM A TOWN OF CHIMNEYS"

DIVISION 2 — 1926-27

							H	A
Middlesbrough	42	27	8	7	122:60	62	2—1	1—3
Portsmouth	42	23	8	11	87:49	54	1—0	2—7
Manchester C.	42	22	10	10	108:61	54	1—2	0—3
Chelsea	42	20	12	10	62:52	52	1—2	0—1
Nottingham F.	42	18	14	10	80:55	50	3—3	1—1
Preston	42	20	9	13	74:72	49	5—1	2—5
Hull	42	20	7	15	63:52	47	1—1	2—1
Port Vale	42	16	13	13	88:78	45	1—3	0—3
Blackpool	42	18	8	16	95:80	44	1—3	0—2
OLDHAM	42	19	6	17	74:84	44	—	—
Barnsley	42	17	9	16	88:87	43	0—4	1—0
Swansea	42	16	11	15	68:72	43	5—2	0—3
Southampton	42	15	12	15	60:62	42	1—1	1—0
Reading	42	16	8	18	64:72	40	3—1	1—6
Wolverhampton	42	14	7	21	73:75	35	2—0	1—1
Notts Co.	42	15	5	22	70:96	35	5—2	2—1
Grimsby	42	11	12	19	74:91	34	3—1	5—2
Fulham	42	13	8	21	58:92	34	2—3	1—1
South Shields	42	11	11	20	71:96	33	3—2	1—4
Clapton Orient	42	12	7	23	60:96	31	5—2	1—3
Darlington	42	12	6	24	79:98	30	3—2	1—0
Bradford C.	42	7	9	26	50:88	23	2—1	1—0

APPEARANCES

Adlam L.W. 35
Armitage J.H. . . . 37
Barnes H. 20
Brelsford B. 8
Crompton N. . . . 1
Goodier E. 9
Gough H. 4
Gray A. 22
Grundy H. 19
Hacking J. 16
Hardy J.J. 2
Hargreaves F. . . 39
Heaton T. 3
Hey C. 11
Ivill E. 35
Jennings A.W. . . 2
King J. 27
Kirkpatrick E. . . 2
Naylor J. 39
Ormston A. 7
Pynegar A. . . . 39
Schofield J. 3
Taylor G. 11
Trotter W. 11
Watson R.H. . . . 37
Wellock M. 5
Wynne S. 19

SCORERS:—Pynegar 18, Watson 15, Hargreaves 9, Taylor 7, Barnes and Wellock each 6, King 4, Armitage 2, Ormston, Kirkpatrick, Schofield, Naylor, Hey, Hamilton (Preston North End) and Rosier (Clapton Orient) each 1.
Total: 74.

"THE TEAM FROM A TOWN OF CHIMNEYS"

DIVISION 2 — 1927-28

							H	A
Manchester C.	42	25	9	8	100:59	59	3—2	1—3
Leeds	42	25	7	10	98:49	57	0—1	0—1
Chelsea	42	23	8	11	75:45	54	2—1	1—2
Preston	42	22	9	11	100:66	53	0—0	1—1
Stoke	42	22	8	12	78:59	52	3—1	0—3
Swansea	42	18	12	12	75:63	48	0—1	0—0
OLDHAM	42	19	8	15	75:51	46	—	—
West Bromwich	42	17	12	13	90:70	46	3—1	0—0
Port Vale	42	18	8	16	68:57	44	4—1	0—1
Nottingham F.	42	15	10	17	83:84	40	4—1	1—2
Grimsby	42	14	12	16	69:83	40	1—0	2—1
Bristol C.	42	15	9	18	76:79	39	4—1	1—2
Barnsley	42	14	11	17	65:85	39	0—1	1—0
Hull	42	12	15	15	41:54	39	5—0	2—2
Notts Co.	42	13	12	17	68:74	38	0—0	1—2
Wolverhampton	42	13	10	19	63:91	36	3—0	1—3
Southampton	42	14	7	21	68:77	35	3—1	2—5
Reading	42	11	13	18	53:75	35	3—2	0—1
Blackpool	42	13	8	21	83:101	34	6—0	2—1
Clapton Orient	42	11	12	19	55:85	34	5—0	0—2
Fulham	42	13	7	22	68:89	33	4—2	1—1
South Shields	42	7	9	26	56:111	23	2—2	3—0

SCORERS:—Pynegar 18, Harris 16, Watson 14, Taylor 11, King 7, Stanton 3, Adlam, Armitage, Jones, Naylor, Trotter and A. Watson (Blackpool) each 1. Total: 75.

APPEARANCES
Adlam L.W. . . . 39
Armitage J.H. . . . 24
Brelsford B. . . . 1
Crompton N. . . . 7
Dyson J. 6
Goodier E. . . . 1
Grundy H. 39
Hacking J. 41
Hargreaves F. . . . 8
Harris N. 31
Ivill E. 42
Jones E. 2
Kellard T. 2
King J. 40
Maddison J.A.B. . 4
Malpas E. 4
Naylor J. 42
Porter W. 9
Prince J. 1
Pynegar A. . . . 40
Stanton C. 7
Taylor G. 31
Trotter W. 3
Watson R.H. . . 38

211

"THE TEAM FROM A TOWN OF CHIMNEYS"

DIVISION 2 — 1928-29

							H	A
Middlesbrough	42	22	11	9	92:57	55	1—3	0—1
Grimsby	42	24	5	13	82:61	53	0—3	0—1
Bradford P.A.	42	22	4	16	88:70	48	2—1	0—2
Southampton	42	17	14	11	74:60	48	3—1	1—2
Notts Co.	42	19	9	14	78:65	47	3—2	0—2
Stoke	42	17	12	13	74:51	46	1—0	1—1
West Bromwich	42	19	8	15	80:79	46	3—0	0—1
Blackpool	42	19	7	16	92:76	45	4—2	0—4
Chelsea	42	17	10	15	64:65	44	1—0	3—2
Tottenham	42	17	9	16	75:81	43	3—1	1—4
Nottingham F.	42	15	12	15	71:70	42	2—0	1—3
Hull	42	13	14	15	58:63	40	0—1	0—1
Preston	42	15	9	18	78:79	39	2—1	2—3
Millwall	42	16	7	19	71:86	39	4—1	3—3
Reading	42	15	9	18	63:86	39	2—1	1—6
Barnsley	42	16	6	20	69:66	38	1—0	1—2
Wolverhampton	42	15	7	20	77:81	37	0—4	0—0
OLDHAM	42	16	5	21	54:75	37	—	—
Swansea	42	13	10	19	62:75	36	2—1	2—3
Bristol C.	42	13	10	19	58:72	36	1—0	0—6
Port Vale	42	15	4	23	71:86	34	1—1	1—2
Clapton Orient	42	12	8	22	45:72	32	1—1	0—2

APPEARANCES

Adlam L. 32
Armitage J.H. . 29
Baker B.H. . . . 1
Brown A. 14
Dyson J. 31
Floyd P. 3
Foster C.L. . . 1
Goodier E. . . 27
Gray M. 24
Green H. 1
Grundy H. . . . 9
Hacking J. . . . 38
Hargreaves F. . 11
Harris N. 8
Hasson W. . . . 16
Ivill E. 42
Jones E. 5
King J. 10
Littlewood S.C. 18
Lowe J. 7
Maddison J.A.B. 2
Naylor J. . . . 15
Ormston A. . . 3
Porter W. . . . 36
Pynegar A. . . 12
Stafford H.E. . 1
Stanton C. . . . 6
Taylor G. . . . 17
Thomas W.E. . 1
Watson R.H. . 21
Worrall F. . . . 20

SCORERS:—Littlewood 12, Dyson 11, Gray 7, Worrall 5, Taylor and Watson each 3, Harris, Jones and Lowe each 2, Goodier, Ivill, King, Porter, Pynegar, Stanton and Matthews (Bradford City) each 1.
Total: 54

"THE TEAM FROM A TOWN OF CHIMNEYS"

DIVISION 2 — 1929-30

							H	A
Blackpool	42	27	4	11	98:67	58	1—2	0—3
Chelsea	42	22	11	9	74:46	55	4—2	1—1
OLDHAM	42	21	11	10	90:51	53	—	—
Bradford P.A.	42	19	12	11	91:70	50	5—1	2—2
Bury	42	22	5	15	78:67	49	2—0	2—0
West Bromwich	42	21	5	16	105:73	47	5—0	3—0
Southampton	42	17	11	14	77:76	45	3—2	0—2
Cardiff	42	18	8	16	61:59	44	4—1	0—5
Wolverhampton	42	16	9	17	77:79	41	6—0	1—1
Nottingham F.	42	13	15	14	55:69	41	0—0	2—1
Stoke	42	16	8	18	74:72	40	5—0	2—0
Tottenham	42	15	9	18	59:61	39	2—0	1—2
Charlton	42	14	11	17	59:63	39	1—0	1—1
Millwall	42	12	15	15	57:73	39	2—2	1—2
Swansea	42	14	9	19	57:61	37	4—1	0—3
Preston	42	13	11	18	65:80	37	0—2	3—0
Barnsley	42	14	8	20	56:71	36	3—2	1—2
Bradford C.	42	12	12	18	60:77	36	6—1	4—2
Reading	42	12	11	19	54:67	35	0—0	1—1
Bristol C.	42	13	9	20	61:83	35	2—2	4—0
Hull	42	14	7	21	51:78	35	3—1	0—1
Notts Co.	42	9	15	18	54:70	33	2—2	1—1

STEWART LITTLEWOOD

APPEARANCES

Adlam L. 42
Cumming L. . . . 25
Dyson J. 19
Goodier E. 38
Gray M. 38
Hacking J. 38
Hargreaves F. . . 2
Hasson W. 40
Hey C. 1
Ivill E. 42
King S. 42
Littlewood S. . . 38
Moss F. 4
Murphy W. . . . 2
Porter W. 41
Seymour T.G. . . 2
Smelt T. 2
Taylor J. 10
Worrall F. 36

SCORERS:—Littlewood 28, Gray 19, Cumming 11, Hasson 9, Worrall 7, Taylor 6, Dyson 4, Adlam 3, Goodier, Murphy and Shaw (Wolverhampton Wanderers) each 1. Total: 90.

"THE TEAM FROM A TOWN OF CHIMNEYS"

DIVISION 2 — 1930-31

						H	A
Everton	42	28	5	9	121:66	61	3–3	4–6
West Bromwich	42	22	10	10	83:49	54	2–2	0–2
Tottenham	42	22	7	13	88:55	51	1–2	0–4
Wolverhampton	42	21	5	16	84:67	47	2–0	0–3
Port Vale	42	21	5	16	67:61	47	3–3	0–2
Bradford P.A.	42	18	10	14	97:66	46	2–0	0–4
Preston	42	17	11	14	83:64	45	2–0	0–1
Burnley	42	17	11	14	81:77	45	3–1	1–6
Southampton	42	19	6	17	74:62	44	2–1	0–1
Bradford C.	42	17	10	15	61:63	44	3–0	0–0
Stoke	42	17	10	15	64:71	44	3–1	0–4
OLDHAM	42	16	10	16	61:72	42	—	—
Bury	42	19	3	20	75:82	41	3–2	3–1
Millwall	42	16	7	19	71:80	39	3–1	0–1
Charlton	42	15	9	18	59:86	39	0–3	1–1
Bristol C.	42	15	8	19	54:82	38	1–3	0–1
Nottingham F.	42	14	9	19	80:85	37	3–1	1–4
Plymouth	42	14	8	20	76:84	36	2–1	1–1
Barnsley	42	13	9	20	59:79	35	0–0	2–1
Swansea	42	12	10	20	51:74	34	2–1	0–0
Reading	42	12	6	24	72:96	30	1–1	3–1
Cardiff	42	8	9	25	47:87	25	4–2	0–0

SCORERS:– Dyson 15, Johnstone 13, Littlewood 8, Gray and Worrall each 6, Adlam and Hasson each 4, Fitton 3, Stanton and Taylor each 1. Total: 61.

Waiting for the ball—soon to go up.

APPEARANCES

Adlam L.	41
Brown A.	4
Burridge B.J.H.	6
Dyson J.	36
Finney W.A.	1
Fitton F.	7
Flavell F.	4
Goodier F.	25
Gray M.	40
Hacking J.	19
Hasson W.	39
Ivill E.	42
Johnstone W.	17
Kennedy F.	4
King J.	3
King S.	42
Littlewood S.C.	21
Moss F.	23
Pears J.	3
Porter W.	38
Stanton C.	5
Taylor J.	2
Thomas E.	1
Worrall F.	39

"THE TEAM FROM A TOWN OF CHIMNEYS"

DIVISION 2 — 1931-32

							H	A
Wolverhampton	42	24	8	10	115:49	56	0—2	1—7
Leeds	42	22	10	10	78:54	54	2—1	0—5
Stoke	42	19*	14	9	69:48	52	1—3	1—1
Plymouth	42	20	9	13	100:66	49	1—3	0—5
Bury	42	21	7	14	70:58	49	1—2	1—2
Bradford P.A.	42	21	7	14	72:63	49	2—1	0—5
Bradford C.	42	16	13	13	80:61	45	1—1	0—2
Tottenham	42	16	11	15	87:78	43	1—2	2—3
Millwall	42	17	9	16	61:61	43	1—1	0—0
Charlton	42	17	9	16	61:66	43	1—0	2—2
Nottingham F.	42	16	10	16	77:72	42	2—4	0—2
Manchester U.	42	17	8	17	71:72	42	1—5	1—5
Preston	42	16	10	16	75:77	42	2—2	3—2
Southampton	42	17	7	18	66:77	41	2—0	1—1
Swansea	42	16	7	19	73:75	39	2—0	0—1
Notts Co.	42	13	12	17	75:75	38	5—2	0—1
Chesterfield	42	13	11	18	64:86	37	6—1	2—0
OLDHAM	42	13	10	19	62:84	36	—	—
Burnley	42	13	9	20	59:87	35	3—1	4—1
Port Vale	42	13	7	22	58:89	33	3—0	1—1
Barnsley	42	12	9	21	55:91	33	2—2	1—3
Bristol C.	42	6	11	25	39:78	23	2—1	1—1

APPEARANCES
Adlam L. 9
Boswell W. 2
Brown A. 15
Dyson J. 30
Finney W.A. . . .28
Fitton F. 2
Goodier F. 14
Gray M. 36
Hacking J. 25
Hallam J. 1
Hasson E. 20
Hope J.R. 4
Ivill E. 42
Johnson H. 10
Johnstone W. . . .35
Jones G.B. 2
King S. 7
Martin J.C. 11
Millward A.C. . . 1
Moss F. 2
Pears J. 24
Pearson H. 14
Pickersgill T. . .17
Porter W. 42
Purcell L. 1
Roscoe J. 19
Seymour T.G. . . 5
Smalley L.W. . .14
Thomas E. 14
Trippier A.W. . . 6
Worrall F. 10

SCORERS:—Johnstone 12, Pears 11, Dyson 9, Roscoe 8, Gray and Hasson each 4, Johnson and Smalley each 3, Worrall 2, Adlam, Boswell, Brown, Fitton, Martin and Trippier each 1.
Total: 62.

DIVISION 2 — 1932-33

							H	A
Stoke	42	25	6	11	78:39	56	0—4	0—4
Tottenham	42	20	15	7	96:51	55	1—5	1—1
Fulham	42	20	10	12	78:65	50	1—3	0—1
Bury	42	20	9	13	84:59	49	2—1	3—3
Nottingham F.	42	17	15	10	67:59	49	1—2	3—2
Manchester U.	42	15	13	14	71:68	43	1—1	0—2
Millwall	42	16	11	15	59:57	43	1—0	1—6
Bradford P.A.	42	17	8	17	77:71	42	1—3	3—1
Preston	42	16	10	16	74:70	42	0—2	2—2
Swansea	42	19	4	19	50:54	42	0—0	0—2
Bradford C.	42	14	13	15	65:61	41	6—1	0—3
Southampton	42	18	5	19	66:66	41	2—0	2—0
Grimsby	42	14	13	15	79:84	41	0—1	1—5
Plymouth	42	16	9	17	63:67	41	3—1	1—2
Notts Co.	42	15	10	17	67:78	40	5—0	1—2
OLDHAM	42	15	8	19	67:80	38	—	—
Port Vale	42	14	10	18	66:79	38	2—1	4—2
Lincoln	42	12	13	17	72:87	37	5—2	3—1
Burnley	42	11	14	17	67:79	36	2—2	1—1
West Ham	42	13	9	20	75:93	35	3—2	2—5
Chesterfield	42	12	10	20	61:84	34	2—0	1—3
Charlton	42	12	7	23	60:91	31	0—0	0—1

APPEARANCES
Agar A. 32
Baldwin W. 1
Brown A. 12
Brunskill N. . . .24
Dickinson J. . . . 4
Gray M. 42
Grice R. 12
Hacking J. 18
Hargreaves F. . . 5
Hasson W. 10
Ivill E. 12
Johnson H. 26
Johnston W.G. . .32
Johnstone W. . . .17
Naylor J. 8
Pears J. 32
Pearson H. 24
Pickersgill T. . .22
Porter W. 40
Reid T. 13
Ridings F. 2
Rowley H. 14
Seymour T.G. . .19
Smalley L.W. . . 6
Stafford H.E. . .15
Steele E. 14
Thomas W.E. . . 6

SCORERS:—Pears 12, Agar and Reid each 10, Johnson 9, Gray and Johnstone each 6, Johnston 4, Hasson and Rowley each 3, Smalley and Steele each 2.
Total: 67.

"THE TEAM FROM A TOWN OF CHIMNEYS"

DIVISION 2 — 1933-34

							H	A
Grimsby	42	27	5	10	103:59	59	1—5	1—2
Preston	42	23	6	13	71:52	52	3—1	0—1
Bolton	42	21	9	12	79:55	51	1—3	0—1
Brentford	42	22	7	13	85:60	51	1—4	1—2
Bradford P.A.	42	23	3	16	86:67	49	1—3	2—4
Bradford C.	42	20	6	16	73:67	46	4—3	2—5
West Ham	42	17	11	14	78:70	45	4—1	4—1
Port Vale	42	19	7	16	60:55	45	5—1	0—2
OLDHAM	42	17	10	15	72:60	44	—	—
Plymouth	42	15	13	14	69:70	43	1—1	0—1
Blackpool	42	15	13	14	62:64	43	2—0	0—0
Bury	42	17	9	16	70:73	43	2—2	1—1
Burnley	42	18	6	18	60:72	42	1—0	1—0
Southampton	42	15	8	19	54:58	38	1—1	0—1
Hull	42	13	12	17	52:68	38	7—0	0—2
Fulham	42	15	7	20	48:67	37	2—2	2—1
Nottingham F.	42	13	9	20	73:74	35	4—1	3—1
Notts Co.	42	12	11	19	53:62	35	2—0	1—1
Swansea	42	10	15	17	51:60	35	0—0	2—2
Manchester U.	42	14	6	22	59:85	34	2—0	3—2
Millwall	42	11	11	20	39:68	33	1—0	0—1
Lincoln	42	9	8	25	44:75	26	3—0	1—1

SCORERS:— Reid 17, Pears 10, Agar and Bailey each 8, Rowley 7, Chadwick and Walsh each 5, Johnston and Pateman each 3, Burke 2, Gray, Hasson, Jeavons and Smith (Nottingham Forest) each 1.
Total: 72.

APPEARANCES

Agar A. 20
Bailey A. 27
Brunskill N. . . 35
Burke P. 37
Chadwick C. . 18
Dickinson J. . . 2
Gray M. 18
Grice R. 5
Hacking J. . . . 28
Hasson W. . . . 10
Jeavons W.H. . 3
Johnson H. . . . 3
Johnston W. . . 26
Pateman G.E. . . 7
Pears J. 32
Porter W. . . . 42
Reid T. 31
Rowley H. . . . 39
Schofield . . . 17
Seymour T.G. . 40
Spink H. 1
Stafford H.E. . . 1
Swift F. 14
Walsh W. 6

DIVISION 2 — 1934-35

							H	A
Brentford	42	26	9	7	93:48	61	1—3	1—2
Bolton	42	26	4	12	96:48	56	1—4	0—2
West Ham	42	26	4	12	80:63	56	1—2	0—2
Blackpool	42	21	11	10	79:57	53	2—3	0—4
Manchester U.	42	23	4	15	76:55	50	3—1	0—4
Newcastle	42	22	4	16	89:68	48	3—2	2—4
Fulham	42	17	12	13	76:56	46	2—1	1—3
Plymouth	42	19	8	15	75:64	46	1—1	0—2
Nottingham F.	42	17	8	17	76:70	42	0—5	0—4
Bury	42	19	4	19	62:73	42	7—2	0—2
Sheffield U.	42	16	9	17	79:70	41	3—2	1—2
Burnley	42	16	9	17	63:73	41	1—2	2—4
Hull	42	16	8	18	63:74	40	5—0	1—1
Norwich	42	14	11	17	71:61	39	4—2	0—0
Bradford P.A.	42	11	16	15	55:63	38	1—1	0—2
Barnsley	42	13	12	17	60:83	38	1—4	0—4
Swansea	42	14	8	20	56:67	36	2—2	1—5
Port Vale	42	11	12	19	55:74	34	2—0	0—2
Southampton	42	11	12	19	46:75	34	0—2	2—2
Bradford C.	42	12	8	22	50:68	32	3—1	0—2
OLDHAM	42	10	6	26	56:95	26	—	—
Notts Co.	42	9	7	26	46:97	25	1—0	1—2

SCORERS:— Walsh 11, Reid 10, Robson 8, Agar 6, Gray 5, Rowley 4, Burke and Murphy each 3, Bailey and Brunskill each 2, Leedham and Spink each 1.
Total: 56.

APPEARANCES

Agar A. 20
Bailey A. 24
Britton F. 1
Brunskill N. . . 36
Buckley A. . . . 6
Burke P. 39
Devlin T. 2
Gray M. 19
Grice R. 9
Hilton W.A. . . 9
Johnston W. . . 6
Leedham F.A. . 11
Murphy J. . . . 7
Porter W. . . . 24
Reid T. 24
Robson J.C. . . 37
Rowley H. . . . 17
Schofield F. . . 24
Seymour T.G. . 42
Sharp A. 1
Shaw J. 1
Spink H. 19
Swift F. 40
Talbot G. 2
Walsh W. 30
White J. 2

"THE TEAM FROM A TOWN OF CHIMNEYS"

DIVISION 3N — 1935-36

							H	A
Chesterfield	42	24	12	6	92:39	60	0—0	0—3
Chester	42	22	11	9	100:45	55	1—3	1—1
Tranmere	42	22	11	9	93:58	55	4—1	4—13
Lincoln	42	22	9	11	91:51	53	2—3	1—2
Stockport	42	20	8	14	65:49	48	1—3	0—2
Crewe	42	19	9	14	80:76	47	0—0	2—2
OLDHAM	42	18	9	15	86:73	45	—	—
Hartlepool	42	15	12	15	57:61	42	2—2	1—0
Accrington	42	17	8	17	63:72	42	3—0	0—1
Walsall	42	16	9	17	79:59	41	2—1	2—1
Rotherham	42	16	9	17	69:66	41	4—1	0—1
Darlington	42	17	6	19	74:79	40	2—0	0—5
Carlisle	42	14	12	16	56:62	40	3—0	1—2
Gateshead	42	13	14	15	56:76	40	2—2	0—0
Barrow	42	13	12	17	58:65	38	3—1	0—3
York	42	13	12	17	62:95	38	6—2	1—3
Halifax	42	15	7	20	57:61	37	3—0	2—4
Wrexham	42	15	7	20	66:75	37	5—2	1—0
Mansfield	42	14	9	19	80:91	37	4—1	0—1
Rochdale	42	10	13	19	58:88	33	3—3	6—2
Southport	42	11	9	22	48:90	31	4—0	1—1
New Brighton	42	9	6	27	43:102	24	6—0	3—1

APPEARANCES

Agar A. 14
Alden N. 1
Bailey A. 2
Brunskill N. . . 38
Buckley A. . . 32
Burke P. 17
Butler C. 13
Chambers W. . 10
Caunce L. . . . 19
Church H. . . 23
Davies T. . . . 16
Gray M. 32
Hilton W. . . . 14
Jones A. 25
Leedham F. . . 30
Milligan G. . . 1
Robson J. . . . 1
Robbins P. . . 11
Ratcliffe B. . . 38
Ridding W. . . 1
Richardson J. . 3
Schofield F. . . 42
Seymour T. . . 18
Shaw J. 1
Talbot R. . . . 13
Walsh W. . . . 41
Williamson T. . 6

SCORERS:—Walsh 32, Buckley 10, Jones and Leedham each 9, Davies 7, Brunskill 5, Agar and Schofield each 3, Bailey and Chambers each 2, Burke, Gray, Ratcliffe and Robbins each 1.
Total: 86.

DIVISION 3N — 1936-37

							H	A
Stockport	42	23	14	5	84:39	60	0—2	1—4
Lincoln	42	25	7	10	103:57	57	1—0	0—2
Chester	42	22	9	11	87:57	53	1—0	1—2
OLDHAM	42	20	11	11	77:59	51	—	—
Hull	42	17	12	13	68:69	46	3—1	0—2
Hartlepool	42	19	7	16	75:69	45	2—0	0—1
Halifax	42	18	9	15	68:63	45	1—0	1—0
Wrexham	42	16	12	14	71:57	44	2—2	1—1
Mansfield	42	18	8	16	91:76	44	1—1	2—1
Carlisle	42	18	8	16	65:68	44	2—1	1—2
Port Vale	42	17	10	15	58:64	44	5—1	0—1
York	42	16	11	15	79:70	43	2—2	1—3
Accrington	42	16	9	17	76:69	41	3—1	1—1
Southport	42	12	13	17	73:87	37	3—3	0—2
New Brighton	42	13	11	18	55:70	37	3—1	2—0
Barrow	42	13	10	19	70:86	36	4—3	2—1
Rotherham	42	14	7	21	78:91	35	4—1	4—4
Rochdale	42	13	9	20	69:86	35	3—0	0—3
Tranmere	42	12	9	21	71:88	33	3—0	3—3
Crewe	42	10	12	20	55:83	32	1—1	2—1
Gateshead	42	11	10	21	63:98	32	4—4	3—0
Darlington	42	8	14	20	66:96	30	1—1	3—0

APPEARANCES

Aspinall J. 2
Brunskill N. . . 10
Buckley A. . . 8
Caunce L. . . . 32
Clarke J. 1
Davis T. 39
Downes P. . . . 36
Diamond J. . . 1
Eaton C. 2
Eaves T. 3
Foster R. . . . 10
Gray M. 12
Hilton W. . . . 34
Jones A. 35
Jones S. 1
Leedham F. . . 7
Milligan G. . . 40
McCormick P. . 28
Price N. 40
Ratcliffe B. . . 39
Robbins P. . . 34
Valentine F. . . 5
Williamson T. . 40
Wiggins J. . . . 3

SCORERS:—Davis 33, A. Jones 11, McCormick 10, Robbins 8, Gray 4, Downes 3, Brunskill and Buckley each 2, Leedham, Williamson, Clarke and Diamond each 1.
Total: 77.

217

"THE TEAM FROM A TOWN OF CHIMNEYS"

DIVISION 3N — 1937-38

							H	A	
Tranmere	42	23	10	9	81:41	56	2—1	1—1	
Doncaster	42	21	12	9	74:49	54	2—1	0—1	
Hull	42	20	13	9	80:43	53	1—1	1—4	
OLDHAM	42	19	13	10	67:46	51	—	—	
Gateshead	42	20	11	11	84:59	51	3—1	0—0	
Rotherham	42	20	10	12	68:56	50	3—1	1—2	
Lincoln	42	19	8	15	66:50	46	2—2	1—0	
Crewe	42	18	9	15	71:53	45	0—0	1—0	
Chester	42	16	12	14	77:72	44	3—2	3—3	
Wrexham	42	16	11	15	58:63	43	2—0	0—1	APPEARANCES
York	42	16	10	16	70:68	42	6—2	0—0	Eaves T.A. 19
Carlisle	42	15	9	18	57:67	39	3—0	1—1	Ferrier R.J. . . 11
New Brighton	42	15	8	19	60:61	38	2—1	0—1	Gray M. 15
Bradford C.	42	14	10	18	66:69	38	1—2	1—1	Hilton W.A. . . 32
Port Vale	42	12	14	16	65:73	38	3—0	2—2	Jones A. 25
Southport	42	12	14	16	53:82	38	2—0	2—2	McCormick P. . 8
Rochdale	42	13	11	18	67:78	37	4—2	1—1	Milligan G.H. . 41
Halifax	42	12	12	18	44:66	36	2—1	1—2	Aspinall J. 2
Darlington	42	11	10	21	54:79	32	3—0	0—1	Blackshaw H.K. 24
Hartlepool	42	10	12	20	53:80	32 •	3—1	0—2	Butler T. 14
Barrow	42	11	10	21	41:71	32	0—0	1—2	Caunce L. 42
Accrington	42	11	7	24	45:75	29	1—0	2—1	Davis T.L. 17

SCORERS:—Diamond 18, Davis 11, Jones and Blackshaw each 6, Robbins 5, Gray 4, McCormick, Williamson and Butler each 3, Milligan and Ferrier each 2, Hilton, Downes, Batey (Carlisle, own goal) and Hartshorne (Lincoln City, own goal) each 1.
Total: 67.

Diamond J.J. . 39
Downes P. ... 15
Price N. 3
Paterson A. ... 6
Ratcliffe B. .. 41
Robbins P. .. 35
Sinkinson F. .. 2
Williamson T. . 41

DIVISION 3N — 1938-39

							H	A	
Barnsley	42	30	7	5	94:34	67	4—2	0—3	
Doncaster	42	21	14	7	87:47	56	0—0	2—3	
Bradford C.	42	22	8	12	89:56	52	2—1	4—1	
Southport	42	20	10	12	75:54	50	2—4	0—0	
OLDHAM	42	22	5	15	76:59	49	—	—	APPEARANCES
Chester	42	20	9	13	88:70	49	1—3	2—4	Aspinall J. 7
Hull	42	18	10	14	83:74	46	4—1	2—0	Butler T. 31
Crewe	42	19	6	17	82:70	44	3—0	2—1	Blackshaw H.K. 35
Stockport	42	17	9	16	91:77	43	3—1	1—3	Caunce L. 41
Gateshead	42	14	14	14	74:67	42	1—3	0—2	Diamond J.J. . 10
Rotherham	42	17	8	17	64:64	42	2—0	1—3	Eaves T.A. 6
Halifax	42	13	16	13	52:54	42	1—0	0—0	Eckersley F. . . 1
Barrow	42	16	9	17	66:65	41	1—0	0—2	Ferrier R.J. . . 32
Wrexham	42	17	7	18	66:79	41	4—2	1—4	Fielden A. 1
Rochdale	42	15	9	18	92:82	39	1—2	2—1	Gray M. 14
New Brighton	42	15	9	18	68:73	39	1—0	1—0	Hayes W. 20
Lincoln	42	12	9	21	66:92	33	1—0	0—1	Hilton W.A. .. 40
Darlington	42	13	7	22	62:92	33	2—0	3—3	Halford D. 26
Carlisle	42	13	7	22	64:111	33	6—0	0—2	Heaton J. 2
York	42	12	8	22	66:92	32	6—0	1—4	Jones A. 13
Hartlepool	42	12	7	23	55:94	31	4—2	0—0	Jones T. 1
Accrington	42	7	6	29	49:103	20	2—0	3—1	McCormick P. . 2

SCORERS:—Ferrier 21, Halford 11, Blackshaw 8, Wright 7, Butler and Taylor each 6, Diamond 4, Hilton and A. Jones each 3, McCormick, Paterson, Gray, Heaton, Fielden, Valentine and opponent each 1.
Total: 76.

Paterson A. ... 15
Ratcliffe B. .. 38
Shipman T.E.R. 40
Taylor J.T. ... 13
Vallance W. .. 1
Valentine A.F. . 2
Williamson T. . 34
Wright E. 37

DIVISION 3N — 1946-47

							H	A
Doncaster	42	33	6	3	123:40	72	0–1	2–4
Rotherham	42	29	6	7	114:53	64	0–1	0–8
Chester	42	25	6	11	95:51	56	1–0	0–2
Stockport	42	24	2	16	78:53	50	0–0	0–4
Bradford C.	42	20	10	12	62:47	50	0–1	0–1
Rochdale	42	19	10	13	80:64	48	3–2	3–1
Wrexham	42	17	12	13	65:51	46	1–5	1–2
Crewe	42	17	9	16	70:74	43	3–1	0–3
Barrow	42	17	7	18	54:62	41	0–1	2–5
Tranmere	42	17	7	18	66:77	41	1–2	2–4
Hull	42	16	8	18	49:53	40	1–2	1–0
Lincoln	42	17	5	20	86:87	39	3–1	3–1
Hartlepool	42	15	9	18	64:73	39	0–0	1–1
Gateshead	42	16	6	20	62:72	38	1–1	0–1
York	42	14	9	19	67:81	37	2–2	0–1
Carlisle	42	14	9	19	70:93	37	0–2	2–1
Darlington	42	15	6	21	68:80	36	2–0	1–1
New Brighton	42	14	8	20	57:77	36	2–2	0–4
OLDHAM	42	12	8	22	55:80	32	—	—
Accrington	42	14	4	24	56:92	32	1–2	3–2
Southport	42	7	11	24	53:85	25	2–4	4–2
Halifax	42	8	6	28	43:92	22	6–1	1–1

SCORERS:—Howe 21, Tomlinson 9, Blackshaw and Ormondy each 5, Burns and Waite each 4, Butler 3, Horton 2, Brierley and Cutting each 1.
Total: 55.

APPEARANCES

Bell T. 25
Blackshaw W. . . . 24
Boothman J. . . . 22
Bowden J. 27
Brierley K. 34
Bunting B. 5
Burns O. 25
Butler T. 30
Cutting J. 4
Ferrier R.J. 2
Harris W. 32
Haslam H. 2
Hayes W. 11
Herbert T. 4
Horton L. 42
Howe F. 30
Hurst J. 15
Goodwin L. 7
Lawton W. 5
Ormandy J. 30
Sawbridge J. . . . 3
Schofield N. 7
Tomlinson F. . . . 27
Waite W.J. 4
Williamson T. . . . 36
Witham R. 5
Wood N. 1
Wright D. 3

DIVISION 3N — 1947-48

							H	A
Lincoln	42	26	8	8	81:40	60	0–0	2–0
Rotherham	42	25	9	8	95:49	59	1–5	1–4
Wrexham	42	21	8	13	74:54	50	1–4	2–1
Gateshead	42	19	11	12	75:57	49	0–1	5–3
Hull	42	18	11	13	59:48	47	0–0	0–1
Accrington	42	20	6	16	62:59	46	1–0	3–2
Barrow	42	16	13	13	49:40	45	2–1	4–2
Mansfield	42	17	11	14	57:51	45	1–1	1–1
Carlisle	42	18	7	17	88:77	43	2–1	1–4
Crewe	42	18	7	17	61:63	43	0–0	2–2
OLDHAM	42	14	13	15	63:64	41	—	—
Rochdale	42	15	11	16	48:72	41	1–1	0–2
York	42	13	14	15	65:60	40	2–2	0–1
Bradford C.	42	15	10	17	65:66	40	3–0	2–0
Southport	42	14	11	17	60:63	39	1–1	0–4
Darlington	42	13	13	16	54:70	39	3–3	6–0
Stockport	42	13	12	17	63:67	38	0–0	0–3
Tranmere	42	16	4	22	54:72	36	0–1	0–1
Hartlepool	42	14	8	20	51:73	36	0–2	1–3
Chester	42	13	9	20	64:67	35	3–1	1–2
Halifax	42	7	13	22	43:76	27	1–1	5–1
New Brighton	42	8	9	25	38:81	25	3–0	2–2

SCORERS:—Blackshaw 17, Haddington 15, Brook 7, Gemmell 6, Tomlinson and Brierley each 4, Fryer 3, Wilson and Jessop each 2, Parnaby, Bowden, Cardwell (Crewe Alexandra) each 1.
Total: 63.

APPEARANCES

Armitage K.J. . . . 5
Bell T. 11
Boothman J. . . . 22
Bowden J. 37
Blackshaw W. . . . 37
Brierley K. 24
Brook L. 11
Bunting B. 27
Divers J. 1
Dowkes T. 1
Fryer J.H. 9
Gemmell E. 19
Haddington R.W. 28
Hayes W. 38
Horton L. 37
Hurst J. 17
Jessop W. 9
Koffman S.J. . . . 3
McManus B. 35
Milne J.B. 13
Naylor T.W. 5
Ogden F. 2
Parnaby T.W. . . . 7
Pollock W. 4
Sawbridge J. . . . 5
Spurdle W. 1
Tilling H.K. 3
Tomlinson F. . . . 24
Walker S. 1
Wilson J. 26

"THE TEAM FROM A TOWN OF CHIMNEYS"

DIVISION 3N — 1948-49

							H	A
Hull	42	27	11	4	93:28	65	1–1	0–6
Rotherham	42	28	6	8	90:46	62	1–3	1–2
Doncaster	42	20	10	12	53:40	50	0–2	0–3
Darlington	42	20	6	16	83:74	46	7–1	1–2
Gateshead	42	16	13	13	69:58	45	0–0	2–2
OLDHAM	42	18	9	15	75:67	45	—	—
Rochdale	42	18	9	15	55:53	45	0–1	2–1
Stockport	42	16	11	15	61:56	43	5–2	2–1
Wrexham	42	17	9	16	56:62	43	1–1	1–1
Mansfield	42	14	14	14	52:48	42	4–0	2–3
Tranmere	42	13	15	14	46:57	41	0–2	1–1
Crewe	42	16	9	17	52:74	41	3–2	4–0
Barrow	42	14	12	16	41:48	40	2–1	1–2
York	42	15	9	18	74:74	39	4–0	0–4
Carlisle	42	14	11	17	60:77	39	1–0	0–2
Hartlepool	42	14	10	18	45:58	38	5–1	2–1
New Brighton	42	14	8	20	46:58	36	4–2	1–0
Chester	42	11	13	18	57:56	35	2–1	2–2
Halifax	42	12	11	19	45:62	35	2–2	1–3
Accrington	42	12	10	20	55:64	34	4–3	1–1
Southport	42	11	9	22	45:64	31	2–1	1–0
Bradford C.	42	10	9	23	48:77	29	1–2	1–2

APPEARANCES
Aston V.W. 7
Bell T. 37
Birkett R. 4
Blackshaw W. .. 6
Bowden J. 8
Brook L. 13
Gemmell E. ... 30
Haddington R. . 33
Hayes W. 22
Hurst J. 34
Hutchinson J.A. 7
Jessop W. 17
Jones J.T. 22
Lawton W. 5
Naylor T.W. ... 2
Ogden F. 20
Pickering W.H. . 42
Smith N.H. ... 1
Spurdle W. ... 35
Stock H. 26
Tomlinson F. .. 39
Watson A. 27
Wilson J. 3
Woodcock E. .. 22

SCORERS:–Gemmell 19, Haddington 18, Tomlinson 14, Stock 7, Jessop 4, Brook and Hutchinson each 3, Spurdle, Woodcock and Hayes each 2, Hurst 1.
Total: 75.

DIVISION 3N — 1949-50

							H	A
Doncaster	42	19	17	6	66:38	55	1–4	1–1
Gateshead	42	23	7	12	87:54	53	1–0	0–2
Rochdale	42	21	9	12	68:41	51	0–0	0–1
Lincoln	42	21	9	12	60:39	51	0–2	2–1
Tranmere	42	19	11	12	51:48	49	2–1	2–4
Rotherham	42	19	10	13	80:59	48	2–2	1–0
Crewe	42	17	14	11	68:55	48	2–1	1–1
Mansfield	42	18	12	12	66:54	48	1–0	1–3
Carlisle	42	16	15	11	68:51	47	1–1	0–3
Stockport	42	19	7	16	55:52	45	3–3	3–1
OLDHAM	42	16	11	15	58:63	43	—	—
Chester	42	17	6	19	70:79	40	0–2	1–1
Accrington	42	16	7	19	57:62	39	0–1	4–3
New Brighton	42	14	10	18	45:63	38	3–0	0–0
Barrow	42	14	9	19	47:53	37	1–3	1–3
Southport	42	12	13	17	51:71	37	2–5	2–3
Darlington	42	11	13	18	56:69	35	2–0	1–1
Hartlepool	42	14	5	23	52:79	33	3–1	2–0
Bradford C.	42	12	8	22	61:76	32	2–1	1–1
Wrexham	42	10	12	20	39:54	32	2–3	1–2
Halifax	42	12	8	22	58:85	32	2–1	1–1
York	42	9	13	20	52:70	31	2–0	1–0

APPEARANCES
Aston V.W. 17
Brook L. 18
Bell T. 9
Clamp E. 3
Campbell C. ... 2
Gemmell E. ... 27
Hayes W. 29
Haddington R.W. 41
Hurst J. 29
Hutchinson J.A. 7
Jessop W. 41
McCormack F.E. 14
Munro J.F. ... 9
McIlvenny R. .. 9
Naylor T.W. .. 27
Ogden F. 39
Ormond W. ... 8
Pickering W.H. . 36
Ramsey D. ... 2
Spurdle W. ... 20
Stock H. 9
Smith L. 18
Stringer E. 1
Tomlinson F. .. 23
Watson A. 14
Woodcock E. .. 7
Wadsworth A.W. 2
Walsh K. 1

SCORERS:–Haddington 19, Gemmell 11, Jessop 8, Stock and Spurdle each 3, Tomlinson, Woodcock and Brook each 2, Hurst, Hayes, Smith, Aston, McIlvenny, Munro Wadsworth and Ormond each 1.
Total: 58.

"THE TEAM FROM A TOWN OF CHIMNEYS"

DIVISION 3N — 1950-51

							H	A
Rotherham	46	31	9	6	103:41	71	4—5	1—3
Mansfield	46	26	12	8	78:48	64	2—0	1—3
Carlisle	46	25	12	9	79:50	62	1—1	0—1
Tranmere	46	24	11	11	83:62	59	3—4	0—1
Lincoln	46	25	8	13	89:58	58	0—0	0—2
Bradford P.A.	46	23	8	15	90:72	54	2—3	1—3
Bradford C.	46	21	10	15	90:63	52	2—2	0—1
Gateshead	46	21	8	17	84:62	50	2—3	2—3
Crewe	46	19	10	17	61:60	48	0—2	1—2
Stockport	46	20	8	18	63:63	48	1—3	4—1
Rochdale	46	17	11	18	69:62	45	2—0	1—0
Scunthorpe	46	13	18	15	58:57	44	3—4	0—1
Chester	46	17	9	20	62:64	43	1—0	1—3
Wrexham	46	15	12	19	55:71	42	2—2	2—0
OLDHAM	46	16	8	22	73:73	40	—	—
Hartlepool	46	16	7	23	64:66	39	5—1	1—0
York	46	12	15	19	66:77	39	2—2	2—2
Darlington	46	13	13	20	59:77	39	2—0	0—0
Barrow	46	16	6	24	51:76	38	0—1	1—2
Shrewsbury	46	15	7	24	43:74	37	2—1	2—2
Southport	46	13	10	23	56:72	36	4—0	4—1
Halifax	46	11	12	23	50:69	34	2—0	0—3
Accrington	46	11	10	25	42:101	32	2—1	2—1
New Brighton	46	11	8	27	40:90	30	3—1	0—2

SCORERS :- Gemmell 20, Haddington 10, Munro and McIlvenny each 8, Hardwick 7, Wadsworth 5, Ormond and Fawley each 4, Jessop 2, Lee, Brook, Thompson (Hartlepools United), Tapscott (Wrexham) and J. Callendar (Gateshead) each 1. Total: 73.

APPEARANCES

Aston V.W.	5
Ball J.A.	7
Bell T.	46
Bradshaw G.F.	1
Brook L.	12
Fawley R.	16
Gemmell E.	41
Goodfellow S.	37
Haddington R.W.	15
Hardwick G.F.M.	23
Hayes W.	6
Hurst J.	3
Jessop W.	27
Lee A.	3
McIlvenny R.	22
Munro J.F.	36
Naylor H.	1
Naylor T.W.	31
Ogden F.	46
Ormond W.	16
Smith L.	32
Stock H.	1
Swallow E.	6
Tomlinson F.	2
Wadsworth A.W.	26
Walsh K.	2
Whyte J.A.	43

"THE TEAM FROM A TOWN OF CHIMNEYS"

DIVISION 3N — 1951-52

							H	A
Lincoln	46	30	9	7	121:52	69	4—1	0—4
Grimsby	46	29	8	9	96:45	66	1—1	1—3
Stockport	46	23	13	10	74:40	59	1—0	0—0
OLDHAM	46	24	9	13	90:61	57	—	—
Gateshead	46	21	11	14	66:49	53	2—0	0—1
Mansfield	46	22	8	16	73:60	52	5—3	1—2
Carlisle	46	19	13	14	62:57	51	2—0	3—3
Bradford P.A.	46	19	12	15	74:64	50	1—2	0—1
Hartlepool	46	21	8	17	71:65	50	5—2	1—1
York	46	18	13	15	73:52	49	2—0	0—5
Tranmere	46	21	6	19	76:71	48	3—0	4—0
Barrow	46	17	12	17	57:61	46	3—1	1—0
Chesterfield	46	17	11	18	65:66	45	3—0	0—1
Scunthorpe	46	14	16	16	65:74	44	2—0	2—2
Bradford C.	46	16	10	20	61:68	42	2—1	2—5
Crewe	46	17	8	21	63:82	42	5—2	1—3
Southport	46	15	11	20	53:71	41	2—1	0—0
Wrexham	46	15	9	22	63:73	39	2—1	0—1
Chester	46	15	9	22	72:85	39	11—2	2—1
Halifax	46	14	7	25	61:97	35	2—0	0—1
Rochdale	46	11	13	22	47:79	35	1—1	2—2
Accrington	46	10	12	24	61:92	32	3—1	2—1
Darlington	46	11	9	26	64:103	31	3—2	2—2
Workington	46	11	7	28	50:91	29	0—1	1—0

SCORERS:—Gemmell 28, McKennan 15, McIlvenny 14, Munro 9, Ormond 5, Hardwick and Johnston each 3, Goodfellow, Smith, Wadsworth and Warner each 2, H. Jackson, Travis, Lee (Chester), Gibson (Tranmere Rovers) and Murphy (Crewe Alexandra) each 1.
Total 90.

APPEARANCES

Aston V.W. . . . 1
Bell T. 40
Broadley P.J. . . . 6
Brook L. 10
Burnett G.G. . . . 24
Fawley R. 2
Gemmell E. . . . 37
Goodfellow S. . . 35
Grainger D. . . . 3
Hardwick G.F.M. 31
Hopkinson E. . . . 3
Jackson H. 2
Jackson R. 6
Johnston T.B. . . . 4
McIlvenny R. . . . 40
McKennan P.S. . . 38
Munro J.F. 41
Naylor T.W. . . . 15
Ogden F. 19
Ormond W. . . . 36
Smith L. 20
Tomlinson F. . . . 1
Travis D. 4
Wadsworth A.W. . 5
Warner J. 35
Whyte J.A. 41
Williams H.D. . . . 1
Williams J.B. . . 1
Wright D. 5

"THE TEAM FROM A TOWN OF CHIMNEYS"

DIVISION 3N — 1952-53

							H	A
OLDHAM	46	22	15	9	77:45	59	—	—
Port Vale	46	20	18	8	67:35	58	0—1	1—1
Wrexham	46	24	8	14	86:66	56	4—2	2—2
York	46	20	13	13	60:45	53	2—1	2—1
Grimsby	46	21	10	15	75:59	52	1—1	1—1
Southport	46	20	11	15	63:60	51	3—0	0—1
Bradford P.A.	46	19	12	15	75:61	50	2—1	0—0
Gateshead	46	17	15	14	76:60	49	1—1	0—1
Carlisle	46	18	13	15	82:68	49	2—4	0—0
Crewe	46	20	8	18	70:68	48	0—1	1—0
Stockport	46	17	13	16	82:69	47	1—1	1—1
Chesterfield	46	18	11	17	65:63	47	1—1	2—1
Tranmere	46	21	5	20	65:63	47	5—2	0—0
Halifax	46	16	15	15	68:68	47	1—0	2—2
Scunthorpe	46	16	14	16	62:56	46	0—1	1—1
Bradford C.	46	14	18	14	75:80	46	2—0	0—0
Hartlepool	46	16	14	16	57:61	46	4—2	1—4
Mansfield	46	16	14	16	55:62	46	1—0	2—0
Barrow	46	16	12	18	66:71	44	3—0	3—4
Chester	46	11	15	20	64:85	37	2—1	1—0
Darlington	46	14	6	26	58:96	34	5—0	5—0
Rochdale	46	14	5	27	62:83	33	1—0	1—3
Workington	46	11	10	25	55:91	32	4—1	1—1
Accrington	46	8	11	27	39:89	27	3—0	2—0

APPEARANCES

Brook L. 35
Burnett G.G. . . . 42
Brierley K. 15
Crawford J.C. . . 14
Clarke A. 20
Fawley R. 1
Gemmell E. . . . 27
Hardwick G.F.M. 30
Houlahan H. . . . 5
Harris J. 12
Jackson H. 1
Jackson R. 3
Lowrie T. 38
McIlvenny R. . . 37
McKennan P.S. . 32
Munro J.F. 33
McGlen W. 11
Naylor T.W. . . . 15
Ogden F. 3
Ormond W. . . . 44
Smith L. 41
Whyte J.A. 46
Whelan R. 1

SCORERS:—Gemmell 24, Ormond and McKennan each 11, McIlvenny 8, Crawford and Clarke each 7, Munro 3, Houlahan and Harris each 2, Brierley and Gill (Chester) each 1.
Total: 77.

"THE TEAM FROM A TOWN OF CHIMNEYS"

DIVISION 2 — 1953-54

							H	A
Leicester	42	23	10	9	97:60	56	0—2	0—1
Everton	42	20	16	6	92:58	56	0—4	1—3
Blackburn	42	23	9	10	86:50	55	1—0	0—4
Nottingham F.	42	20	12	10	86:59	52	1—3	1—2
Rotherham	42	21	7	14	80:67	49	2—3	0—7
Luton	42	18	12	12	64:59	48	1—2	4—4
Birmingham	42	18	11	13	78:58	47	2—3	1—2
Fulham	42	17	10	15	98:85	44	2—3	1—3
Bristol R.	42	14	16	12	64:58	44	0—0	0—1
Leeds	42	15	13	14	89:81	43	4—2	1—2
Stoke	42	12	17	13	71:60	41	1—0	1—0
Doncaster	42	16	9	17	59:63	41	2—2	0—1
West Ham	42	15	9	18	67:69	39	3—1	1—0
Notts Co.	42	13	13	16	54:74	39	1—3	0—2
Hull	42	16	6	20	64:66	38	0—0	0—8
Lincoln	42	14	9	19	65:83	37	1—0	1—3
Bury	42	11	14	17	54:72	36	0—0	0—1
Derby	42	12	11	19	64:82	35	0—0	1—3
Plymouth	42	9	16	17	65:82	34	1—1	0—5
Swansea	42	13	8	21	58:82	34	2—2	0—4
Brentford	42	10	11	21	40:78	31	2—0	1—3
OLDHAM	42	8	9	25	40:89	25	—	—

SCORERS:—McIlvenny, Lowrie and Scrine each 5, Hardwick 4, Clarke and Ormond each 3, McKennan, Adams, Gemmell, Harris and Brierley each 2, McGlen, H. Jackson, Lewin, Crawford and Green (Birmingham) each 1.
Total: 40.

APPEARANCES
Adams R.M. 23
Brierley K. 37
Brook L. 13
Burnett G.G. . . . 24
Clarke A. 23
Crawford J.C. . . . 10
Crook G. 1
Fawley R. 8
Gemmell E. 13
Hardwick G.F.M. 34
Harris J. 15
Houlahan H. . . . 1
Jackson H. 4
Jackson R. 1
Lowrie T. 29
Lewin D.J. 9
McGlen W. 9
McIlvenny R. . . 31
McKennan P.S. . . 8
McShane H. . . . 13
Naylor T.W. 7
Ogden F. 18
Ormond W. . . . 18
Scrine F.H. . . . 17
Smith L. 39
Thompson J. . . . 4
Walker T.J. . . . 15
Whyte J.A. 38

LATICS CHRISTMAS BUMPER

Old HARDWICK Hubbard,
went to the cupboard,
to get poor LATICS MᶜADAM.
When she got there,
the cupboard was bare,
NOT ENOUGH DOUGH . . . . .
SHE'D HAD 'IM.

DIVISION 3N — 1954-55

							H	A
Barnsley	46	30	5	11	86:46	65	4–1	2–2
Accrington	46	25	11	10	96:67	61	0–1	0–4
Scunthorpe	46	23	12	11	81:53	58	1–1	1–6
York	46	24	10	12	92:63	58	3–2	1–2
Hartlepool	46	25	5	16	64:49	55	0–1	0–2
Chesterfield	46	24	6	16	81:70	54	4–1	3–1
Gateshead	46	20	12	14	65:69	52	1–2	2–2
Workington	46	18	14	14	68:55	50	2–1	0–3
Stockport	46	18	12	16	84:70	48	1–1	2–3
OLDHAM	46	19	10	17	74:68	48	—	—
Southport	46	16	16	14	47:44	48	1–0	0–1
Rochdale	46	17	14	15	69:66	48	0–0	1–2
Mansfield	46	18	9	19	65:71	45	1–1	3–1
Halifax	46	15	13	18	63:67	43	1–2	0–0
Darlington	46	14	14	18	62:73	42	3–1	2–0
Bradford P.A.	46	15	11	20	56:70	41	5–0	2–0
Barrow	46	17	6	23	70:89	40	3–2	1–3
Wrexham	46	13	12	21	65:77	38	2–1	1–2
Tranmere	46	13	11	22	55:70	37	2–1	1–2
Carlisle	46	15	6	25	78:89	36	2–1	2–5
Bradford C.	46	13	10	23	47:55	36	1–0	1–1
Crewe	46	10	14	22	68:91	34	4–0	1–4
Grimsby	46	13	8	25	47:78	34	4–0	1–1
Chester	46	12	9	25	44:77	33	2–1	0–0

APPEARANCES

Bollands J.F. . . . 7
Brook L. 14
Brierley 15
Brunskill J. . . . 12
Burnett G. 10
Chaytor K. 18
Crook G. 18
D'Arcy M.E. . . 25
Fawley R. 8
Garland R. 1
Hardwick G.F.M. 38
Hobson W. . . . 28
Jackson H. 2
Jackson R. 20
Kerr J. 18
King D. 7
Lewin J. 1
Lowrie T. 12
McGlen W. . . . 36
McShane H. . . . 28
Naylor T.W. . . 16
O'Donnell J. . . . 5
Ogden F. 4
Scrine F.H. . . . 41
Smith L. 10
Travis D. 40
Walker T.J. . . . 42
Whyte J.A. . . . 30

SCORERS :—Travis 30, Scrine 10, Chaytor 8, Walker 6, McShane 5, Kerr 3, Brierley, Brunskill, Crook, and McGlenn each 2, Hardwick, Jackson, Murray (Stockport County), and Lees (Crewe Alexandra) each 1. Total: 74.

DIVISION 3N — 1955-56

							H	A
Grimsby	46	31	6	9	76:29	68	1–1	1–5
Derby	46	28	7	11	110:55	63	1–1	0–2
Accrington	46	25	9	12	92:57	59	1–3	2–2
Hartlepool	46	26	5	15	81:60	57	3–2	0–1
Southport	46	23	11	12	66:53	57	1–1	1–1
Chesterfield	46	25	4	17	94:66	54	2–2	0–1
Stockport	46	21	9	16	90:61	51	3–2	0–0
Bradford C.	46	18	13	15	78:64	49	1–1	0–0
Scunthorpe	46	20	8	18	75:63	48	2–1	1–2
Workington	46	19	9	18	75:63	47	0–1	3–4
York	46	19	9	18	85:72	47	2–2	0–2
Rochdale	46	17	13	16	66:84	47	2–2	4–4
Gateshead	46	17	11	18	77:84	45	1–2	3–1
Wrexham	46	16	10	20	66:73	42	1–1	1–1
Darlington	46	16	9	21	60:73	41	3–3	1–2
Tranmere	46	16	9	21	59:84	41	4–1	3–0
Chester	46	13	14	19	52:82	40	4–1	2–3
Mansfield	46	14	11	21	84:81	39	1–1	0–2
Halifax	46	14	11	21	66:76	39	1–3	1–5
OLDHAM	46	10	18	18	76:86	38	—	—
Carlisle	46	15	8	23	71:95	38	2–2	1–3
Barrow	46	12	9	25	61:83	33	6–1	1–4
Bradford P.A.	46	13	7	26	61:122	33	5–1	1–4
Crewe	46	9	10	27	50:105	28	1–1	2–1

APPEARANCES

Anderson S. . . . 5
Betts E. 2
Bollands J.F. . . 16
Brook L. 27
Burns L.F. 4
Chaytor K. . . . 30
Crook G. 21
Darcy M.E. . . . 20
Fawley R. 18
Garland R. 8
Hardwick G.F.M. 34
Hobson W. . . . 40
Jackson H. 1
Kerr J. 16
King D. 15
McGlen W. . . . 12
Naylor T.W. . . 11
Neale P. 45
Ogden F. 5
O'Donnell J. . . 10
Outhwaite G. . . 4
Scrine F.H. . . . 20
Sharratt H. . . . 1
Smith L. 18
Thompson J. . . 4
Travis D. 37
Walker T.J. . . . 46
Whyte J.A. . . . 36

SCORERS :—Travis 15, Walker 11, Chaytor 11, King 7, Scrine 6, Fawley 6, Crook 5, O'Donnell 3, Garland 3, Neale 3, Hobson 1, Thomson 1, Kerr 1, Opponents 3. Total: 76.

"THE TEAM FROM A TOWN OF CHIMNEYS"

DIVISION 3N — 1956-57

						H	A
Derby	46	26	11	9	111:53	63	1—2 2—3
Hartlepool	46	25	9	12	90:63	59	0—0 1—4
Accrington	46	25	8	13	95:64	58	2—4 2—2
Workington	46	24	10	12	93:63	58	1—0 0—0
Stockport	46	23	8	15	91:75	54	2—0 1—2
Chesterfield	46	22	9	15	96:79	53	3—3 0—1
York	46	21	10	15	75:61	52	3—1 1—2
Hull	46	21	10	15	84:69	52	1—3 1—2
Bradford C.	46	22	8	16	78:68	52	1—1 1—4
Barrow	46	21	9	16	76:62	51	0—1 1—2
Halifax	46	21	7	18	65:70	49	4—3 1—1
Wrexham	46	19	10	17	97:74	48	1—2 4—4
Rochdale	46	18	12	16	65:65	48	0—1 2—0
Scunthorpe	46	15	15	16	71:69	45	1—1 0—0
Carlisle	46	16	13	17	76:85	45	2—2 2—2
Mansfield	46	17	10	19	91:90	44	1—1 4—2
Gateshead	46	17	10	19	72:90	44	1—2 3—2
Darlington	46	17	8	21	82:95	42	3—2 0—1
OLDHAM	46	12	15	19	66:74	39	— —
Bradford P.A.	46	16	3	27	66:93	35	3—1 2—2
Chester	46	10	13	23	55:84	33	0—0 0—1
Southport	46	10	12	24	52:94	32	2—1 0—2
Tranmere	46	7	13	26	51:91	27	1—0 1—2
Crewe	46	6	9	31	43:110	21	2—0 2—2

APPEARANCES

Bazley J. 13
Betts E. 24
Brook L. 36
Campbell J. . . . 36
Cassidy L. 4
Chaytor K. . . . 5
Crook G. 16
Duffy G. 6
Fawley R. 20
Ferguson J. . . . 1
Hartley E. 1
Hitchen T. 3
Hobson W. . . . 44
Jackson N. . . . 2
Lawless T. 9
Murphy E. 39
Murray K. 10
Naylor W. 40
Neale P. 23
Pearson D. 25
Ross A. 3
Stenner A. 3
Teece J. 11
Thompson J. . . . 42
Torrance G. . . . 4
Travis D. 32
Walker T. 17
Williams D. . . . 28
Worthington F. . 10
Wright T. 8

SCORERS :—Travis 14, Pearson 12, Neale 7, Crook 6, Betts 6, Campbell 5, Walker 3, Thompson 3, Wright 2, Murray 2, Worthington 1, Chaytor 1, Brook 1, Opponents 3. Total: 66.

"THE TEAM FROM A TOWN OF CHIMNEYS"

DIVISION 3N — 1957-58

							H	A
Scunthorpe	46	29	8	9	88:50	66	2—1	1—1
Accrington	46	25	9	12	83:61	59	0—3	1—1
Bradford C.	46	21	15	10	73:49	57	1—1	0—0
Bury	46	23	10	13	94:62	56	1—3	0—4
Hull	46	19	15	12	78:67	53	1—1	0—9
Mansfield	46	22	8	16	100:92	52	1—1	4—4
Halifax	46	20	11	15	83:69	51	2—4	0—4
Chesterfield	46	18	15	13	71:69	51	2—1	1—2
Stockport	46	18	11	17	74:67	47	2—4	0—3
Rochdale	46	19	8	19	79:67	46	0—0	3—1
Tranmere	46	18	10	18	82:76	46	1—0	1—1
Wrexham	46	17	12	17	61:63	46	4—1	2—2
York	46	17	12	17	68:76	46	2—3	2—2
Gateshead	46	15	15	16	68:76	45	0—0	0—1
OLDHAM	46	14	17	15	72:84	45	—	—
Carlisle	46	19	6	21	80:78	44	1—0	1—1
Hartlepool	46	16	12	18	73:76	44	4—0	1—4
Barrow	46	13	15	18	66:74	41	1—1	2—2
Workington	46	14	13	19	72:81	41	4—1	2—4
Darlington	46	17	7	22	78:89	41	2—2	1—3
Chester	46	13	13	20	73:81	39	5—1	0—0
Bradford P.A.	46	13	11	22	68:95	37	4—2	3—1
Southport	46	11	6	29	52:88	28	3—2	1—2
Crewe	46	8	7	31	47:93	23	1—0	2—0

The lower 12 clubs of Divisions 3N & 3S formed the new Division 4 Athletic were founder members.

SCORERS:—Duffy 16, Neale 16, Spurdle 13, Murray 12, Thompson 4, Walker 4, Over 2, Bazley 1, Crossley 1, Opponents 3. Total: 72.

APPEARANCES

Bazley J. 10
Chaytor K. 5
Crook G. 1
Crossley T. 2
Dryburgh T. 1
Duffy G. 32
Farmer W. 5
Fawley R. 20
Fox R. 1
Gaynor L. 5
Hall A. 4
Hobson W. 30
Melville L. 2
Muir I. 35
Murphy E. 13
Murray K. 24
Naylor W. 38
Neale P. 38
Over E. 21
Phoenix P. 6
Sharpe G. 1
Shimwell E. 7
Smith S. 4
Spurdle W. . . . 35
Stephenson L. . . 8
Teece D. 41
Thompson J. . . 40
Walker T. 36
West E. 41

DIVISION 4 — 1958-59

							H	A
Port Vale	46	26	12	81	10:58	64	0—2	0—0
Coventry	46	24	12	10	84:47	60	2—0	0—1
York	46	21	18	7	73:52	60	0—1	1—3
Shrewsbury	46	24	10	12	101:63	58	3—1	0—0
Exeter	46	23	11	12	87:61	57	2—1	2—3
Walsall	46	21	10	15	95:64	52	1—4	0—3
Crystal Palace	46	20	12	14	90:71	52	3—0	0—4
Northampton	46	21	9	16	85:78	51	2—1	1—2
Millwall	46	20	10	16	76:69	50	1—3	2—4
Carlisle	46	19	12	15	62:65	50	2—0	0—3
Gillingham	46	20	9	17	82:77	49	3—1	2—3
Torquay	46	16	12	18	78:77	44	1—0	1—2
Chester	46	16	12	18	72:84	44	3—5	2—5
Bradford P.A.	46	18	7	21	75:77	43	1—0	1—2
Watford	46	16	10	20	81:79	42	3—5	1—2
Darlington	46	13	16	17	66:68	42	1—3	1—1
Workington	46	12	17	17	63:78	41	1—0	0—2
Crewe	46	15	10	21	70:82	40	2—1	0—5
Hartlepool	46	15	10	21	74:88	40	1—0	0—4
Gateshead	46	16	8	22	56:85	40	3—0	1—2
OLDHAM	46	16	4	26	59:84	36	—	—
Aldershot	46	14	7	25	63:97	35	0—1	3—1
Barrow	46	9	10	27	51:104	28	2—0	1—2
Southport	46	7	12	27	41:86	26	2—0	1—1

SCORERS:—Phoenix 13, Thompson 10, Bourne 6, John 5, Bazley 4, Duffy 4, Hall 4, Mallon 4, Robinson 3, Neale 2, Stringfellow 2, Spurdle 1, Opponents 1. Total: 59.

APPEARANCES

Bazley J. 33
Bourne A. 18
Beswick I. 21
Chaytor K. 15
Clark R. 4
Duffy G. 20
Hall A.S. 37
Hobson W. . . . 29
John R.C. 19
Murphy E. 19
Mallon J.G. . . . 12
McReady B. . . . 7
Naylor T.W. . . . 18
Neale P. 11
Phoenix P.P. . . 40
Robinson K. . . 25
Spurdle W. . . . 26
Stringfellow P. . 14
Teece D.A. . . . 39
Thompson J. . . 20
Taylor W.B. . . . 42
Walker T.J. . . . 2
West E. 35

227

"THE TEAM FROM A TOWN OF CHIMNEYS"

DIVISION 4 — 1959-60

							H	A
Walsall	46	28	9	9	102:60	65	2—4	1—2
Notts Co.	46	26	8	12	107:69	60	0—3	1—3
Torquay	46	26	8	12	84:58	60	0—2	1—4
Watford	46	24	9	13	92:67	57	0—0	0—6
Millwall	46	18	17	11	84:61	53	1—1	1—0
Northampton	46	22	9	15	85:63	53	0—1	1—8
Gillingham	46	21	10	15	74:69	52	3—1	2—2
Crystal Palace	46	19	12	15	84:64	50	1—0	2—3
Exeter	46	19	11	16	80:70	49	1—2	3—4
Stockport	46	19	11	16	58:54	49	0—0	1—3
Bradford P.A.	46	17	15	14	70:68	49	2—0	0—2
Rochdale	46	18	10	18	65:60	46	1—0	0—2
Aldershot	46	18	9	19	77:74	45	0—1	0—2
Crewe	46	18	9	19	79:88	45	2—4	2—2
Darlington	46	17	9	20	63:73	43	1—3	3—1
Workington	46	14	14	18	68:60	42	2—2	0—2
Doncaster	46	16	10	20	69:76	42	1—1	0—0
Barrow	46	15	11	20	77:87	41	1—0	0—2
Carlisle	46	15	11	20	51:66	41	0—1	1—0
Chester	46	14	12	20	59:77	40	0—0	0—0
Southport	46	10	14	22	48:92	34	0—1	0—1
Gateshead	46	12	9	25	58:86	33	1—1	0—2
OLDHAM	46	8	12	26	41:83	28	—	—
Hartlepool	46	10	7	29	59:109	27	1—2	2—2

SCORERS:—Stringfellow 11, Bazley 7, Birch 4, Bourne 4, Mallon 4, Spurdle 3, Phoenix 3, McGill 2, Walters 2, Scott 1.
Total: 41.

APPEARANCES

Bazley J. 27
Beswick I. 14
Birch B. 19
Bourne A. . . . 17
Chaytor K. . . . 4
Corbett P. . . . 10
Ferguson C. . . 45
Ferguson J. . . 36
Hall A. 17
Jarvis B. 30
John R. 13
Mallon J. . . . 19
Marsh J. 2
McGill J. 39
O'Loughlin B. . 12
Phoenix P. . . . 32
Player R. . . . 2
Richardson S. . 22
Robinson K. . 12
Stringfellow P. 31
Scott R. 9
Spurdle W. . . 36
Taylor W. . . . 8
Walters G. . . . 13
West E. 37

DIVISION 4 — 1960-61

							H	A
Peterborough	46	28	10	8	134:65	66	1—1	2—2
Crystal Palace	46	29	6	11	110:69	64	4—3	1—2
Northampton	46	25	10	11	90:62	60	1—2	0—1
Bradford P.A.	46	26	8	12	84:74	60	4—0	1—5
York	46	21	9	16	80:60	51	3—1	0—1
Millwall	46	21	8	17	97:86	50	2—3	1—0
Darlington	46	18	13	15	78:70	49	3—3	1—0
Workington	46	21	7	18	74:76	49	3—5	1—1
Crewe	46	20	9	17	61:67	49	1—0	1—2
Aldershot	46	18	9	19	79:69	45	0—2	0—4
Doncaster	46	19	7	20	76:78	45	1—1	1—2
OLDHAM	46	19	7	20	79:88	45	—	—
Stockport	46	18	9	19	57:66	45	3—0	1—0
Southport	46	19	6	21	69:67	44	3—2	0—2
Gillingham	46	15	13	18	64:66	43	1—1	3—2
Wrexham	46	17	8	21	62:56	42	0—2	2—2
Rochdale	46	17	8	21	60:66	42	0—2	0—3
Accrington	46	16	8	22	74:88	40	5—2	1—5
Carlisle	46	13	13	20	61:79	39	5—2	0—3
Mansfield	46	16	6	24	71:78	38	3—1	2—1
Exeter	46	14	10	22	66:94	38	5—2	0—3
Barrow	46	13	11	22	52:79	37	3—1	2—1
Hartlepool	46	12	8	26	71:103	32	2—1	1—5
Chester	46	11	9	26	61:104	31	4—1	1—3

SCORERS:—Lister 14, Johnstone 11, Frizzell 10, Liddell 9, Rackley 7, Birch 6, Phoenix 5, Bazley 5, Stringfellow 3, Branagan 2, Jarvis 2, Davies 1, Hall 1, Robinson 1, Spurdle 1, Opponents 1.
Total: 79.

APPEARANCES

Bazley J. 26
Beswick I. . . . 11
Birch B. 16
Branagan K. . . 34
Davies E. 2
Ferguson C. . . 12
Frizzell J. . . . 40
Greenhall G. . 25
Hall A. 16
Hardie J. . . . 17
Jarvis B. 20
Johnstone R. . 30
Liddell J. . . . 18
Lister H. 23
McCue J. . . . 35
McCurley K. . . 1
O'Loughlin W. 15
Phoenix P. . . 44
Rackley R. . . 19
Robinson K. . . 3
Rollo J. 29
Smith B. 1
Spurdle W. . . 28
Stringfellow P. 9
Wann A. 19
Warhurst R. . . 8
West E. 4
White G. 1

"THE TEAM FROM A TOWN OF CHIMNEYS"

DIVISION 4 — 1961-62

							H	A
Millwall	44	23	10	11	87:62	56	4—2	0—2
Colchester	44	23	9	12	104:71	55	2—2	1—5
Wrexham	44	22	9	13	96:56	53	1—1	1—2
Carlisle	44	22	8	14	64:63	52	5—0	0—2
Bradford C.	44	21	9	14	94:86	51	2—2	1—1
York	44	20	10	14	84:53	50	1—0	1—4
Aldershot	44	22	5	17	81:60	49	2—1	1—3
Workington	44	19	11	14	69:70	49	0—2	2—0
Barrow	44	17	14	13	74:58	48	3—2	1—3
Crewe	44	20	6	18	79:70	46	2—0	5—3
OLDHAM	44	17	12	15	77:70	46	—	—
Rochdale	44	19	7	18	71:71	45	2—2	1—3
Darlington	44	18	9	17	61:73	45	0—1	0—3
Mansfield	44	19	6	19	77:66	44	2—3	0—2
Tranmere	44	20	4	20	70:81	44	2—0	1—3
Stockport	44	17	9	18	70:69	43	0—0	1—1
Southport	44	17	9	18	61:71	43	2—1	5—0
Exeter	44	13	11	20	62:77	37	1—1	3—3
Chesterfield	44	14	9	21	70:87	37	3—1	3—2
Gillingham	44	13	11	20	73:94	37	1—1	2—0
Doncaster	44	11	7	26	60:85	29	3—1	0—0
Hartlepool	44	8	11	25	52:101	27	5—2	1—1
Chester	44	7	12	25	54:96	26	4—1	0—1
Accrington								

Accrington Stanley resigned from the League after playing 33 matches, results declared void.

SCORERS:—Frizzell 24, Lister 17, Johnstone 10, Shackleton 7, Colquhoun 6, Phoenix 4, Bazley 2, Dickinson 2, Branagan 1, Ford 1, Jarvis 1, Liddell 1, Spurdle 1. Total: 77.

APPEARANCES
Ackerley S. . . . 2
Bazley J.A. . . 21
Branagan J.K. . 37
Bollands J.F. . 23
Colquhoun J. . 41
Dickinson L. . 5
Ford K. 5
Frizzell J.L. . . 41
Greaves I.D. . . 17
Horsburgh J.J. 1
Hodkinson D. . 2
Jarvis B.J. . . . 24
Johnstone R. . 40
Liddell J.C. . . 5
Lister H.F. . . 32
McCue J.W. . . 21
Phoenix P.P. . 35
Robinson J. . . 3
Rollo J.S. . . . 20
Spurdle W. . . 15
Scott J.J. . . . 43
Shackleton A. . 10
Williams A. . . 41

"THE TEAM FROM A TOWN OF CHIMNEYS"

DIVISION 4 — 1962-63

							H	A
Brentford	46	27	8	11	98:64	62	2—1	1—2
OLDHAM	46	24	11	11	95:60	59	—	—
Crewe	46	24	11	11	86:58	59	2—2	3—2
Mansfield	46	24	9	13	108:69	57	3—2	2—4
Gillingham	46	22	13	11	71:49	57	2—1	3—4
Torquay	46	20	16	10	75:56	56	1—1	0—2
Rochdale	46	20	11	15	67:59	51	5—1	1—1
Tranmere	46	20	10	16	81:67	50	1—1	2—1
Barrow	46	19	12	15	82:80	50	2—1	2—3
Workington	46	17	13	16	76:68	47	2—2	1—0
Aldershot	46	15	17	14	73:69	47	2—0	1—1
Darlington	46	19	6	21	72:87	44	1—0	1—1
Southport	46	15	14	17	72:106	44	11—0	1—2
York	46	16	11	19	67:62	43	3—2	2—5
Chesterfield	46	13	16	17	70:64	42	2—1	0—0
Doncaster	46	14	14	18	64:77	42	4—0	1—1
Exeter	46	16	10	20	57:77	42	1—2	1—2
Oxford	46	13	15	18	70:71	41	2—0	1—1
Stockport	46	15	11	20	56:70	41	2—1	1—2
Newport	46	14	11	21	76:90	39	3—2	0—0
Chester	46	15	9	22	51:66	39	2—0	0—1
Lincoln	46	13	9	24	68:89	35	4—1	2—1
Bradford C.	46	11	10	25	64:93	32	2—1	3—1
Hartlepool	46	7	11	28	56:104	25	6—1	1—0

SCORERS:—Lister 30, Whitaker 17, Colquhoun 13, Ledger 8, Bowie 5, Frizzell 5, Williams 5, McCall 4, Johnstone 5, Opponents 3.
Total: 95.

APPEARANCES
Bollands J. 36
Bowie J. 14
Branagan K. ...46
Colquhoun J. ..46
Frizzell J. 22
Greaves I. 5
Jarvis B. 14
Johnstone R. ..28
Ledger R. 46
Lister H. 39
Marshall W. ...38
McCall P. 46
Phoenix P. 4
Rollo J. 10
Spurdle W. 4
Scott J. 29
Whitaker C. ...33
Williams A. ...46

DIVISION 3 — 1963-64

							H	A
Coventry	46	22	16	8	98:61	60	2—0	1—4
Crystal Palace	46	23	14	9	73:51	60	3—1	3—1
Watford	46	23	12	11	79:59	58	1—0	1—2
Bournemouth	46	24	8	14	79:58	56	2—4	0—1
Bristol C.	46	20	15	11	84:64	55	1—2	1—3
Reading	46	21	10	15	79:62	52	3—1	1—0
Mansfield	46	20	11	15	76:62	51	1—0	1—1
Hull	46	16	17	13	73:68	49	1—1	1—0
OLDHAM	46	20	8	18	73:70	48	—	—
Peterborough	46	18	11	17	75:70	47	4—2	0—0
Shrewsbury	46	18	11	17	73:80	47	2—4	0—2
Bristol R.	46	19	8	19	91:79	46	2—2	1—0
Port Vale	46	16	14	16	53:49	46	1—0	0—1
Southend	46	15	15	16	77:78	45	0—3	2—2
Q.P.R.	46	18	9	19	76:78	45	2—1	2—3
Brentford	46	15	14	17	87:80	44	4—1	0—2
Colchester	46	12	19	15	70:68	43	2—2	3—2
Luton	46	16	10	20	64:80	42	0—1	2—1
Walsall	46	13	14	19	59:76	40	2—4	1—1
Barnsley	46	12	15	19	68:94	39	2—0	2—2
Millwall	46	14	10	22	53:67	38	1—2	1—2
Crewe	46	11	12	23	50:77	34	3—2	0—1
Wrexham	46	13	6	27	75:107	32	3—2	4—0
Notts Co.	46	9	9	28	45:92	27	2—0	2—4

SCORERS:—Lister 14, Whitaker 12, Ledger 10, Johnstone 9, Colquhoun 7, Bowie 6, Sievwright 4, Williams 4, Craig 3, Frizzell 2, Barlow 1, McCall 1.
Total: 73.

APPEARANCES
Barlow C. 6
Bollands J. ...40
Bowie J. 26
Branagan K. ...28
Burdess J. 2
Colquhoun J. ..35
Craig R. 10
Frizzell J. 34
Halsall A. 2
Jackson A. 2
Johnstone R. ..34
Ledger R. 45
Lister H. 29
McCall P. 26
McGinn W. 3
Marshall W. ...19
Sievwright G. ..37
Scott J. 4
Swinburne A. .. 4
Taylor B. 40
Whitaker C. ...39
Williams A. ...41

"THE TEAM FROM A TOWN OF CHIMNEYS"

DIVISION 3 — 1964-65

							H	A
Carlisle	46	25	10	11	76:53	60	2—3	0—2
Bristol C.	46	24	11	11	92:55	59	7—3	0—2
Mansfield	46	24	11	11	95:61	59	2—1	1—4
Hull	46	23	12	11	91:57	58	2—1	1—2
Brentford	46	24	9	13	83:55	57	1—1	2—2
Bristol R.	46	20	15	11	82:58	55	1—2	0—0
Gillingham	46	23	9	14	70:50	55	2—0	1—2
Peterborough	46	22	7	17	85:74	51	3—1	0—5
Watford	46	17	16	13	71:64	50	2—0	2—3
Grimsby	46	16	17	13	68:67	49	1—5	1—3
Bournemouth	46	18	11	17	72:63	47	1—1	0—0
Southend	46	19	8	19	78:71	46	0—2	1—6
Reading	46	16	14	16	70:70	46	1—2	0—1
Q.P.R.	46	17	12	17	72:80	46	5—3	1—1
Workington	46	17	12	17	58:69	46	0—2	0—0
Shrewsbury	46	15	12	19	76:84	42	1—3	3—1
Exeter	46	12	17	17	51:52	41	2—0	1—2
Scunthorpe	46	14	12	20	65:72	40	2—1	1—1
Walsall	46	15	7	24	55:80	37	1—3	2—1
OLDHAM	46	13	10	23	61:83	36	—	—
Luton	46	11	11	24	51:94	33	0—2	0—2
Port Vale	46	9	14	23	41:76	32	0—1	1—2
Colchester	46	10	10	26	50:89	30	3—1	2—2
Barnsley	46	9	11	26	54:90	29	1—1	1—0

SCORERS:—Frizzell 11, Bartley 9, Harris 7, Colquhoun 6, Quixall 6, Bowie 4, Ledger 4, Martin 4, Lister 2, Branagan 2, Craig 1, Jackson 1, Opponents 4. Total: 61.

APPEARANCES

Bartley A. 31
Bollands J. . . . 19
Bowie J. 35
Branagan K. . . . 24
Burdess J. 1
Cameron A. . . . 15
Colquhoun J. . . 41
Craig R. 8
Dearden W. . . . 11
Frizzell J. 42
Harris J. 26
Jackson A. . . . 6
Johnstone R. . . 11
Lawson A. . . . 7
Ledger R. 35
Lister H. 12
Martin B. 42
McCall P. 36
McGinn W. . . . 20
Quixall A. 13
Swan R. 27
Williams A. . . . **44**

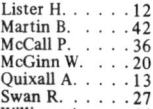

"THE TEAM FROM A TOWN OF CHIMNEYS"

DIVISION 3 — 1965-66

							H	A
Hull	46	31	7	8	109:62	69	2—2	1—5
Millwall	46	27	11	8	76:43	65	0—2	0—1
Q.P.R.	46	24	9	13	95:65	57	0—2	1—1
Scunthorpe	46	21	11	14	80:67	53	1—3	1—1
Workington	46	19	14	13	67:57	52	1—1	1—0
Gillingham	46	22	8	16	62:54	52	5—3	0—3
Swindon	46	19	13	14	74:48	51	1—1	1—0
Reading	46	19	13	14	70:63	51	2—2	2—3
Walsall	46	20	10	16	77:64	50	1—2	2—2
Shrewsbury	46	19	11	16	73:64	49	0—1	1—3
Grimsby	46	17	13	16	68:62	47	1—4	1—3
Watford	46	17	13	16	55:51	47	0—1	0—4
Peterborough	46	17	12	17	80:66	46	2—4	1—0
Oxford	46	19	8	19	70:74	46	3—0	3—3
Brighton	46	16	11	19	67:65	43	1—0	1—3
Bristol R.	46	14	14	18	64:64	42	2—0	0—4
Swansea	46	15	11	20	81:96	41	1—0	1—4
Bournemouth	46	13	12	21	38:56	38	2—2	0—1
Mansfield	46	15	8	23	59:89	38	1—1	0—1
OLDHAM	46	12	13	21	55:81	37	—	—
Southend	46	16	4	26	54:83	36	1—0	2—0
Exeter	46	12	11	23	53:79	35	3—1	0—4
Brentford	46	10	12	24	48:69	32	1—1	0—0
York	46	9	9	28	53:106	27	3—0	2—2

APPEARANCES

Asprey W. 28
Bartley A. 20
Bollands J. ... 17
Blore R. 28
Bowie J. 45
Branagan K. ... 8
Bryan P. 7
Dearden W. ... 21
Frizzell J. 46
Hall J. 2
Harris J. 2
Holden S. 34
Holt R. 16
Jackson A. ... 16
Lawson A. 26
Large F. 20
Ledger R. 46
McGinn W. ... 16
McCarthy P. ... 2
McGowan G. .. 5
McIlroy J. 12
Pennington J. .. 27
Quixall A. 25
Stevens D. 29
Swan R. 35
Towers I. 22
Wood I. 1

SCORERS: — Large 8, Towers 8, Holden 5, Quixall 5, Bartley 4, Frizzell 4, Ledger 4, Bowie 3, Jackson 3, Dearden 2, Harris 2, Blore 3, Asprey 1, McGowan 1, Lawson 1, Opponents 2. Total: 55.

DIVISION 3 — 1966-67

							H	A
Q.P.R.	46	26	15	5	103:38	67	0—1	1—0
Middlesbrough	46	23	9	14	87:64	55	0—1	2—0
Watford	46	20	14	12	61:46	54	1—1	2—2
Reading	46	22	9	15	76:57	53	1—3	1—2
Bristol R.	46	20	13	13	76:67	53	3—0	1—2
Shrewsbury	46	20	12	14	77:62	52	4—1	1—3
Torquay	46	21	9	16	73:54	51	5—0	0—4
Swindon	46	20	10	16	81:59	50	1—0	3—6
Mansfield	46	20	9	17	84:79	49	0—0	4—2
OLDHAM	46	19	10	17	80:63	48	—	—
Gillingham	46	15	16	15	58:62	46	2—1	0—1
Walsall	46	18	10	18	65:72	46	6—2	1—1
Colchester	46	17	10	19	76:73	44	4—0	2—3
Leyton Orient	46	13	18	15	58:68	44	3—1	2—2
Peterborough	46	14	15	17	66:71	43	1—0	1—3
Oxford	46	15	13	18	61:66	43	1—1	1—3
Grimsby	46	17	9	20	61:68	43	0—1	0—1
Scunthorpe	46	17	8	21	58:73	42	2—0	1—1
Brighton	46	13	15	18	61:71	41	4—1	0—2
Bournemouth	46	12	17	17	39:57	41	1—1	1—2
Swansea	46	12	15	19	85:89	39	4—1	0—3
Darlington	46	13	11	22	47:81	37	4—0	3—2
Doncaster	46	12	8	26	58:117	32	1—0	0—1
Workington	46	12	7	27	55:89	31	3—0	1—1

APPEARANCES

Asprey W. 36
Bebbington K. 38
Best D. 39
Blair R. 17
Blore R. 32
Bowie J. 43
Chapman L. ... 15
Collins J. 20
Foster A. 5
Frizzell J. 35
Hunter A. 11
Johnston W. ... 6
Knighton K. ... 23
Lawson A. 14
Ledger R. 38
Makin J. 3
McIlroy J. 21
Nolan M. 1
Towers I. 46
Wood I. 14

SCORERS: — Towers 27, *Large 12, Collins 8, *Kinnell 8, Bowie 7, Blore 7, Wood 4, Bebbington 3, Asprey 2, Johnston 1, McIlroy 1. Total: 80.   *Transferred during season.

232

"THE TEAM FROM A TOWN OF CHIMNEYS"

DIVISION 3 — 1967-68

							H	A
Oxford	46	22	13	11	69:47	57	3—1	1—3
Bury	46	24	8	14	91:65	56	1—2	1—3
Shrewsbury	46	20	15	11	61:49	55	0—0	2—4
Torquay	46	21	11	14	60:56	53	0—1	1—2
Reading	46	21	9	16	70:60	51	1—3	1—0
Watford	46	21	8	17	74:50	50	2—0	2—1
Walsall	46	19	12	15	74:61	50	0—3	1—3
Barrow	46	21	8	17	65:54	50	3—1	1—4
Swindon	46	16	17	13	74:51	49	0—2	0—0
Brighton	46	16	16	14	57:55	48	3—0	1—0
Gillingham	46	18	12	16	59:63	48	0—1	0—1
Bournemouth	46	16	15	15	56:51	47	1—1	0—0
Stockport	46	19	9	18	70:75	47	4—1	2—0
Southport	46	17	12	17	65:65	46	2—0	0—1
Bristol R.	46	17	9	20	72:78	43	3—5	3—4
OLDHAM	46	18	7	21	60:65	43	—	—
Northampton	46	14	13	19	58:72	41	2—0	2—1
Orient	46	12	17	17	46:62	41	2—2	2—0
Tranmere	46	14	12	20	62:74	40	2—1	0—1
Mansfield	46	12	13	21	51:67	37	1—0	1—1
Grimsby	46	14	9	23	52:69	37	2—1	1—0
Colchester	46	9	15	22	50:87	33	2—1	0—0
Scunthorpe	46	10	12	24	56:87	32	3—4	0—2
Peterborough	46	20	10	16	79:67	31	0—2	1—2

SCORERS:—Towers 10, Ledger 10, Magee 6, Bebbington 6, Blore 5, Sheffield 6, Johnston 5, Knighton 3, Wood 3, Asprey 1, Blair 1, Chapman 1, Frizzell 1, Hunter 1. Opponents 1. Total: 60.

APPEARANCES

Asprey W.	17
Bebbington K.	36
Best D.	46
Blair R.	25
Blore R.	40
Bowie J.	26
Chapman L.	11
Doyle A.	13
Frizzell J.	32
Hunter A.	29
Johnston W.	18
Joyce W.	27
Knighton K.	22
Lawson A.	20
Ledger R.	33
Magee E.	24
McIlroy J.	2
Nolan M.	1
Philpott A.	15
Sheffield L.	16
Towers I.	29
Wood I.	24

"THE TEAM FROM A TOWN OF CHIMNEYS"

DIVISION 3 — 1968-69

						H	A
Watford	46	27	10	9	74:34	64	0—3 0—2
Swindon	46	27	10	9	71:35	64	2—3 1—5
Luton	46	25	11	10	74:38	61	0—1 0—4
Bournemouth	46	21	9	16	60:45	51	2—0 1—3
Plymouth	46	17	15	14	53:49	49	0—2 1—1
Torquay	46	18	12	16	54:46	48	3—1 1—3
Tranmere	46	19	10	17	70:68	48	1—2 2—6
Southport	46	17	13	16	71:64	47	0—1 1—3
Stockport	46	16	14	16	67:68	46	5—2 0—0
Barnsley	46	16	14	16	58:63	46	1—1 1—0
Rotherham	46	16	13	17	56:50	45	0—0 2—1
Brighton	46	16	13	17	72:65	45	2—0 0—6
Walsall	46	14	16	16	50:49	44	1—0 1—2
Reading	46	15	13	18	67:66	43	1—1 1—4
Mansfield	46	16	11	19	58:62	43	2—2 0—4
Bristol R.	46	16	11	19	63:71	43	2—1 0—1
Shrewsbury	46	16	11	19	51:67	43	2—2 1—0
Orient	46	14	14	18	51:58	42	3—1 0—3
Barrow	46	17	8	21	56:75	42	0—1 1—2
Gillingham	46	13	15	18	54:63	41	1—0 0—2
Northampton	46	14	12	20	54:61	40	1—1 1—1
Hartlepool	46	10	19	17	40:70	39	1—2 2—0
Crewe	46	13	9	24	52:76	35	3—0 0—3
OLDHAM	46	13	9	24	50:83	35	— —

SCORERS:—Bebbington 12, Spence 12, Chapman 7, Blore 3, Bowie 3, Colquhoun 3, Magee 3, Joyce 2, Blair 1, Down 1, Philpott 1, Opponents 2. Total: 50.

APPEARANCES

Aitken B. 1
Bebbington K. . . 44
Best D. 15
Blair R. 27
Blore R. 44
Bowie J. 27
Bright D. 11
Chapman I. . . . 44
Colquhoun J. . . 29
Down D. 10
Doyle A. 22
Frizzell J. 16
Gordine B. 25
Hunter A. 44
Johnston B. . . . 4
Joyce W. 37
Lawson A. 35
Magee E. 17
Molyneux B. . . . 9
Philpott A. 11
Spence A. 23
Smith R. 1
Wood I. 41

"THE TEAM FROM A TOWN OF CHIMNEYS"

DIVISION 4 — 1969-70

							H	A
Chesterfield	46	27	10	9	77:32	64	1—0	1—3
Wrexham	46	26	9	11	84:49	61	2—3	1—1
Swansea	46	21	18	7	66:45	60	0—1	0—4
Port Vale	46	20	19	7	61:33	59	2—3	0—1
Brentford	46	20	16	10	58:39	56	4—1	1—1
Aldershot	46	20	13	13	78:65	53	4—2	0—1
Notts Co.	46	22	8	16	73:62	52	5—0	0—0
Lincoln	46	17	16	13	66:52	50	1—1	1—0
Peterborough	46	17	14	15	77:69	48	4—2	1—8
Colchester	46	17	14	15	64:63	48	1—2	1—3
Chester	46	21	6	19	58:66	48	5—0	1—2
Scunthorpe	46	18	10	18	67:65	46	1—3	1—2
York	46	16	14	16	55:62	46	3—1	0—0
Northampton	46	16	12	18	64:55	44	0—2	0—0
Crewe	46	16	12	18	51:51	44	2—1	1—1
Grimsby	46	14	15	17	54:58	43	0—2	1—4
Southend	46	15	10	21	59:85	40	3—0	0—1
Exeter	46	14	11	21	57:59	39	1—1	2—0
OLDHAM	46	13	13	20	60:65	39	—	—
Workington	46	12	14	20	46:64	38	1—2	0—1
Newport	46	13	11	22	53:74	37	3—0	1—2
Darlington	46	13	10	23	53:73	36	1—1	1—1
Hartlepool	46	10	10	26	42:82	30	1—0	1—1
Bradford P.A.	46	6	11	29	41:96	23	0—0	0—0

SCORERS:— Beardall 11, Fryatt 11, (2 League for Blackburn), Shaw 11, Bebbington 7, Bowie 5, Bingham 3, Colquhoun 3, Blore 2, McNeill 2, Chapman 1, Robins 1, Wood 1, Woodall 1, Opponents 1.
Total: 60.

APPEARANCES

Beardall	21
Bebbington	37
Blair	9
Bowie	44
Bright	8
Blore	30
Bingham	16
Bryceland	1
Chapman	9
Colquhoun	39
Faulkner	1
Fitton	2
Frizzell	4
Fryatt	16
Gordine	41
Hoolickin	5
Joyce	3
Lawson	39
McNeill	20
Robins	3
Spence	3
Schofield	1
Shaw	34
Taylor	2
Thomson	18
Wilson	25
Whittle	26
Wood	46
Woodall	3

"THE TEAM FROM A TOWN OF CHIMNEYS"

DIVISION 4 — 1970-71

							H	A
Notts Co.	46	30	9	7	89:36	69	1—3	0—2
Bournemouth	46	24	12	10	81:46	60	2—2	0—5
OLDHAM	46	24	11	11	88:63	59	—	—
York	46	23	10	13	78:54	56	1—1	1—0
Chester	46	24	7	15	69:55	55	1—1	1—0
Colchester	46	21	12	13	70:54	54	4—0	2—1
Northampton	46	19	13	14	63:59	51	1—1	3—1
Southport	46	21	6	19	63:57	48	2—4	4—1
Exeter	46	17	14	15	67:68	48	2—1	2—0
Workington	46	18	12	16	48:49	48	1—3	0—0
Stockport	46	16	14	16	49:65	46	1—1	1—1
Darlington	46	17	11	18	58:57	45	3—1	1—3
Aldershot	46	14	17	15	66:71	45	5—2	1—1
Brentford	46	18	8	20	66:62	44	5—1	1—1
Crewe	46	18	8	20	75:76	44	5—3	1—0
Peterborough	46	18	7	21	70:71	43	3—0	1—2
Scunthorpe	46	15	13	18	56:61	43	1—1	3—2
Southend	46	14	15	17	53:66	43	2—0	0—3
Grimsby	46	18	7	21	57:71	43	1—0	1—4
Cambridge	46	15	13	18	51:66	43	4—1	1—3
Lincoln	46	13	13	20	70:71	39	4—2	1—2
Newport	46	10	8	28	55:85	28	4—0	4—1
Hartlepool	46	8	12	26	34:74	28	2—0	1—0
Barrow	46	7	8	31	51:90	22	2—1	1—1

SCORERS:—Fryatt 24, Shaw 23, Bryceland 10, Bebbington 10, McNeill 7, Whittle 3, Wood 2, Mundy 2, Hartle 2, Cranston 1, Thomson 1, Heath 1, Opponents 2. Total: 88.

APPEARANCES
Bebbington K. . 43
Bowie I. 46
Bryceland T. . 45
Cranston W. . . 36
Dowd H. 24
Fryatt J. 45
Gordine V. . . 17
Hartle B. 8
Heath D. 32
Marsland G. . . 1
McNeill A. . . . 39
Mundy J. . . . 3
Shaw D. 45
Short M. 5
Sweeney A. . . 7
Thomson A. . . 9
Turner B. . . . 10
Whittle M. . . . 46
Wood I. 45

"THE TEAM FROM A TOWN OF CHIMNEYS"

DIVISION 3 — 1971-72

							H	A
Aston Villa	46	32	6	8	85:32	70	0—6	0—1
Brighton	46	27	11	8	82:47	65	2—4	1—0
Bournemouth	46	23	16	7	73:37	62	3—1	0—2
Notts Co.	46	25	12	9	74:44	62	0—1	0—2
Rotherham	46	20	15	11	69:52	55	5—1	1—3
Bristol R.	46	21	12	13	75:56	54	3—2	0—1
Bolton	46	17	16	13	51:41	50	2—2	1—2
Plymouth	46	20	10	16	74:64	50	0—1	0—0
Walsall	46	15	18	13	62:57	48	1—3	3—2
Blackburn	46	19	9	18	54:57	47	1—1	1—0
OLDHAM	46	17	11	18	59:63	45	—	—
Shrewsbury	46	17	10	19	73:65	44	1—4	4—2
Chesterfield	46	18	8	20	57:57	44	1—1	1—0
Swansea	46	17	10	19	46:59	44	1—0	0—0
Port Vale	46	13	15	18	43:59	41	1—0	0—1
Wrexham	46	16	8	22	59:63	40	0—2	1—3
Halifax	46	13	12	21	48:61	38	0—0	0—0
Rochdale	46	12	13	21	57:83	37	3—2	1—1
York	46	12	12	22	57:66	36	1—0	0—0
Tranmere	46	10	16	20	50:71	36	3—1	2—2
Mansfield	46	8	20	18	41:63	36	2—1	1—2
Barnsley	46	9	18	19	32:64	36	6—0	1—2
Torquay	46	10	12	24	41:69	32	1—0	2—0
Bradford City	46	11	10	25	45:77	32	0—2	2—2

SCORERS:—Shaw 18, Robins 9, Fryatt 5, McNeill 5, Whittle 5, Bebbington 4, Bowie 3, Garwood 3, Wood 2, Heath 1, Jones 1, Mulvaney 1, Sweeney 1, Opponents 1. Total: 59.

APPEARANCES

Bebbington K. . . 41
Bowie J. 36
Bryceland T. . . . 20
Buckley I. 5
Clements P. 26
Cranston W. 28
Crumblehulme K. . 3
Dowd H. 41
Fryatt J. 15
Garwood C. . . . 9
Heath D. 12
Hicks K. 3
Hoolickin S. 1
Jones C. 3
McNeill A. 36
Mulvaney R. . . 44
Ogden C. 5
Robins I. 23
Shaw D. 45
Sleeuwenhoek J. . 2
Spence D. 3
Sweeney A. . . . 14
Whittle M. 45
Wood I. 46

237

"THE TEAM FROM A TOWN OF CHIMNEYS"

DIVISION 3 — 1972-73

							H	A
Bolton	46	25	11	10	73:39	61	2—0	1—2
Notts Co.	46	23	11	12	67:47	57	1—1	4—2
Blackburn	46	20	15	11	57:47	55	1—2	1—1
OLDHAM	46	19	16	11	72:54	54	—	—
Bristol R.	46	20	13	13	77:56	53	3—0	3—3
Port Vale	46	21	11	14	56:69	53	1—0	2—0
Bournemouth	46	17	16	13	66:44	50	1—1	0—2
Plymouth	46	20	10	16	74:66	50	7—1	3—1
Grimsby	46	20	8	18	67:61	48	1—2	2—6
Tranmere	46	15	16	15	56:52	46	3—1	1—0
Charlton	46	17	11	18	69:67	45	0—1	2—4
Wrexham	46	14	17	15	55:54	45	2—2	1—1
Rochdale	46	14	17	15	48:54	45	0—0	0—0
Southend	46	17	10	19	61:54	44	0—1	1—0
Shrewsbury	46	15	14	17	46:54	44	2—1	2—2
Chesterfield	46	17	9	20	57:61	43	3—0	1—4
Walsall	46	18	7	21	56:66	43	2—1	0—3
York	46	13	15	18	42:46	41	1—1	0—0
Watford	46	12	17	17	43:48	41	2—1	1—2
Halifax	46	13	15	18	43:53	41	1—1	3—0
Rotherham	46	17	7	22	51:65	41	1—0	3—2
Brentford	46	15	7	24	51:69	37	1—1	1—1
Swansea	46	14	9	23	51:73	37	2—0	0—0
Scunthorpe	46	10	10	26	33:82	30	3—0	0—0

SCORERS:—Shaw 17, Garwood 12, Robins 11, Whittle 6, McVitie 5, Blair 4, McNeill 4, Edwards 3, Wood 2, Lester 2, Hicks 1, Morrissey 1, Sweeney 1.
Opponents 3.
Total: 72.

APPEARANCES
Blair R. 29
Clements P. . . . 6
Collins R. 6
Cranston W. . . . 34
Dowd H. 37
Edwards P. . . . 16
Garwood C. . . . 35
Hicks K. 46
Hoolickin S. . . . 2
Jones C. 3
Lester M. 15
McNeill A. 42
McVitie G. 25
Morrissey J. . . . 6
Mulvaney R. . . . 18
Ogden C. 9
Robins I. 36
Shaw D. 31
Spence D. 2
Sweeney A. . . . 16
Whittle M. 46
Wood I. 46

"THE TEAM FROM A TOWN OF CHIMNEYS"

DIVISION 3 — 1973-74

							H	A
OLDHAM	46	25	12	9	83:47	62	—	—
Bristol R.	46	22	17	7	65:33	61	1—1	2—1
York	46	21	19	6	67:38	61	2—1	1—1
Wrexham	46	22	12	12	63:43	56	0—0	2—1
Chesterfield	46	21	14	11	55:42	56	0—0	0—1
Grimsby	46	18	15	13	67:50	51	3—1	1—2
Watford	46	19	12	15	64:56	50	0—3	1—0
Aldershot	46	19	11	16	65:52	49	2—0	1—0
Halifax	46	14	21	11	48:51	49	3—2	0—0
Huddersfield	46	17	13	16	56:55	47	6—0	1—2
Bournemouth	46	16	15	15	54:58	47	4—2	3—0
Southend	46	16	14	16	62:62	46	2—0	2—2
Blackburn	46	18	10	18	62:64	46	2—3	1—0
Charlton	46	19	8	19	66:73	46	0—2	1—4
Walsall	46	16	13	17	57:48	45	2—1	1—1
Tranmere	46	15	15	16	50:44	45	2—2	2—0
Plymouth	46	17	10	19	59:54	44	1—0	0—0
Hereford	46	14	15	17	53:57	43	1—1	4—3
Brighton	46	16	11	19	52:58	43	0—1	2—1
Port Vale	46	14	14	18	52:58	42	1—1	0—3
Cambridge	46	13	9	24	48:81	35	6—1	1—1
Shrewsbury	46	10	11	25	41:62	31	3—0	2—0
Southport	46	6	16	24	35:82	28	6—0	2—0
Rochdale	46	2	17	27	38:94	21	3—1	3—1

SCORERS:—Garwood 16, Blair 11, Jones 10, Lochhead 10, McVitie 9, Whittle 9 (7 pens), Groves 4, Robins 4, Edwards 2, Hicks 2, Bailey 1, Hateley 1, Mulvaney 1, Wood 1. Opponents 2. Total: 83.

APPEARANCES

Bailey A.D.	14
Blair R.V.	41
Dowd H.	20
Edwards P.F.	23
Garwood C.A.	26
Groves A.J.	18
Hateley	1
Hicks K.	44
Jones G.A.	26
Lester M.	11
Lochhead A.L.	41
McNeill A.A.	13
McVitie G.J.	46
Mulvaney R.	23
Ogden C.	26
Robins I.	43
Whittle M.	46
Wood I.	44

"THE TEAM FROM A TOWN OF CHIMNEYS"

DIVISION 2 — 1974-75

							H	A
Manchester U.	42	26	9	7	66:30	61	1—0	2—3
Aston Villa	42	25	8	9	69:32	58	1—2	0—5
Norwich	42	20	13	9	58:37	53	2—2	0—1
Sunderland	42	19	13	10	65:35	51	0—0	2—2
Bristol C.	42	21	8	13	47:33	50	2—0	1—3
West Bromwich	42	18	9	15	54:42	45	0—0	0—1
Blackpool	42	14	17	11	38:33	45	1—0	0—1
Hull	42	15	14	13	40:53	44	0—1	1—1
Fulham	42	13	16	13	44:39	42	1—0	0—0
Bolton	42	15	12	15	45:41	42	1—0	1—1
Oxford	42	15	12	15	41:51	42	1—1	0—1
Orient	42	11	20	11	28:39	42	0—0	1—3
Southampton	42	15	11	16	53:54	41	1—1	0—1
Notts Co.	42	12	16	14	49:59	40	1—0	0—1
York	42	14	10	18	51:55	38	2—3	0—0
Nottingham F.	42	12	14	16	43:55	38	2—0	0—1
Portsmouth	42	12	13	17	44:54	37	2—0	1—1
OLDHAM	42	10	15	17	40:48	35	—	—
Bristol R.	42	12	11	19	42:64	35	3—4	1—2
Millwall	42	10	12	20	44:56	32	1—1	0—0
Cardiff	42	9	14	19	36:62	32	4—0	1—3
Sheffield W.	42	5	11	26	29:64	21	2—1	1—1

SCORERS:—Robins 9, Young 7, Jones 4, McVitie 4, Whittle 4 (3 pens), Garwood 3, Groves 3, Blair 1, Edwards 1, McNeill 1, Treacy 1, Opponents 2.
Total: 40.

APPEARANCES
Bailey 12
Bell 32
Blair 36
Branagan . . . 3
Chapman . . . 24
Edwards 17
Garwood . . . 13
Groves 35
Hicks 32
Holt 21
Jones 19
Lochhead . . . 3
McNeill 4
McVitie 29
Mulvaney . . . 3
Ogden 42
Robins 36
Treacy 3
Whittle 37
Wood 37
Young 21

"THE TEAM FROM A TOWN OF CHIMNEYS"

DIVISION 2 — 1975-76

							H	A
Sunderland	42	24	8	10	67:36	56	1—1	0—2
Bristol C.	42	19	15	8	59:35	53	2—4	0—1
West Bromwich	42	20	13	9	50:33	53	0—1	1—1
Bolton	42	20	12	10	64:38	52	2—1	0—4
Notts Co.	42	19	11	12	60:41	49	2—2	1—5
Southampton	42	21	7	14	66:50	49	3—2	2—3
Luton	42	19	10	13	61:51	48	1—1	3—2
Nottingham F.	42	17	12	13	55:40	46	0—0	3—4
Charlton	42	15	12	15	61:72	42	2—0	1—3
Blackpool	42	14	14	14	40:49	42	1—0	1—1
Chelsea	42	12	16	14	53:54	40	2—1	3—0
Fulham	42	13	14	15	45:47	40	2—2	0—1
Orient	42	13	14	15	37:39	40	1—1	0—2
Hull	42	14	11	17	45:49	39	1—0	0—3
Blackburn	42	12	14	16	45:50	38	2—1	1—4
Plymouth	42	13	12	17	48:54	38	3—2	1—2
OLDHAM	42	13	12	17	57:68	38	—	—
Bristol R.	42	11	16	15	38:50	38	2—0	0—1
Carlisle	42	12	13	17	45:59	37	2—2	1—2
Oxford	42	11	11	20	39:59	33	1—1	1—1
York	42	10	8	24	39:71	28	2—0	0—1
Portsmouth	42	9	7	26	32:61	25	5—2	1—1

SCORERS:—Shaw 13, Whittle 8, Jones 7, Robins 6, Blair 4, Young 4, Hicks 3, Groves 3, Bell 3, Chapman 2, Wood 2, McVitie 1, Opponents 1. Total: 57.

APPEARANCES

Bell G. 40
Blair R. 35
Branagan J. . . 13
Carroll J. . . . 5
Chapman L. . . 41
Dungworth J. . . 5
Edwards P. . . . 29
Groves A. . . . 40
Hicks K. 30
Holt D. 37
Jones G. 15
McVitie G. . . 10
Ogden C. . . . 18
Platt J. 24
Robins I. . . . 38
Shaw D. 29
Whittle M. . . . 39
Wood I. 37
Young A. . . . 19

241

"THE TEAM FROM A TOWN OF CHIMNEYS"

DIVISION 2 — 1976-77

							H	A
Wolverhampton	42	22	13	7	84:45	57	0—2	0—5
Chelsea	42	21	13	8	73:53	55	0—0	3—4
Nottingham F.	42	21	10	11	77:43	52	1—0	0—3
Bolton	42	20	11	11	74:54	51	2—2	0—3
Blackpool	42	17	17	8	58:42	51	1—0	2—0
Luton	42	23	6	15	67:48	48	1—2	0—1
Charlton	42	16	16	10	71:58	48	1—1	1—2
Notts Co.	42	19	10	13	65:60	48	1—1	0—1
Southampton	42	17	10	15	72:67	44	2—1	0—4
Millwall	42	17	13	14	57:53	43	2—1	1—2
Sheffield U.	42	14	12	16	54:63	40	1—2	1—2
Blackburn	42	15	9	18	42:54	39	2—0	0—2
OLDHAM	42	14	10	18	52:64	38	—	—
Hull	42	10	17	15	45:53	37	3—0	1—0
Bristol R.	42	12	13	17	53:68	37	4—0	0—0
Burnley	42	11	14	17	46:64	36	3—1	0—1
Fulham	42	11	13	18	44:61	35	1—0	0—5
Cardiff	42	12	10	20	56:67	34	3—2	1—3
Orient	42	9	16	17	37:55	34	0—0	2—0
Carlisle	42	11	12	19	49:75	34	4—1	1—1
Plymouth	42	8	16	18	46:65	32	2—2	2—2
Hereford	42	8	15	19	57:78	31	3—5	0—1

SCORERS:— Halom 18 (1 pen.), Shaw 8, Irving 6 (1 pen.), Bell 4, Chapman 3, Robins 3, Whittle 3 (1 pen.), Valentine 2, Young 2, Groves 1, Hicks 1, Wood 1. Total: 52.

APPEARANCES

Bell G.T.A.	36
Blair R.V.	26
Branagan J.P.	9
Chapman L.	42
Edwards P.F.	6
Groves A.J.	31
Halom V.L.	37
Hicks K.	24
Holt D.	17
Hoolickin G.J.	1
Hurst J.	38
Irving D.	17
Ogden C.J.	15
Platt J.R.	27
Robins I.	33
Shaw G.D.	26
Valentine C.H.	12
Whittle M.	24
Wood I.T.	30
Young A.F.	11

"THE TEAM FROM A TOWN OF CHIMNEYS"

DIVISION 2 — 1977-78

							H	A
Bolton	42	24	10	8	63:33	58	2—2	0—1
Southampton	42	22	13	7	70:39	57	1—1	2—2
Tottenham	42	20	16	6	83:49	56	1—1	1—5
Brighton	42	22	12	8	63:38	56	1—1	1—1
Blackburn	42	16	13	13	56:60	45	0—2	2—4
Sunderland	42	14	16	12	67:59	44	1—1	1—3
Stoke	42	16	10	16	53:49	42	1—1	0—3
OLDHAM	42	13	16	13	54:58	42	—	—
Crystal Palace	42	13	15	14	50:47	41	1—1	0—0
Fulham	42	14	13	15	49:49	41	2—0	2—0
Burnley	42	15	10	17	56:64	40	2—0	1—4
Sheffield U.	42	16	8	18	62:73	40	3—0	0—1
Luton	42	14	10	18	54:52	38	1—0	1—0
Orient	42	10	18	14	43:49	38	2—1	3—5
Notts Co.	42	11	16	15	54:62	38	2—1	2—3
Millwall	42	12	14	16	49:57	38	2—2	0—2
Charlton	42	13	12	17	55:68	38	1—1	2—2
Bristol R.	42	13	12	17	61:77	38	4—1	0—0
Cardiff	42	13	12	17	51:71	38	1—1	0—1
Blackpool	42	12	13	17	59:60	37	2—1	1—1
Mansfield	42	10	11	21	49:69	31	0—1	2—0
Hull	42	8	12	22	34:52	28	2—1	1—0

SCORERS:—Taylor 20, Halom 11, Young 7, Chapman 4, Valentine 4, Blair 1, Hurst 1, Irving 1, Gardner 1, Wood 1, Heaton 1, Opponents 2. Total: 54.

APPEARANCES

Bell G.T.A. . . . 36
Bernard M.P. . . . 4
Blair R.V. 24
Chapman L. . . . 38
Edwards P.F. . . 18
Edwards S.G. . . 5
Gardner S.D. . . 17
Groves A.J. . . . 12
Halom V.L. . . . 31
Heaton P.J. . . . 1
Hicks K. 25
Hilton M.G.J. . . 4
Holt D. 31
Hoolickin G.J. . 17
Hurst J. 31
Irving D. 1
Ogden C.J. . . . 12
Platt J.R. 30
Taylor S.J. . . . 32
Valentine C.H. . 32
Wood I.T. 33
Young A.F. . . . 28

243

"THE TEAM FROM A TOWN OF CHIMNEYS"

DIVISION 2 — 1978-79

							H	A
Crystal Palace	42	19	19	4	51:24	57	0—0	0—1
Brighton	42	23	10	9	72:39	56	1—3	0—1
Stoke	42	20	16	6	58:31	56	1—1	0—4
Sunderland	42	22	11	9	70:44	55	0—0	0—3
West Ham	42	18	14	10	70:39	50	2—2	0—3
Notts Co.	42	14	16	12	48:60	44	3—3	0—0
Preston	42	12	18	12	59:57	42	2—0	1—1
Newcastle	42	17	8	17	51:55	42	1—3	1—1
Cardiff	42	16	10	16	56:70	42	2—1	3—1
Fulham	42	13	15	14	50:47	41	0—2	0—1
Orient	42	15	10	17	51:51	40	0—0	0—0
Cambridge	42	12	16	14	44:52	40	4—1	3—3
Burnley	42	14	12	16	51:62	40	2—0	0—1
OLDHAM	42	13	13	16	52:61	39	—	—
Wrexham	42	12	14	16	45:42	38	1—0	0—2
Bristol R.	42	14	10	18	48:60	38	3—1	0—0
Leicester	42	10	17	15	43:52	37	2—1	0—2
Luton	42	13	10	19	60:57	36	2—0	1—6
Charlton	42	11	13	18	60:69	35	0—3	0—2
Sheffield U.	42	11	12	19	52:69	34	1—1	2—4
Millwall	42	11	10	21	42:61	32	4—1	3—2
Blackburn	42	10	10	22	41:72	30	5—0	2—0

SCORERS:— Young 10, Heaton 5, Stainrod 5, Taylor 5, Hicks 4, Halom 4, Steel 4, Chapman 3, Hilton 3, Bell 2, Wood 2, Blair 1, Hurst 1, Valentine 1, Hoolickin 1, Opponents 1. Total: 52.

APPEARANCES

Atkinson P. 1
Bernard M. 2
Bell G. 23
Blair R. 35
Chapman L. . . . 42
Edwards S. . . . 32
Gardner S. 33
Halom V. 31
Heaton P. 29
Hicks K. 35
Hilton M. 20
Holt D. 5
Hoolickin G. . . 2
Hurst J. 41
Jordan T. 12
Keegan G. 20
McDonnell P. . . 42
Sinclair N. 1
Stainrod S. . . . 14
Steel J. 21
Taylor S. 16
Valentine C. . . 12
Wood I. 36
Young A. 37

"THE TEAM FROM A TOWN OF CHIMNEYS"

DIVISION 2 — 1979-80

							H	A
Leicester	42	21	13	8	58:38	55	1—1	1—0
Sunderland	42	21	12	9	69:42	54	3—0	2—4
Birmingham	42	21	11	10	58:38	53	1—0	0—2
Chelsea	42	23	7	12	66:52	53	1—0	0—3
Q.P.R.	42	18	13	11	75:53	49	0—0	3—4
Luton	42	16	17	9	66:45	49	2—1	0—0
West Ham	42	20	7	15	54:43	47	0—0	0—1
Cambridge	42	14	16	12	61:53	44	1—1	3—3
Newcastle	42	15	14	13	53:49	44	1—0	2—3
Preston	42	12	19	11	56:52	43	3—2	1—0
OLDHAM	42	16	11	15	49:53	43	—	—
Swansea	42	17	9	16	48:53	43	4—1	0—2
Shrewsbury	42	18	5	19	60:53	41	0—2	1—0
Orient	42	12	17	13	48:54	41	1—0	1—1
Cardiff	42	16	8	18	41:48	40	0—3	0—1
Wrexham	42	16	6	20	40:49	38	2—3	1—1
Notts Co.	42	11	15	16	51:52	37	1—0	1—1
Watford	42	12	13	17	39:46	37	1—1	0—1
Bristol R.	42	11	13	18	50:64	35	2—1	0—2
Fulham	42	11	7	24	42:74	29	0—1	1—0
Burnley	42	6	15	21	39:73	27	2—1	1—1
Charlton	42	6	10	26	39:78	22	4—3	1—2

SCORERS:—Stainrod 11, Steel 10, Halom 8, Atkinson 6, Wylde 4, Heaton 3, Kowenicki 3, Clements, Valentine, Wood and Holt each 1. Total: 49.

APPEARANCES
Atkinson P.G. . . 39
Blair R.V. 27
Clements K.H. . 36
Edwards S.G. . . 13
Gardner S.D. . . 4
Halom V.L. . . . 25
Heaton P.J. . . . 22
Hicks K. 6
Hilton M.G.J. . . 24
Hoolickin G.J. . 4
Holt D. 31
Hurst J. 26
Jordon T.E. . . . 1
Keegan G.A. . . 22
Kowenicki R. . . 24
McDonnell P.A. 34
Platt J.R. 8
Steel W.J. . . . 33
Stainrod S.A. . 37
Valentine C.H. 21
Wood I. 37
Wylde R. . . . 10

"THE TEAM FROM A TOWN OF CHIMNEYS"

DIVISION 2 — 1980-81

							H	A
West Ham	42	28	10	4	79:29	66	0—0	1—1
Notts Co.	42	18	17	7	49:38	53	0—1	2—0
Swansea	42	18	14	10	64:44	50	2—2	0—3
Blackburn	42	16	18	8	42:29	50	1—0	0—1
Luton	42	18	12	12	61:46	48	0—0	2—1
Derby	42	15	15	12	57:52	45	0—2	1—4
Grimsby	42	15	15	12	44:42	45	1—2	0—0
Q.P.R.	42	15	13	14	56:46	43	1—0	0—2
Watford	42	16	11	15	50:45	43	2—1	1—2
Sheffield W.	42	17	8	17	53:51	42	2—0	0—3
Newcastle	42	14	14	14	30:45	42	0—0	0—0
Chelsea	42	14	12	16	46:41	40	0—0	0—1
Cambridge	42	17	6	17	53:65	40	2—2	1—3
Shrewsbury	42	11	17	14	46:47	39	0—0	2—2
OLDHAM	42	12	15	15	39:48	39	—	—
Wrexham	42	12	14	16	43:45	38	1—3	2—3
Orient	42	13	12	17	52:56	38	0—1	3—2
Bolton	42	14	10	18	61:66	38	1—1	0—2
Cardiff	42	12	12	18	44:60	36	2—0	2—0
Preston	42	11	14	17	41:62	36	1—1	2—1
Bristol C.	42	7	16	19	29:51	30	2—0	1—1
Bristol R.	42	5	13	24	34:65	23	1—0	0—0

APPEARANCES
Atkinson P.G. . . . 28
Blair R.V. 42
Clements K.H. . . 40
Edwards S.G. . . . 12
Futcher P. 36
Gardner S.D. . . . 4
Heaton P.J. 15
Hilton M.G.J. . . . 10
Hoolickin G.J. . . 13
Hurst J. 34
Keegan G.A. . . . 41
Kowenicki R. . . . 16
McDonnell P.A. . . 22
McDonough D.K. 13
Nuttall M. 7
Palmer R.N. 21
Platt J.R. 20
Sinclair N.J.T. . . 21
Stainrod S.A. . . . 18
Steel W.J. 21
Wylde R. 28

SCORERS:—Wylde 12, Palmer 6, Stainrod 5, Steel 3, McDonough 3, Keegan 2, Kowenicki 2, Heaton 2, Atkinson 2, Futcher and Nuttall one each.
Total: 39.

"THE TEAM FROM A TOWN OF CHIMNEYS"

DIVISION 2 — 1981-82

							H	A
Luton	42	25	13	4	86:46	88	1—1	0—2
Watford	42	23	11	8	76:42	80	1—1	1—1
Norwich	42	22	5	15	64:50	71	2—0	2—1
Sheffield Wed.	42	20	10	12	55:51	70	0—3	1—2
Q.P.R.	42	21	6	15	65:43	69	2—0	0—0
Barnsley	42	19	10	13	59:41	67	1—1	1—3
Rotherham	42	20	7	15	66:54	67	0—3	2—1
Leicester	42	18	12	12	56:48	66	1—1	1—2
Newcastle	42	18	8	16	52:50	62	3—1	0—2
Blackburn	42	16	11	15	47:43	59	0—3	0—0
OLDHAM	42	15	14	13	50:51	59	—	—
Chelsea	42	15	12	15	60:60	57	1—0	2—2
Charlton	42	13	12	17	50:65	51	1—0	1—3
Cambridge	42	13	9	20	48:53	48	2—0	0—0
Crystal Palace	42	13	9	20	34:45	48	0—0	0—4
Derby	42	12	12	18	53:68	48	1—1	0—1
Grimsby	42	11	13	18	53:65	46	3—1	1—2
Shrewsbury	42	11	3	18	37:57	46	1—1	1—2
Bolton	42	13	7	22	39:61	46	1—1	2—0
Cardiff	42	12	8	22	45:61	44	2—2	1—0
Wrexham	42	11	11	20	40:56	44	2—1	3—0
Orient	42	10	9	23	39:61	39	3—2	3—0

SCORERS: Wylde 16, Heaton 12, Steel 7, Palmer 7, Keegan 3, Bowden 2, McDonough 1, Clements 1, Opponents 1.
Total: 50.

APPEARANCES
Atkinson............33
Anderson............1
Bowden..............3
Clements...........27
Edwards............20
Firm................9
Futcher............37
Goram...............3
Heaton.............38
Hoolickin..........28
Keegan.............40
McDonough..........33
McDonnell..........39
Nuttall.............1
Palmer.............35
Ryan...............37
Sinclair............9
Steel..............35
Wylde..............34

"THE TEAM FROM A TOWN OF CHIMNEYS"

DIVISION 2 — 1982-83

							H	A
Q.P.R.	42	26	7	9	77:36	85	0—1	0—1
Wolves	42	20	15	7	68:44	75	4—1	0—0
Leicester	42	20	10	12	72:44	70	1—2	1—2
*Fulham	42	20	9	13	64:47	69	1—0	3—0
Newcastle	42	18	13	11	75:53	67	2—2	0—1
Sheffield Wed.	42	16	15	11	60:47	63	1—1	1—1
OLDHAM	42	14	19	9	64:47	61	—	—
Leeds	42	13	21	8	51:46	60	2—2	0—0
Shrewsbury	42	15	14	13	48:48	59	1—0	0—0
Barnsley	42	14	15	13	57:55	57	1—1	1—1
Blackburn	42	15	12	15	58:58	57	0—0	2—2
Cambridge	42	13	12	17	42:60	51	3—0	4—1
*Derby	42	10	19	13	49:58	49	2—2	2—2
Carlisle	42	12	12	18	68:70	48	4—3	0—0
Crystal Palace	42	12	12	18	43:52	48	2—0	0—1
Middlesbrough	42	11	15	16	46:67	48	3—0	1—1
Charlton	42	13	9	20	63:86	48	2—2	1—4
Chelsea	42	11	14	17	51:61	47	2—2	0—2
Grimsby	42	12	11	19	45:70	47	1—1	2—0
Rotherham	42	10	15	17	45:68	45	1—1	3—1
Burnley	42	12	8	22	56:66	44	3—0	2—1
Bolton	42	11	11	20	42:61	44	2—3	3—2

*Game between Derby and Fulham abandoned after 88 minutes but result allowed to stand at 1-0.

SCORERS: Wylde 19, Palmer 15, McDonough 10, Ryan 8, Heaton 3, Atkinson 3, Steel 2, Sinclair 1, Henry 1, Opponents 2. Total: 64.

APPEARANCES

Atkinson 42
Anderson 3
Bowden 26
Clements 37
Edwards 7
Futcher 25
Goram 38
Hodge 4
Heaton 19
Hoolickin 30
Hudson 4
Henry 11
Humphreys 2
Jones 2
Keegan 20
McDonough 38
McMahon 2
Palmer 42
Ryan 40
Sinclair 23
Steel 6
Taylor 4
Wylde 37

248

"THE TEAM FROM A TOWN OF CHIMNEYS"

DIVISION 2 — 1983-84   H   A

Chelsea	42	25	13	4	90:40	89	1—1	0—3
Sheffield Wed.	42	26	10	6	72:34	89	1—3	0—3
Newcastle	42	24	8	10	85:53	80	1—2	0—3
Manchester City	42	20	10	12	66:48	70	2—2	0—2
Grimsby	42	19	13	10	60:47	70	2—1	0—3
Blackburn	42	17	16	9	57:46	67	0—0	1—3
Carlisle	42	16	16	10	48:41	64	2—3	0—2
Shrewsbury	42	17	10	15	49:53	61	0—1	0—2
Brighton	42	17	9	16	69:60	60	1—0	0—4
Leeds	42	16	12	14	55:56	60	3—2	0—2
Fulham	42	15	12	15	60:53	57	3—0	0—3
Huddersfield	42	14	15	13	56:49	57	0—3	1—0
Charlton	42	16	9	17	53:64	57	0—0	1—2
Barnsley	42	15	7	20	57:53	52	1—0	1—0
Cardiff	42	15	6	21	53:66	51	2—1	0—2
Portsmouth	42	14	7	21	73:64	49	3—2	4—3
Middlebrough	42	12	13	17	41:47	49	2—1	2—3
Crystal Palace	42	12	11	19	42:52	47	3—2	1—2
OLDHAM	42	13	8	21	47:73	47	—	—
Derby	42	11	9	22	36:72	42	3—0	2—2
Swansea	42	7	8	27	36:85	29	3—3	0—0
Cambridge	42	4	12	26	28:77	24	0—0	1—2

SCORERS: Palmer 13, Cross 6, Ward 6, Quinn 5, McBride 4, Henry 4, Heaton 2, Parker 2, Hoolickin 1, Bowden 1, Colville 1, Hodkinson 1, Opponents 1. Total: 47.

APPEARANCES

Bowden 31
Bromage 2
Buchan 24
Clements 41
Cross 18
Colville 4
Goram 22
Grew 5
Heaton 10
Hoolickin 34
Hudson 12
Henry 39
Humphreys 5
Hodkinson 3
Jones 2
McDonough 38
McBride 19
Parkin 5
Palmer 42
Parker 22
Quinn 14
Sinclair 18
Ward 42
Wealands 10

"THE TEAM FROM A TOWN OF CHIMNEYS"

DIVISION 2 — 1984-85

						H	A
Oxford	42	25	9	8	84:36	84	0—0 2—5
Birmingham	42	25	7	10	59:33	82	0—1 1—0
Manchester City	42	21	11	10	66:40	74	0—2 0—0
Portsmouth	42	20	14	8	69:50	74	0—2 1—5
Blackburn	42	21	10	11	66:41	73	2—0 1—1
Brighton	42	20	12	10	58:34	72	1—0 0—2
Leeds	42	19	12	11	66:43	69	1—1 0—6
Shrewsbury	42	18	11	13	66:53	65	0—1 0—3
Fulham	42	19	8	15	68:64	65	2—1 1—3
Grimsby	42	18	8	16	72:64	62	2—0 1—4
Barnsley	42	14	16	12	42:42	58	2—1 1—0
Wimbledon	42	16	10	16	71:75	58	0—1 0—1
Huddersfield	42	15	10	17	52:64	55	2—2 1—2
OLDHAM	42	15	8	19	49:67	53	— —
Crystal Palace	42	12	12	18	46:65	48	1—0 0—3
Carlisle	42	13	8	21	50:67	47	2—3 5—2
Charlton	42	11	12	19	51:63	45	2—1 1—2
Sheffield United	42	10	14	18	54:66	44	2—2 0—2
Middlesbrough	42	10	10	22	41:57	40	2—0 2—1
Notts Co.	42	10	7	25	45:73	37	3—2 0—0
Cardiff	42	9	8	25	47:79	35	0—1 2—2
Wolves	42	8	9	25	37:79	33	3—2 3—0

SCORERS: Quinn 18, Palmer 9, Parker 9, Ward 6, Henry 3, McBride 1, Colville 1, McGuire 1, Harrison 1. Total: 49.

APPEARANCES

Bowden.................13
Buchan....................4
Barlow..................31
Bullock....................6
Clements.............23
Colville...................3
Donachie..............39
Goram..................41
Hoolickin.............31
Henry...................40
Hodkinson.............1
Harrison.................5
Jones......................3
McDonough.........32
McGuire...............20
McBride.................9
O'Callaghan...........9
Palmer.................35
Parker..................32
Parkin....................1
Quinn...................40
Sinclair...................1
Ward....................42

250

"THE TEAM FROM A TOWN OF CHIMNEYS"

DIVISION 2 — 1985-86

							H	A
Norwich	42	25	9	8	84:39	84	1–3	0–1
Charlton	42	22	11	9	78:45	77	2–1	1–1
Wimbledon	42	21	13	8	58:37	76	2–1	0–0
Portsmouth	42	22	7	13	69:41	73	2–0	2–1
Crystal Palace	42	19	9	14	57:52	66	2–0	2–3
Hull	42	17	13	12	65:55	64	3–1	2–4
Sheffield United	42	17	11	14	64:63	62	1–5	0–2
OLDHAM	42	17	9	16	62:61	60	—	—
Millwall	42	17	8	17	64:65	59	0–0	1–0
Stoke	42	14	15	13	48:50	57	2–4	0–2
Brighton	42	16	8	18	64:64	56	4–0	1–1
Barnsley	42	14	14	14	47:50	56	1–1	0–1
Bradford	42	16	6	20	51:63	54	0–1	0–1
Leeds	42	15	8	19	56:72	53	3–1	1–3
Grimsby	42	14	10	18	58:62	52	2–1	4–1
Huddersfield	42	14	10	18	51:67	52	1–1	0–2
Shrewsbury	42	14	9	19	52:64	51	4–3	0–2
Sunderland	42	13	11	18	47:61	50	2–2	3–0
Blackburn	42	12	13	17	53:62	49	3–1	0–0
Carlisle	42	13	7	22	47:71	46	2–1	1–3
Middlesbrough	42	12	9	21	44:53	45	1–0	2–3
Fulham	42	10	6	26	45:69	36	2–1	2–2

SCORERS: Futcher 17, Palmer 15, Quinn 11, Henry 7, McGuire 2, Colville 2, Atkinson 1, Fairclough 1, Williams 1, Jones 1, Linighan 1, Milligan 1, Opponents 2. Total: 62.

APPEARANCES

Atkinson 26
Barlow 26
Bullock 4
Colville 13
Donachie 33
Futcher 40
Fairclough 6
Goram 41
Gorton 1
Hoolickin 32
Henry 40
Jones 18
Linighan 15
McDonough 20
McGuire 40
Milligan 5
O'Callaghan 1
Palmer 41
Quinn 24
Ryan 19
Smith 14
Williams 3

"THE TEAM FROM A TOWN OF CHIMNEYS"

DIVISION 2 — 1986-87

							H	A
Derby County	42	25	9	8	64:38	84	1–4	1–0
Portsmouth	42	23	9	10	53:28	78	0–0	0–3
OLDHAM	42	22	9	11	65:44	75	—	—
Leeds	42	19	11	12	58:44	68	0–1	2–0
Ipswich	42	17	13	12	59:43	64	2–1	1–0
Crystal Palace	42	19	5	18	51:53	62	1–0	1–2
Plymouth	42	16	13	13	62:57	61	2–1	2–3
Stoke	42	16	10	16	63:53	58	2–0	2–0
Sheffield United	42	15	13	14	50:49	58	3–1	0–2
Bradford	42	15	10	17	62:62	55	2–1	3–0
Barnsley	42	14	13	15	49:52	55	2–0	1–1
Blackburn	42	15	10	17	45:55	55	3–0	0–1
Reading	42	14	11	17	52:59	53	4–0	3–2
Hull	42	13	14	15	41:55	53	0–0	0–1
West Bromwich	42	13	12	17	51:49	51	2–1	0–2
Millwall	42	14	9	19	39:45	51	2–1	0–0
Huddersfield	42	13	12	17	54:61	51	2–0	4–5
Shrewsbury	42	15	6	21	41:53	51	3–0	0–2
Birmingham	42	11	17	14	47:59	50	2–2	3–1
Sunderland	42	12	12	18	49:59	48	1–1	2–0
Grimsby	42	10	14	18	39:59	44	1–1	2–2
Brighton	42	9	12	21	37:54	39	1–1	2–1

APPEARANCES

Barlow 27
Colville 2
Callaghan 1
Cecere 12
Donachie 33
Edmonds 1
Ellis 3
Futcher 25
Goram 41
Gorton 1
Hoolickin 18
Henry 35
Irwin 41
Jones 14
Linighan 40
McDonough 4
McGuire 5
Moore 13
Milligan 37
Ormondroyd 8
Palmer 42
Ryan 1
Williams 30
Wright 28

SCORERS: Palmer 16, Futcher 13, Williams 9, Wright 7, Henry 6, Cecere 4, Linighan 3, Barlow 2, Milligan 2, Irwin 1, Moore 1, Ormondroyd 1.
Total: 65.

PLAY-OFFS

Promotion and relegation play-offs were introduced in 1986/7 involving all four divisions. They were used, in part, to reduce the First Division to 20 clubs over two seasons.

Leeds 1 Oldham 0
Oldham 2 Leeds 1 (aet)

"THE TEAM FROM A TOWN OF CHIMNEYS"

DIVISION 2 — 1987-88

							H	A
Millwall	44	25	7	12	72:52	82	0—0	1—1
Aston Villa	44	22	12	10	68:41	78	0—1	2—1
Middlesbrough	44	22	12	10	63:36	78	3—1	0—1
Bradford City	44	22	11	11	74:54	77	0—2	3—5
Blackburn	44	21	14	9	68:52	77	4—2	0—1
Crystal Palace	44	22	9	13	86:59	75	1—0	1—3
Leeds United	44	19	12	13	61:51	69	1—1	1—1
Ipswich	44	19	9	16	61:52	66	3—1	0—2
Manchester City	44	19	8	17	80:60	65	1—1	2—1
OLDHAM	44	18	11	15	72:64	65	—	—
Stoke City	44	17	11	16	50:57	62	5—1	2—2
Swindon	44	16	11	17	73:60	59	4—3	0—2
Leicester City	44	16	11	17	62:61	59	2—0	1—4
Barnsley	44	15	12	17	61:62	57	1—0	1—1
Hull City	44	14	15	15	54:60	57	1—2	0—1
Plymouth Argyle	44	16	8	20	65:67	56	0—1	0—1
Bournemouth	44	13	10	21	56:68	49	2—0	2—2
Shrewsbury	44	11	16	17	42:54	49	2—2	3—2
Birmingham City	44	11	15	18	41:66	48	1—2	3—1
West Bromwich	44	12	11	21	50:69	47	2—1	0—0
Sheffield United	44	13	7	24	45:74	46	3—2	5—0
Reading	44	10	12	22	44:70	42	4—2	0—3
Huddersfield	44	6	10	28	41:100	28	3—2	2—2

SCORERS: Ritchie 19, Palmer 17, Bunn 9, Wright 9, T. Henry 4, Ellis 3, Linighan 2, Callaghan 2, Cecere 2, Milligan 1, Flynn 1, Williams 1, Opponents 2. Total: 72.

APPEARANCES

Atkinson 3
Barlow 19
Barrett 16
Bunn 21
Cecere 14
Callaghan 10
Donachie 30
Edmonds 2
Ellis 2
Flynn 29
Goram 9
Gorton 24
Henry N. 3
Henry. T. 20
Irwin 43
Keeley 10
Kelly J. 10
Linighan 32
Marshall 10
Milligan 39
Palmer 42
Ritchie 36
Rhodes 11
Williams 9
Wright 40

253

"THE TEAM FROM A TOWN OF CHIMNEYS"

DIVISION 2 — 1988-89

							H	A
Chelsea	46	29	12	5	96:50	99	1—4	2—2
Manchester City	46	23	13	10	77:53	82	0—1	4—1
Crystal Palace	46	23	12	11	71:49	81	2—3	0—2
Watford	46	22	12	12	74:48	78	3—1	1—3
Blackburn	46	22	11	13	74:59	77	1—1	1—3
Swindon Town	46	20	16	10	68:53	76	2—2	2—2
Barnsley	46	20	14	12	66:58	74	1—1	3—4
Ipswich Town	46	22	7	17	71:61	73	4—0	1—2
West Bromwich	46	18	18	10	65:41	72	1—3	1—3
Leeds United	46	17	16	13	59:50	67	2—2	0—0
Sunderland	46	16	15	15	60:60	63	2—2	2—3
Bournemouth	46	18	8	20	53:62	62	2—0	2—2
Stoke City	46	15	14	17	57:72	59	2—2	0—0
Bradford City	46	13	17	16	52:59	56	1—1	0—2
Leicester City	46	13	16	7	56:63	55	1—1	2—1
OLDHAM	46	11	21	14	75:72	54	—	—
Oxford United	46	14	12	20	62:70	54	3—0	1—1
Plymouth Argyle	46	14	12	20	55:66	54	2—2	0—3
Brighton	46	14	9	23	57:66	51	2—1	0—2
Portsmouth	46	13	12	21	53:62	51	5—3	1—1
Hull City	46	11	14	21	52:68	47	2—2	1—1
Shrewsbury Town	46	8	18	20	40:67	42	3—0	0—0
Birmingham City	46	8	11	27	31:76	35	4—0	0—0
Walsall	46	5	16	25	41:80	31	3—0	2—2

APPEARANCES

Adams 9
Barlow 15
Barrett 43
Bunn 25
Blundell 2
Cecere 9
Donachie 4
Flynn 7
Henry N. 14
Holden 13
Hartford 3
Hallworth 16
Irwin 39
Kelly J. 41
Litchfield 3
Marshall 40
Milligan 38
Morgan 1
Palmer 45
Philliskirk 3
Ritchie 29
Rhodes 26
Skipper 26
Williams 2
Warhurst 2
Wright 37

SCORERS: Palmer 15, Ritchie 14, Bunn 12, Wright 7, Milligan 6, J. Kelly, 6, Marshall 4, Holden 4, Irwin 2, Cecere 2, Williams 1, Skipper 1, Opponents 1.
Total: 75.

"THE TEAM FROM A TOWN OF CHIMNEYS"

DIVISION 2 — 1989-90

							H	A
Leeds United	46	24	13	9	79:52	85	3—1	1—1
Sheffield United	46	24	13	9	78:58	85	0—2	1—2
Newcastle	46	22	14	10	80:55	80	1—1	1—2
Swindon	46	20	14	12	79:59	74	2—2	2—3
Blackburn	46	19	17	10	74:59	74	2—0	0—1
*Sunderland	46	20	14	12	70:64	74	2—1	3—2
West Ham	46	20	12	14	80:57	72	3—0	2—0
OLDHAM	46	19	14	13	70:57	71	—	—
Ipswich	46	19	12	15	67:66	69	4—1	1—1
Wolves	46	18	13	15	67:60	67	1—1	1—1
Port Vale	46	15	16	15	62:57	61	2—1	0—2
Portsmouth	46	15	16	15	62:65	61	3—3	1—2
Leicester	46	15	14	17	67:79	59	1—0	0—3
Hull	46	14	16	16	58:65	58	3—2	0—0
Watford	46	14	15	17	58:60	57	1—1	0—3
Plymouth	46	14	13	19	58:63	55	3—2	0—2
Oxford	46	15	9	22	57:66	54	4—1	1—0
Brighton	46	15	9	22	56:72	54	1—1	1—1
Barnsley	46	13	15	18	49:71	54	2—0	0—1
West Bromwich	46	12	15	19	67:71	51	2—1	2—2
Middlesbrough	46	13	11	22	52:63	50	2—0	0—1
Bournemouth	46	12	12	22	57:76	48	4—0	0—2
Bradford	46	9	14	23	44:68	41	2—2	1—1
Stoke	46	6	19	21	35:63	37	2—0	2—1

*Also promoted

SCORERS: Palmer 16, Ritchie 15, R. Holden 9, Milligan 7, Bunn 5, Adams 4, Marshall 3, Barrett 2, Redfearn 2, McGarvey 1, Barlow 1, Irwin 1, Warhurst 1, Opponents 3. Total: 70.

APPEARANCES

Adams 18
Barlow 43
Barrett 46
Bunn 28
Donachie 7
Henry N 40
Holden R 45
Hallworth 15
Heseltine 1
Holden A 6
Irwin 42
Moulden 5
Marshall 23
Milligan 41
McGarvey 2
Palmer 33
Ritchie 37
Rhodes 31
Redfearn 15
Williams 1
Warhurst 30

OLDHAM ATHLETIC 1990/91 FIRST TEAM SQUAD

Top Row – left to right: Chris Halstead, Jason Fisk, Ian Thompstone, John Smith, Jon Hallworth, Andy Holden, Steve Morgan, Chris Blundell, Andy Ritchie
Middle Row: Billy Urmson (Coach), Ronnie Evans (Kit Manager), Rick Holden, Roger Palmer, Paul Warhurst, Willie Donachie (Player Coach), Mike Milligan, Wayne Heseltine, Darren Huyton, Ian Liversedge (Physio)
Front Row: Neil Redfearn, Nick Henry, Ian Marshall, Paul Moulden, Joe Royle (Manager), Earl Barrett, Frank Bunn, Andy Barlow, Neil Adams

"THE TEAM FROM A TOWN OF CHIMNEYS"

F.A. Cup Record ~ 1906 * 1990

SEASON	ROUND	RESULTS	SCORERS
1906/07	Qual.	Athletic 5, Hyde 0	
		Athletic 4, Newton Heath 1	
		Buxton 1, Athletic 3	
		Atherton 1, Athletic 1	
	Replay	Athletic 4, Atherton 1	
		Athletic 9, Southbank 1	
	1	Athletic 5, Kidderminster 0	
	2	Athletic 0, Liverpool 1	
1907/08	Qual.	Athletic 8, Darwen 1	
	1	Athletic 2, Leeds City 1	Newton, Whaites
	2	Athletic 0, Everton 0	
	Replay	Everton 6, Athletic 1	Whaites
1908/09	1	Athletic 1, Leeds City 1	Hamilton
	Replay	Leeds City 2, Athletic 0	
1909/10	1	Athletic 1, Aston Villa 2	Toward
1910/11	1	Birmingham City 1, Athletic 1	Toward
	Replay	Athletic 2, Birmingham City 0	Wilson, Woodger
	2	Hull City 1, Athletic 0	
1911/12	1	Athletic 1 Hull City 1	Wilson
	Replay	Hull City 0, Athletic 1	Woodger
	2	Manchester City 0, Athletic 1	Woodger
	3	Athletic 0, Everton 2	
1912/13	1	Athletic 2, Bolton W. 0	Tummon (2)
	2	Athletic 5, Nottingham Forest 1	Kemp (2), Tummon, Walter, Woodger
	3	Athletic 0, Manchester U. 0	
	Replay	Manchester U. 1, Athletic 2	Gee, Toward

Manchester Evening Chronicle, Saturday 22nd February 1913
ATHLETIC v MANCHESTER UNITED, F.A. CUP THIRD ROUND

A DEADLY CONTEST.

THE SNAKE CHARMER: "I'm very much afraid that one of them is going to swallow the other. I wonder which it will be!"

[Oldham Athletic and Manchester United have been drawn together in the English Cup. They meet at Oldham next Saturday in the third round of the competition].

257

"THE TEAM FROM A TOWN OF CHIMNEYS"

SEASON	ROUND	RESULTS	SCORERS
1912/13	4	Everton 0, Athletic 1	Gee
	Semi F.	Athletic 0, Aston Villa 1 (at Blackburn)	
1913/14	1	Athletic 1, Brighton 1	Donnachie
	Replay	Brighton 1, Athletic 0 (After extra time)	
1914/15	1	Croydon Common 0, Athletic 3	Wilson, Kemp, Tummon
	2	Athletic 3, Rochdale 0	Kemp, Gee, Donnachie
	3	Birmingham City 2, Athletic 3	Kemp, Chasmore, Pilkington
	4	Athletic 0, Sheffield U. 0	
	Replay	Sheffield U. 3, Athletic 0 (After extra time)	

NO COMPETITION DURING WORLD WAR 1

1919/20	1	Cardiff City 2, Athletic 0	
1920/21	1	Brighton 4, Athletic 1	Marshall
1921/22	1	Gillingham 1, Athletic 3	Broadbent (2), Taylor
	2	Barnsley 3, Athletic 1	Broadbent
1922/23	1	Athletic 0, Middlesbrough 1	
1923/24	1	Athletic 2, Sunderland 1	Staniforth, Blair
	2	Swindon Town 2, Athletic 0	
1924/25	1	Blackburn Rovers 1, Athletic 0	
1925/26	1	Athletic 10, Lytham 1	Barnes (3), Watson (2), Pynegar (2), Ormston (2), Naylor
	2	Stockton 4, Athletic 6	Watson (4), Pynegar, Wynne (pen.)
	3	Millwall 1, Athletic 1	Douglas
	Replay	Athletic 0, Millwall 1	

Manchester Evening Chronicle, Wednesday 26th February 1913
MANCHESTER UNITED v ATHLETIC, F.A. CUP THIRD ROUND REPLAY

A NEW VERSION OF AN OLD RHYME.

There was a young man of Old Trafford. Who went for a ride on a bafford;

They returned from that ride with the fellow inside And a smile on the face of the bafford!

[N.B.—A bafford is a newly-discovered animal, scientifically known as Oldhama Athletica. It is very fierce, and possesses great powers of endurance. It has been tamed, but the words "Manchester" and "cup-tie" invariably lash it into a state of great fury. It lives mainly on cotton, but likes an occasional change of diet.]

"THE TEAM FROM A TOWN OF CHIMNEYS"

SEASON	ROUND	RESULTS	SCORERS
1926/27	3	Athletic 2, Brentford 1 (Abandoned)	Pynegar (pen.), Watson
	Replay	Athletic 2, Brentford 4	Barnes, Pynegar
1927/28	3	Blackpool 1, Athletic 4	Watson (2), King, Stanton
	4	Tottenham 3, Athletic 0	
1928/29	3	Bolton W. 2, Athletic 0	
1929/30	3	Athletic 1, Wolverhampton W. 0	Goodier
	4	Athletic 3, Sheffield W. 4	Littlewood (2), Adlam
1930/31	3	Athletic 1, Watford 3	Fitton
1931/32	3	Athletic 1, Huddersfield T. 1	Ivill
	Replay	Huddersfield T. 6, Athletic 0	
1932/33	3	Athletic 0, Tottenham 6	
1933/34	3	Reading 1, Athletic 2	Rowley, Bailey
	4	Athletic 1, Sheffield W. 1	Bailey
	Replay	Sheffield W. 6, Athletic 1	
1934/35	3	Sheffield W. 3, Athletic 1	Walsh
1935/36	1	Athletic 6, Ferryhill Ath. 1	Davis (2), Buckley, Brunskill, Agar, Walsh
	2	Bristol R. 1, Athletic 1	Walsh
	Replay	Athletic 1, Bristol R. 4	Robson
1936/37	1	Athletic 1, Tranmere R. 0	Davis
	2	Lincoln City 2, Athletic 3	McCormick (2), Davis
	3	Exeter City 3, Athletic 0	
1937/38	1	Wrexham 2, Athletic 1	Hilton
1938/39	1	Athletic 2, Crewe Alex. 2	Halford, Blackshaw
	Replay	Crewe Alex. 1, Athletic 0	

NO COMPETITION DURING WORLD WAR 2

1945/46	1L(1)	Southport 1, Athletic 2	Chapman (2)
	2L	Athletic 3, Southport 1	Standring (2), Lawton
	1L(2)	Athletic 2, Accrington S. 1	Standring, West
	2L	Accrington S. 3, Athletic 1	Ferrier
1946/47	1	Athletic 1, Tranmere R. 0	Tomlinson
	2	Athletic 1, Doncaster R. 2	Bowden
1947/48	1	Athletic 6, Lancaster C. 0	Haddington (2), Wilson, Horton, Gemmell, Brierley
	2	Athletic 0, Mansfield T. 1	
1948/49	1	Wrexham 0, Athletic 3	Gemmell, Stock, Jessup
	2	Walthamstow A. 2, Athletic 2	Gemmell, Tomlinson
	Replay	Athletic 3, Walthamstow A. 1	Haddington (2), Gemmell
	3	Athletic 2, Cardiff City 3	Gemmell, Haddington
1949/50	1	Athletic 4, Stockton 0	Haddington (2), Gemmell Spurdle
	2	Crewe Alec. 1, Athletic 1	Jessop
	Replay	Athletic 0, Crewe Alex 0	
	Sec. Rep.	Athletic 3, Crewe Alex. 0 (at Maine Road)	Haddington (2), Spurdle
	3	Athletic 2, Newcastle U. 7	
1950/51	1	Bradford City 2, Athletic 2	Gemmell (2)
	Replay	Athletic 2, Bradford City 1	Munro, Goodfellow
	2	Hartlepool U. 1, Athletic 2	Newton (o.g.), Ormond
	3	Manchester U. 4, Athletic 1	Smith
1951/52	1	Nelson 0, Athletic 4	McKennan (3), Gemmell
	2	Southend U. 5, Athletic 0	

"THE TEAM FROM A TOWN OF CHIMNEYS"

SEASON	ROUND	RESULTS	SCORERS
1952/53	1	Boston U. 1, Athletic 2	McKennan, Clarke
	2	Port Vale 0, Athletic 3	Gemmell (2), Ormond
	3	Athletic 1, Birmingham C. 3	McKennan
1953/54	3	Ipswich T. 3, Athletic 3	McIlvenny (2), Clarke
	Replay	Athletic 0, Ipswich T. 1	
1954/55	1	Athletic 1, Crewe Alex. 0	McShane
	2	Bournemouth 1, Athletic 0	
1955/56	1	Bradford City 3, Athletic 1	Scrine
1956/57	1	Halifax T. 2, Athletic 3	Neale (2), Pearson
	2	Accrington S. 2, Athletic 1	Betts
1957/58	1	Athletic 2, Bradford PA 0	Fawley, Duffy
	2	Athletic 1, Workington 5	Murray
1958/59	1	Denaby U. 0, Athletic 2	Thompson (2)
	2	Athletic 2, South Shields 0	Bourne, Phoenix
	3	Stoke City 5, Athletic 1	Duffy
1959/60	1	Shildon 1, Athletic 1	Spurdle
	Replay	Athletic 3, Shildon 0	McGill, Bazley, Walters
	2	Bury 2, Athletic 1	Phoenix
1960/61	1	Rhyl 0, Athletic 1	Lister
	2	Chesterfield 4, Athletic 4	Lister (2), Johnstone, Phoenix
	Replay	Athletic 0, Chesterfield 3	
1961/62	1	Athletic 5, Shildon 2	Lister (3), Jarvis, Johnstone (pen.)
	2	Chesterfield 2, Athletic 2	Lister, Colquhoun
	Replay	Athletic 4, Chester 2	Colquhoun (2), Johnstone (pen.), Powell (o.g.)
	3	Bristol R. 1, Athletic 1	Phoenix
	Replay	Athletic 2, Bristol R. 0	Colquhoun (2)
	4	Athletic 1, Liverpool 2	Colquhoun
1962/63	1	Athletic 2, Bradford C. 5	Frizzell, Whittaker
1963/64	1	Athletic 3, Mansfield T. 2	Colquhoun, Ledger, Whittaker
	2	Athletic 2, Bradford C. 0	Bowie, Scoular (o.g.)
	3	Ipswich T. 6, Athletic 3	Lister (2), Bowie
1964/65	1	Athletic 4, Hereford 0	Colquhoun (3), Lister
	2	Crook Town 0, Athletic 1	Bartley
	3	Middlesbrough 6, Athletic 2	Williams, Martin
1965/66	1	Mansfield T. 1, Athletic 3	Holden (2), Jackson
	2	Darlington 0, Athletic 1	Dearden
	3	Athletic 2, West Ham 2	Blore (2)
	Replay	West Ham 2, Athletic 1	Pennington
1966/67	1	Athletic 3, Notts County 1	Collins, Large, Asprey (pen.)
	2	Grantham 0, Athletic 4	Collins (2), Wood, Bebbington
	3	Athletic 2, Wolverhampton W. 2	Bebbington (2)
	Replay	Wolverhampton W. 4, Athletic 1	Bebbington
1967/68	1	Barrow 2, Athletic 0	
1968/69	1	Wrexham 4, Athletic 2	Bebbington, Chapman
1969/70	1	Athletic 3, Grantham 1	Colquhoun, Wood, Bingham (pen.)
	2	South Shields 0, Athletic 0	
	Replay	Athletic 1, South Shields 2	Bebbington

260

SEASON	ROUND	RESULTS	SCORERS
1970/71	1	Rochdale 2, Athletic 0	
1971/72	1	Chesterfield 3, Athletic 0	
1972/73	1	Athletic 1, Scarborough 1	Shaw
	Replay	Scarborough 2, Athletic 1	Collins
1973/74	1	Formby 0, Athletic 2	Jones (2)
	2	Halifax T. 0, Athletic 1	McVitie
	3	Cambridge U. 2, Athletic 2	Simmons (o.g.), Lochhead
	Replay	Athletic 3, Cambridge U. 3 (After extra time)	Robins (2), McVitie
	Sec. Rep.	Athletic 2, Cambridge U. 1 (at Nottingham Forest)	Jones, Garwood
	4	Athletic 1, Burnley 4	Whittle (pen.)
1974/75	3	Athletic 0, Aston Villa 3	
1975/76	3	Sunderland 2, Athletic 0	
1976/77	3	Athletic 3, Plymouth A. 0	Halom, Robins, Whittle
	4	Northwich V. 1, Athletic 3 (at Manchester City)	Halom (2), Valentine
	5	Liverpool 3, Athletic 1	Shaw
1977/78	3	Luton Town 1, Athletic 1	Taylor
	Replay	Athletic 1, Luton Town 2	Young
1978/79	3	Stoke City 2, Athletic 0 (Abandoned)	
	Replay	Stoke City 0, Athletic 1	Wood
	4	Athletic 3, Leicester City 1	Young (3)
	5	Athletic 0, Tottenham 1	
1979/80	3	Athletic 0, Coventry C. 1	
1980/81	3	Wimbledon 0, Athletic 0	
	Replay	Athletic 0, Wimbledon 1	
1981/82	3	Gillingham 2, Athletic 1	Heaton
1982/83	3	Athletic 0, Fulham 2	
1983/84	3	Shrewsbury Town 3, Athletic 0	
1984/85	3	Athletic 2, Brentford 1	Quinn, Harrison
	4	Sheffield Wed. 5, Athletic 1	Bowden
1985/86	3	Athletic 1, Orient 2	Palmer
1986/87	3	Athletic 1, Bradford City 1	McGuire
	Replay	Bradford 5, Athletic 1	Wright
1987/88	3	Athletic 2, Tottenham 4	Wright, Cecere
1988/89	3	Charlton Athletic 2, Athletic 1	Milligan
1989/90	3	Birmingham 1, Athletic 1	Bunn
	Replay	Athletic 1, Birmingham 0	R. Holden
	4	Athletic 2, Brighton 1	Ritchie, McGarvey
	5	Athletic 2, Everton 2	Ritchie (Pen), Palmer
	Replay	Everton 1, Athletic 1	Marshall
	2nd Replay	Athletic 2, Everton 1	Palmer, Marshall (Pen)
	6	Athletic 3, Aston Villa 0	Redfearn, R. Holden Price (O.G.)
	Semi	Athletic 3, Manchester Utd. 3 (At Maine Road)	Barrett, Marshall, Palmer
	Replay	Athletic 1, Manchester Utd. 2 (At Maine Road)	Ritchie

"THE TEAM FROM A TOWN OF CHIMNEYS"

GOALSCORERS FOR ATHLETIC IN THE F.A. CUP
(up to and including 1989/90)

11 — Colquhoun; 10 — Gemmell, Lister, Haddington; 9 — Watson; 6 — Bebbington; 5 — McKennan, Pynegar, Kemp; 4 — Phoenix, Young, Davis, Barnes, Tummon, Palmer, Woodger, Spurdle, Halom. 3 — Johnstone, Toward, Wilson, Gee, Robins, Jones, Ritchie, Marshall, Broadbent, Walsh, Standring; 2 — Clarke, McIlvenney, Neale, Duffy, Thompson, Bowie, Whittaker, Holden, Blore, Wood, Shaw, Whaites, Donnachie, Ormston, Littlewood, Bailey, Ormond, McVitie, Whittle, Wright, R. Holden.
1 each: Newton, Hamilton, Walters, Cashmore, Pilkington, Marshall, Taylor, Staniforth, Blair, Naylor, Wynne, Douglas, King, Stanton, Goodier, Adlam, Fitton, Ivill, Rowley, Buckley, Brunskill, Agar, Robson, McCormick, Hilton, Halford, Blackshaw, Lawton, West, Ferrier, Tomlinson, Bowden, Wilson, Horton, Brierley, Stock, Jessup, Munro, Tomlinson, Pennington, Goodfellow, Smith, McShane, Scrine, Pearson, Betts, Fawley, Murray, Bourne, Walters, McGill, Bazley, Jarvis, Frizzell, Ledger, Bartley, Martin, Williams, Jackson, Dearden, Chapman L., Bingham, Collins, Valentine, Taylor, Jessop, Lochhead, Garwood, Heaton, Quinn, Harrison, Bowden, McGuire, Cecere, Milligan, Bunn, McGarvey, Barrett and Redfearn.

MANCHESTER UNITED v ATHLETIC
(F.A. Cup Semi-Final) April 8th 1990

Roger Palmer scores the sixth and final goal in a tremendous Semi-Final

HAT-TRICK'S FOR ATHLETIC IN THE F.A. CUP
1907/08 Hancock v. Darwen (H) won 8-1
1925-26 Barnes v. Lytham (H) won 10-1
1925-26 Watson (4) v. Stockton (A) won 6-4
1951-52 McKennan v. Nelson (A) won 4-0
1961-62 Lister v. Shildon (H) won 5-2
1964-65 Colquhoun v. Hereford United (H) won 4-0
1978-79 Young v. Leicester City (H) won 3-1

H. Hancock   *A. Young*

"THE TEAM FROM A TOWN OF CHIMNEYS"

League Cup Record ~ 1960 * 1990

SEASON	ROUND	RESULT	SCORERS
1960/61	1	Athletic 2, Hartlepool Utd. 1	Liddell, Birch
	2	Norwich City 6, Athletic 2	Lister (2)
1961/62	1	Athletic 1, Charlton Athletic 4	Frizzell
1962/63	1	Crewe Alexandra 2, Athletic 3	Lister 2, Colquhoun
	2	Sunderland 7, Athletic 1	Lister
1963/64	1	Athletic 3, Workington Town 5	Bowie (2), Lister
1964/65	1	Grimsby Town 3, Athletic 1	Craig
1965/66	1	Athletic 3, Tranmere Rovers 2	Bowie, Bartley, Quixall
	2	Athletic 1, Portsmouth 2	Holden
1966/67	1	Barrow 2, Athletic 1	Dearden
1967/68	1	Workington Town 1, Athletic 1	Blore
	Replay	Athletic 1, Workington Town 1 (After extra time)	Foster
	Sec. Rep.	Workington Town 2, Athletic 1	Magee
1968/69	1	Preston 1, Athletic 1	Blair
	Replay	Athletic 0, Preston 1	
1969/70	1	Southport 5, Athletic 1	Spence
1970/71	1	Bury 1, Athletic 3	Shaw, Fryatt, Bryceland
	2	Athletic 2, Middlesbrough 4	Fryatt, Bebbington
1971/72	1	Athletic 1, Bury 0	Clements
	2	Torquay 2, Athletic 1	Shaw
1973/74	1	Bury 0, Athletic 0	
	Replay	Athletic 2, Bury 3	Robins (2)
1974/75	1	Bury 2, Athletic 0	
1975/76	1L(1)	Athletic 3, Workington 0	G. Jones (3)
	2nd Leg	Workington 1, Athletic 3	Holt, Groves, Chapman
	2	Aston Villa 2, Athletic 0	
1976/77	1L(1)	Bradford City 1, Athletic 1	Chapman
	2nd Leg	Athletic 1, Bradford City 3	Halom
1977/78	2	Brighton 0, Athletic 0	
	Replay	Athletic 2, Brighton 2 (After extra time)	Halom, P. Edwards
	Sec. Rep.	Athletic 2, Brighton 1	Chapman, Irving
	3	Hull City 2, Athletic 0	
1978/79	2	Athletic 0, Notts. Forest 0	
	Replay	Notts. Forest 4, Athletic 2	Halom, Taylor
1979/80	1L(2)	Northampton T. 3, Athletic 0	
	2nd Leg	Athletic 3, Northampton T. 1	Hilton, Wood, Heaton
1980/81	2	Athletic 3, Portsmouth 2	Keegan, Kowenicki, Stainrod
	2nd Leg	Portsmouth 1, Athletic 0 (After extra time) Portsmouth won on away goals	
1981/82	1L(1)	Bolton W. 2, Athletic 1	Atkinson
	2nd Leg	Athletic 4, Bolton W. 2 (After extra time)	Palmer (2), Wylde, Heaton
	1L(2)		
		Athletic 1, Newport C. 0	Palmer
	2nd Leg	Newport C 0, Athletic 0	
	3	Athletic 1, Fulham 1	Steel
	Replay	Fulham 3, Athletic 0	

263

"THE TEAM FROM A TOWN OF CHIMNEYS"

SEASON	ROUND	RESULTS	SCORERS
1982/83	2L(1)	Gillingham 2, Athletic 0	
	2nd Leg	Athletic 1, Gillingham 0	McDonough
1983/84	2L(1)	Stockport 0, Athletic 2	McDonough, Parker
	2nd Leg	Athletic 2, Stockport 2	McDonough, Palmer
	3	Wimbledon 3, Athletic 1	Cross
1984/85	1L(1)	Bolton 2, Athletic 1	Parker
	2nd Leg	Athletic 4, Bolton 4 (After Extra Time)	T. Henry, Quinn 2, Parker
1985/86	2L(1)	Liverpool 3, Athletic 0	
	2nd Leg	Athletic 2, Liverpool 5	Fairclough 2
1986/87	2L(1)	Athletic 3, Leeds United 2	Futcher 2, Linighan
	2nd Leg	Leeds United 0, Athletic 1	Palmer
	3	Coventry City 2, Athletic 1	Hoolickin
1987/88	2L(1)	Carlisle United 4, Athletic 3	Henry T., Irwin, Ritchie
	2nd Leg	Athletic 4, Carlisle United 1	Palmer 3, Linighan
	3	Leeds United 2, Athletic 2	Wright, Williams (Pen)
	Replay	Athletic 4, Leeds United 2	Keeley, Williams, Irwin, Wright
	4	Everton 2, Athletic 1	Irwin
1988/89	2L(1)	Darlington 2, Athletic 0	
	2nd Leg	Athletic 4, Darlington 0	Williams, Bunn, Ritchie, Philliskirk
	3	Everton 1, Athletic 1	Ritchie
	Replay	Athletic 0, Everton 2	
1989/90	2L(1)	Athletic 2, Leeds United 1	Ritchie, R. Holden
	2nd Leg	Leeds United 1, Athletic 2	Bunn, Ritchie
	3	Athletic 7, Scarborough 0	Bunn 6, Ritchie
	4	Athletic 3, Arsenal 1	Ritchie 2, N. Henry
	5	Southampton 2, Athletic 2	Ritchie 2
	Replay	Athletic 2, Southampton 0	Ritchie, Milligan
	Semi(1)	Athletic 6, West Ham 0	Ritchie 2, Palmer, Adams, R. Holden, Barrett
	Semi(2)	West Ham 3, Athletic 0	
	Final	Nottingham Forest 1, Athletic 0 (At Wembley Stadium)	

GOALSCORERS FOR ATHLETIC IN THE LEAGUE/LITTLEWOODS CUP
(up to and including the 1989-1990 Season)

13 — Ritchie; 9 — Palmer; 8 — Bunn; 6 — Lister; 3 — Bowie, Jones, McDonough, Chapman, Paker, Irwin, Williams, Halom; 2 — Heaton, Shaw, Fryatt, Robins, Fairclough, Henry T., Quinn, Futcher, Linighan, Wright.
1 each: Liddell, Birch, Frizzell, Colquhoun, Craig, Bartley, Quixall, Holden S., Dearden, Blore, Foster, Magee, Blair, Spence, Bryceland, Bebbington, Clements P. Holt, Groves, Edwards P., Irving, Taylor, Hilton, Wood, Keegan, Stainrod, Kowenicki, Atkinson, Wylde, Steel, Cross, Hoolickin, Philliskirk, Henry N., Milligan, Adams, Barrett.

HAT-TRICK SCORERS FOR ATHLETIC IN THE LEAGUE/LITTLEWOODS CUP
1975-76, Jones v Workington Town (H) won 3-0
1987-88, Palmer v Carlisle United (H) won 4-1
1989-90, Bunn (6) v Scarborough (H) won 7-0

Frankie Bunn *George Jones*

"THE TEAM FROM A TOWN OF CHIMNEYS"

ATHLETIC v NOTTINGHAM FOREST
(Littlewoods Cup Final) 29th April 1990
A match winning save as Forest's keeper Steve Sutton dives full length to keep out a goal-bound header from Roger Palmer

Paul Warhurst sends a shot wide of the Forest goal

A moment to savour for Manager Joe Royle and his skipper Mike Milligan as thousands of fans gathered in Oldham town centre to pay tribute to the Athletic players

Supporters lined the streets as Athletic's open-top bus and escort of eight mounted policemen moved towards the civic centre

"THE TEAM FROM A TOWN OF CHIMNEYS"

Odds & Sods

"THE TEAM FROM A TOWN OF CHIMNEYS"

ATHLETIC'S TOUR OF RHODESIA & MALAWI, 1967

June 18th
v St. Paul's (Rhodesia National Champions) — in Salisbury.
Won 6-0 ... Towers (3), Bebbington, Magee, Knighton.
Attendance: 20,000.

June 21st
v Rio Tinto — in Que Que.
Lost 2-3 ... Blore, Asprey (penalty).
Attendance: 4,777.

June 24th
v F A R XI (Football Association of Rhodesia) — in Bulawayo.
Won 3-1 ... Towers, Wood, Magee.
Attendance: 13,700.

June 25th
v Dynamos (National League [North Zone] leaders) — in Salisbury.
Won 4-2 ... Blore, Asprey (penalty), Foster, Hunter.
Attendance: 4,200.

June 28th
v Mangula — in Mangula.
Won 4-0 ... Wood (3), Knighton.
Attendance: 4,000.

July 1st
v Great Dykes Association XI — in Mtoroshanga.
Won 7-3 ... Foster (6), Knighton (penalty).
Attendance: 6,300.

July 1st
v Tornados — in Salisbury.
Won 3-2 ... Towers, Hunter, Manuel (own goal).
Attendance: 2,700.

July 2nd
v Manicaland XI — in Umtali.
Won 2-1 ... Blore, Foster.
Attendance: 15,000.

July 4th
v Salisbury Callies — in Salisbury.
Won 5-2 ... Bebbington (3), Towers, Wood.
Attendance: 5,400.

July 6th
v Malawi F.A. — in Blantyre.
Won 3-2 ... Magee, Towers, Blore.
Attendance: 45,000.

July 8th
v Blantyre Sports Club — in Blantyre.
Won 6-2 ... Foster (3), Towers (2), Wood.
Attendance: 3,000.

RECORD:

Pl	W	D	L	F	Agt.
11	10	0	1	45	18

'MORE OFFICIAL ENGAGEMENTS' — RHODESIA, 1967

"THE TEAM FROM A TOWN OF CHIMNEYS"

"THE TEAM FROM A TOWN OF CHIMNEYS"

During Athletic's tour of Rhodesia in 1967, the local witch doctors were reported to have spread voodoo powders along the home teams goal lines to prevent Athletic scoring. Not that this had any effect as 45 goals passed over them in the 11 matches played.

Oldham Athletic and the Oldham R.L. Club, both bidding for promotion, joined forces on Sunday, January 10th, 1982 to create local sporting history. With the Rugby League ground frost bound, their 'Home Game' against Batley took place at Boundary Park where the pitch is protected by undersoil heating. Oldham won this first ever Rugby League match at Boundary Park by 17-9.

Mr. Harry Massey, the Athletic chairman in 1962, offered the Latic's players a £5 per goal bonus prior to a game against Southport on Boxing Day 1962. Athletic won the game by 11-0, Mr. Massey payed out, but withdrew his offer for subsequent matches!

Paul Heaton scored Athletic's 4,000th Football League goal on Saturday, December 19th 1981 in a Second Division fixture against Orient. Athletic won the match 3-2.

ATHLETIC V CHELSEA, 1981/82, Division 2
A Jet Ranger Helicopter delivers the match ball

Athletic opened their 1939/40 campaign with a 3-1 win at home to Carlisle United. The team that day read: Caunce, Hilton, Shipman, Williamson, Ratcliffe (Capt.), Hayes, Chapman, Ferrier, Valentine, Blackshaw, Halford. This same day saw Roosevelt's peace appeal to Hitler.

Manchester Evening News — August 1939:—

The 1939/40 season is going to be a troublous voyage, if it is not stopped altogether. It is a good job that we Englishmen can meet trouble and danger with humour and resignation. Humour carried us through the last conflict, and it accounted for the fact that in Union Street, Oldham just a few days ago a news lad's rather feeble shout, "War averted, Hitler signs for Latics!" was met with general laughter. These things relieve tension, and it will be sad if football has to go by the board.

September 4, 1939 — Britain at war with Germany

Mr. Robert Mellor, Athletic's secretary, this morning informed the Boundary Park players that their contracts had been terminated. He had the Captain B. Ratcliffe, and the Vice Captain W. Hilton before him, and explained the position to them.

The players, realising that such a position could not be avoided, accepted it philosophically. Mr. Mellor had also been in touch with the Football League, and was informed that all footballers' contracts terminated as from the week ending September 1st, 1939.

Latic's were playing Kidderminster in an F.A. Cup tie back in 1907 and the referee awarded a penalty against them. When the official had placed the ball on the spot he turned round to find there was no goalkeeper. Hewitson was behind the goal among the fans laying the odds that they would not score — and they didn't!

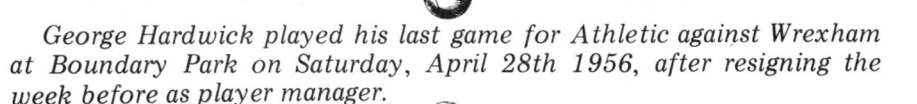

George Hardwick played his last game for Athletic against Wrexham at Boundary Park on Saturday, April 28th 1956, after resigning the week before as player manager.

A dramatic challenge to the Oldham Athletic shareholders, who were urging swift action to sign the England and Middlesbrough player, Wilf Mannion, was delivered on October 29th 1948 by veteran director Arthur Barlow, a former chairman of the club. He stated that he was prepared to lend the club, free of interest £2,000, for an unspecified period, on condition that 15 other supporters each make an equal loan. Middlesbrough were willing to transfer him for £25,000. The arrangement never materialised and the deal fell through.

Plaque commemorating Athletic's promotion to Division One - 1910 showing the Club directors.

Former Athletic full-back Sam Wynne was the first player to die during a first-class fixture, when on Saturday 30th April 1927 he collapsed while taking a free-kick after 40 mins of a Bury v Sheffield United Division 1 game. He died in the dressing room and a post-mortem showed he had been suffering from pneumonia. The game was abandoned and replayed the following Thursday, with all receipts going to Wynne's widow.

Sam Wynne scored with a penalty and a free-kick for his own side, Oldham Athletic, on Saturday 6th October 1923 and also scored two own goals for Manchester United. Athletic won the Division 2 fixture 3-2.

"THE TEAM FROM A TOWN OF CHIMNEYS"

Founders and Pioneers of Oldham Athletic AFC, 1900

E. Schofield, H. Anderson, T. Johnston, W. Shone, A. Grey, W. C. Brierley, R. Brierley, A. Tetlow, E. C. Perritt, A. Pellowe, J. W. Mayall, H. Jones, D. Heywood. W. Sharpe, J. Sankey, F. Sinkinson, H. Lees, Jim Schofield, J. W. Bolton, J. Winterbottom, S. Lee, S. Parkin, T. Dunkerley, H. Chadwick, A. Barlow, James Schofield. J. Bell, W. Taylor, F. Brooks, H. Garland, F. Marsland, G. Worsley, T. Worsley, O. Field, S. Simpson, H. M. Jones, E. Holt, H. Nuttall. Joe Schofield, G. Fenton, H. Dickenson, J. Eastwood, J. Brooks, W. Platt, G. Travis, J. Finney, W. Catterall. W. Hughes. J. Perkins. H. Green.

David Ashworth and his 'Billy Pot'

Mr. Ashworth (Oldham Athletic's manager) had a very "high" opinion of his team last Saturday.

An amusing incident concerned manager David Ashworth during a game with Leeds City in 1908. He always watched the matches from the Flat Stand, Broadway side, running up and down with his 'Billy Pot' on, keeping up with play. This day he was running down with F. Hesham and nearly ran off the end of the stand, ending in an undignified sitting position.

"THE TEAM FROM A TOWN OF CHIMNEYS"

AT BOUNDARY PARK — A WELCOME TO NEWCASTLE UNITED — SEPTEMBER 10th 1910

Crowds o' faces line th' enclosure,
Quips an' jokes are bandied free,
Th' 'Latics' prospects folk discussin':
" What's th' result o' th' match to be?
Is this team fro' th' Tyne as mighty
As some footbo' judges say?
Han we lost afore we'en started?
Han we heck! We'st win to-day!

" We'n a team o' gradely triers —
As they fund deawn Ashton-road —
An' fro' th' top o' th' League to th' bottom
We're noan as feeart as what they're coed.

" Thoose 'at beeat us on eawr mettle,
Waint ha't' throw a chance away —
Hello! Tere are th' Latics comin'!
Good owd Owdham! Hip, Hooray!"

A crowd of 34,000 attended the Newcastle game and this gate remained a record for a league match at Boundary Park until a game against Blackpool in the 2nd Division on April 21st 1930, when a crowd of 45,120 paid receipts of £2,458. 17s. 6d. Why such a gap should occur, heaven knows, but one thing is certain, this record will in modern days never be bettered as the crowd limit has been drastically slashed.

In season 1906/07 Athletic were members of the Lancashire Combination and played Liverpool, a first division club, in the 1st round of the F.A. Cup and lost 1-0. Athletic's goalkeeper Daw let the ball roll between his legs in the last three mins in front of a crowd of 21,000 spectators.

During Athletic's second season in the First Division, Hodson and Fay were given a joint benefit in the match against Liverpool at Boundary Park, each player had a guarantee of £250.

In season 1911/12 Jimmy Fay left Athletic to join Bolton Wanderers because he was not allowed to live in Southport. When Fay left, and D. Walders was reaching the end of a distinguished career, the old half-back line of Fay, Walders & Wilson was disbanded and Oldham paid their record fee (at the time) of £1,250 to Aston Villa for George Hunter who joined in January 1912.

— LET THERE BE LIGHT —

Floodlights were switched on at Boundary Park for the first time on Tuesday, October 3, 1961, for a friendly match against Burnley which attracted a crowd of 15,520 and ended in a 3-3 draw. The Latics goals came from Lister, Johnstone and Liddell.

The lights were paid for by voluntary donation and were switched on by Mr. John Clayton who had done a tremendous amount of work to get the project off the ground.

The four towers are 115 feet total height. Almost 1½ miles of cable, mostly in underground trenches, was used and the installation was carried out by local electricians.

The installation includes amenity lighting and associated secondary lighting which is automatically switched on in the event of supply failure.

— ROYAL VISIT —

H.R.H. The Prince of Wales visited Boundary Park on Wednesday, July 6, 1921 . . . and drew one of the best crowds ever seen at the ground!

More than 40,000 ex-servicemen, disabled soldiers, factory workers and schoolchildren crammed the terraces for a view of The Prince.

A special low stand was erected in the centre of the ground for The Prince to receive the presentees; flags fluttered from every quarter; streamers of coloured buntings added to the gaiety of the scene — and the old Press box even had a fresh coat of green paint for the occasion.

Boundary Park from the air — 1933

"THE TEAM FROM A TOWN OF CHIMNEYS"

The first Sunday games played by first-class clubs were during the power crisis of 1973/74. The first game ever was a third round F.A. Cup tie at Cambridge on the morning of 6th January 1974 when 8,479 people saw Cambridge United draw 2-2 with Oldham Athletic.

In 1976/77 Northwich Victoria were forced to transfer their home fourth round F.A. Cup tie against Oldham Athletic to Maine Road when it was discovered that they had sold more tickets than their official capacity allowed. Athletic won the tie 3-1.

Ford Sporting League: Sponsored by the Motor Company, this lasted for only one season — 1970/71, and was based on points for good behaviour and goals scored. Oldham Athletic won it easily and received £70,000 for their efforts. The rules of the competition said Athletic must spend the money on ground improvements, which they did, while at the same time they had to approach the local council for financial help in running the team and club.

Aston Villa's one goal victory over Oldham Athletic in the F.A. Cup semi-final of 1913 meant that for the only time in the history of the competition, the finalists — Villa and Sunderland were also the clubs that finished first and second in Division 1. Villa's one goal victory in the final robbed Sunderland of a rare League and Cup double.

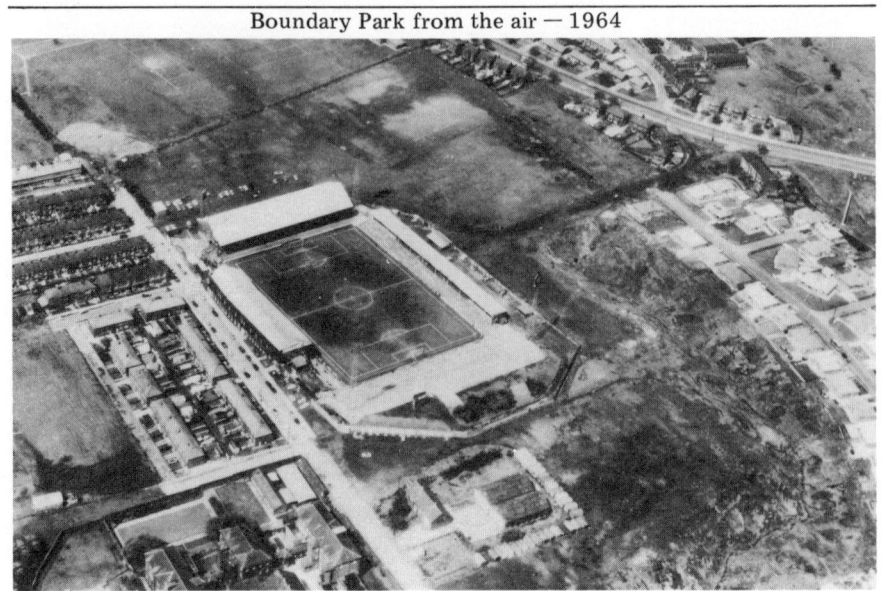

Boundary Park from the air — 1964

"THE TEAM FROM A TOWN OF CHIMNEYS"

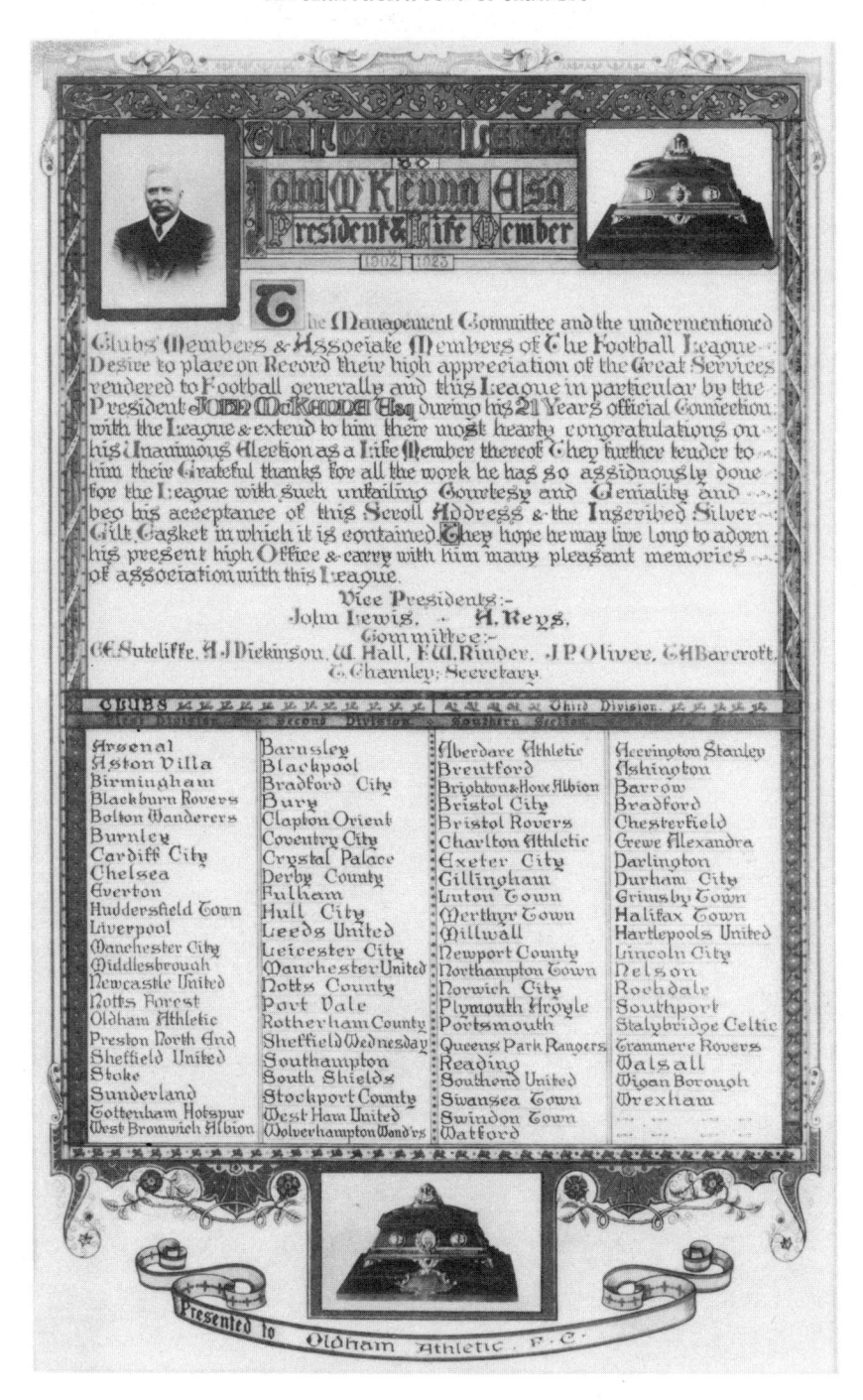

OLDHAM ATHLETIC'S FIRST EUROPEAN TOUR OF AUSTRIA AND HUNGARY 1911
BUDAPEST 25th MAY 1911 · FARENEVAROSI TORNA CLUB 2 · OLDHAM ATHLETIC 2

Back Row (left to right): A.N. Other · Broad · Fay · Montgomery · Donnachie · Woodger · Wilson · MacDonald · Moffat · Jones · D. Walders · Cope
Front Row: Farenevarosi Torna Club Team

November 1975 — Eric Sykes accepted an invitation to join the Board of Oldham Athletic.

Mr. Sykes, apart from being a noted script-writer, is a star of stage, films and television; but his association with Athletic goes back to his school-days, when he lived locally in Ward Street and attended the local school. Shortly after his appointment to the Board, it was clear he retained fond memories of seeing Latics in action.

August 1977 — Eric Sykes resigned from Athletic's Board. Due to outside pressures of work, he felt he couldn't justify his position.

1978/79 Season, Athletic suffered their 1000th League defeat since joining the Football League in 1907.

Athletic and Blackburn Rovers created a piece of Football League history on Boxing Day 1981. Their Second Division game was switched from Ewood Park to Boundary Park after it became obvious that Blackburn's ground could not be saved from the big freeze that decimated the holiday fixtures. Although many F.A. Cup Tie venues had been switched in the past, it was the first time a League fixture had been reversed. Blackburn won the match by 3-0 in front of 15,400 spectators. Gate receipts of just under £24,000 produced a new club record.

In September 1946, former Athletic and England goalkeeper Jack Hacking, then Accrington Stanley's manager, transferred his own son, Jack Hacking Jnr., also a goalkeeper, to Stockport County.

Athletic achieved 30 points in 23 away Division Three matches in 1973/74. They won 12 and drew six of their games.

When Athletic visited Barrow in a Division Three (North) match on 14 September 1957, only outside-left Ron Fawley retained his position from the previous game in which Oldham had lost 4-1 at Hartlepools United. Oldham drew 2-2, and at the end of the season Fawley was granted a free transfer.

Jimmy Fay's first appearance for Athletic was at Hudson Fold in season 1905-06, against Atherton in the Lancashire Combination 'A' Division. This match also marked the first appearance of Jimmy Hodson.

ATHLETIC V MANCHESTER UNITED, 28th December 1975

The famous goal that never was 'scored' by Athletics Ronnie Blair (hidden) The man who 'waved play-on' was referee T.D. Spencer (Wilts)

"THE TEAM FROM A TOWN OF CHIMNEYS"

The first ever F.A. Cup tie played in Oldham was between Oldham County and Oswaldtwistle Rovers on Saturday, October 31st 1896. This first round qualifying match was won by Oldham County by 7-0. The home team was: Mackay, Gaskell, Mellors, Foster, Errentz (Capt.), Stevenson, Carmen, Cunliffe, Furniss, Sharpe, Wilson.

In Athletic's first season at Boundary Park they won the Lancashire Combination Championship and the second team won the Lancashire Alliance League Cup.

A heavy, muddy ground in a Boundary Park F.A. Cup replay with Crewe Alexandra in December 1949 meant that the Athletic players went through 24 pairs of shorts and 26 jerseys during the game — an abnormal number.

Middlesbrough v Oldham Athletic in Division 1 on Saturday 3 April 1915. This game, the most celebrated incident of it's kind, was abandoned after 55 minutes when Athletic's full-back William Cook refused to accept the referee's decision to dismiss him. Oldham had gone to Middlesbrough needing a win to effectively secure the League Championship. When Cook was sent off, Oldham were 4-1 down and, as he refused to leave the field, the referee abandoned the game. The League ordered the result to stand and Cook was banned for a year — no great hardship as by then the League had been abandoned for the duration of the Great War.

The best individual scoring record for one season with Athletic was Tommy Davies's 35 League and Cup goals in 1936-37.
In later years, Don Travis came closest to the record with 34 in 1954-55. Next comes Bert Lister with 33 in 1962-63.

Athletic's first match at their new ground, Boundary Park, was on September 1, 1906. The game against Colne, was watched by 3,454 people, producing gate receipts of £51.13s.6d.

A memory of Manchester League days when Joe Stafford and Aron Hulme were Athletic's full-backs, when opposing teams were pressing, seeing Stafford tearing across the pitch and bashing the ball towards Pine Mill Lodge when the team played at Hudson Fold. Of taking jam jars back to the shop to get 1d for entrance money, gaining admission at the bottom of Westhulme Hospital wall.

"THE TEAM FROM A TOWN OF CHIMNEYS"

SATURDAY, MARCH 15, 1930.

A Talkie

Eleven Sound Arguments why Oldham Athletic should go into the First Division

For instance, there's Littlewood, a leader who likes to 'have a pop at (and in) goal.

Crafty Cummng & cunning Hasson run well together.

Worrall, the worrier, & Gray, the graceful, also spell danger

Leslie will have his bonus, and

where is there a goodier than Goodier?

Gentlemen: the King and a real ruler too.

Where can you find a better "Port-er in a storm? and then there's Ivill.

Last, but not least, there's Hacking, who plays for his King & Country

This incident concerns Jimmy Fay the Athletic captain during a match with Leeds City at Boundary Park on Saturday November 30th 1907. After the interval with the score 1-1, Oldham were late coming on to the field, the referee blew his whistle two or three times, but no Latics. It was Leeds to kick off the second half and they were playing towards the Rochdale Road end. Just as Athletic were taking the field the referee blew his whistle to start the game. The ball was passed straight to the left wing to the speedy Leeds wingman Croot. To have seen Jimmy Fay run down the steps was amazing, all records were broken as he caught Croot cutting in from the wing, but failed to stop the cross which Leeds inside left Gemmell converted. This put the Athletic team firmly on their mettle, and the grit and determination they showed was reflected in the final score of Oldham 4, Leeds City 2.

Athletic's last opponents in First Division football were Cardiff City whom they beat 3-1 at Boundary Park in 1923.

"THE TEAM FROM A TOWN OF CHIMNEYS"

When Jimmy Fay came to see the Oldham officials to sign, they offered him 2s. 6d., less wage than he wanted and they refused to alter their decision. After 10 mins he walked out of the public house where the meeting was being held. One of the officials, who had seen Fay play, told the club they had not only lost a good half-back but also a good inside-forward. They told this official that if he was as good as that he should go after him and sign him. He was caught just before entering Werneth Station on Featherstall Road, and he signed at the entrance to the station.

Some time after, a tailor's shop in Yorkshire Street offered an overcoat to any player who scored a hat-trick within a limited time. Jimmy Fay obliged and received free overcoats for himself and for the man who signed him on Athletic's books.

Jimmy Fay performed the hat-trick for Oldham Athletic against Barnsley.
(Manchester Chronicle 26/2/1910)

283

The fastest ever goal in first-class soccer was scored by ex Oldham Athletic centre forward Jim Fryatt then playing for Bradford Park Avenue on 25 April 1964. Just 4 seconds after the kick-off, Tranmere Rovers found themselves a goal down.

The 1-0 victory over Blackburn Rovers at Boundary Park on November 11th 1980 was Athletic's 1,000th victory in the Football League.

1958/59 season saw Athletic apply for re-election to the Football League for the first time in their History.

Tony Smyth was appointed club secretary of Athletic on 1st March 1973 and resigned two days later because of ill-health, making him the shortest serving club secretary in Football League history.

Athletic joined the select band of clubs to install undersoil heating on the pitch in 1980.

With the help of local business sponsorship and lottery money, work started in mid-May.

The "Meltaway" under-pitch soilwarming system was installed by a Swedish company at an approximate cost of £60,000.

Operating from an oil-fired boiler, 16 miles of plastic cable under the playing area circulates water at a temperature of $20^{o}C$, to prevent the surface freezing in winter.

The system was completed and ready for use in early December 1980 and was used for the first time for the match against Grimsby Town on December 27.

J.W. Lees Brewers became controlling shareholders of the club in 1975, and Mr. Harry Wilde became club chairman, when they bought out the interest of the two sons of former chairman Mr. John Lowe.

Mr. Lowe had joined the board in December 1969 when he arranged to buy the controlling interest of former chairman Mr. Ken Bates. He served as executive director for 18 months and took the chair in 1972 following the resignation of Mr. Harry Massey. Sadly, Mr. Lowe died in January 1974, aged 66, and thus missed the promotion push of that year into the Second Division.

Mr. William Shore became chairman for a short time but resigned in December 1974. He was followed by Mr. Arthur Hudson and his vice-chairman Mr. Dick Schofield, until Mr. Wilde took over.

ATHLETIC v LIVERPOOL (F.A. Cup 4th Round) January 1962
Chadderton Road End crash barriers collapse as Ian St. John (inset) puts Liverpool into a 1-0 lead

Boundary Park in the 1937-38 season, showing the rear of the Main Stand and Official Entrance

Athletic's Frank Bunn smashed the Littlewoods Cup individual record for most goals in a match by hitting six during Athletic's 7-0 victory over Scarborough Latic's sponsors, Bovis, sent Frank six crystal glasses (one for each goal) – October 1989

A painting of Boundary Park by Pop Star/Actor Tommy Steele (1970)

"THE TEAM FROM A TOWN OF CHIMNEYS"

READING v ATHLETIC (Division 2, 1927/28)
Latics players being introduced to H.R.H. Prince Arthur of Connaught at Elm Park

Athletic Captain George Hardwick attends a Supporters Club Meeting in 1951

The first wartime match was played on September 4th 1915, Athletic v. Manchester United at Boundary Park, Oldham winning by 3-2. The home team was: Matthews, Goodwin, Lester, Moffatt, Pilkington, Birks, Holbrook, Walters, Gee, A. Wolstenholme, Bertenshaw. Holbrook was a former Oldham Rugby player. There was a crowd of 4,420 with takings of £99 at a 'Tanner' a time.

Athletic left Hudson Fold and Mr. David Ashworth first became manager in the same year, 1906.

The first broadcasts of match reports to local hospitals from Boundary Park were made in 1952.

"THE TEAM FROM A TOWN OF CHIMNEYS"